Get started in Gujarati

Rachel Dwyer

Revised by Emilia Bachrach

First published in Great Britain in 1995 by Hodder & Stoughton.
An Hachette UK company.

First published in US 1995 by NTC Publishing Group, 4255 West Touhy Avenue Lincolnwood (Chicago), Illinois 60646 -1975 U.S.A.

This edition published 2013

This edition published in US in 2013 by The McGraw-Hill Companies, Inc.

British Library Cataloguing in Publication Data: a catalogue record for this title is available from the British Library.

Library of Congress Catalog Card Number: on file.

10 9 8 7 6 5 4 3 2 1

Typeset by Cenveo® Publisher Services.

Printed and bound in United Kingdom by Cox and Wyman.

Hodder & Stoughton Ltd

338 Euston Road

London NW1 3BH

www.hodder.co.uk

Contents

Meet the author

Rachel Dwyer is professor of Indian Cultures and Cinema at the School of Oriental and African Studies (SOAS), University of London. She took her BA in Sanskrit at SOAS, followed by an MPhil in General Linguistics and Comparative Philology at the University of Oxford. Her PhD research was on the Gujarati lyrics of Dayaram (1777–1852) and she is currently working on popular culture in India. She teaches courses on the literatures of South Asia and on Indian cinema and society.

ACKNOWLEDGEMENTS

I should like to thank in particular Monisha Shah for her help in writing the dialogues. For their detailed observations, corrections and suggestions I should like to thank Professor Harivallabh Bhayani, Dr Raghuveer Chaudhari, Kornelius Krumpelmann and Professor Christopher Shackle. Thanks are due also to Dr Ian Raeside, Dr Rupert Snell and Professor J.C. Wright for their general comments. The students who attended Gujarati I classes studied this course in manuscript form and made many suggestions for improvements. I should like to mention in particular Vijayalakshmi Bhanap, Aanal Chandaria, Christine Chojnacki Udita Jhunjhunwala, Steve Neumann, Rakesh Odedra, Kanaiya Parekh Prerana Patel, Viren Patel and Priya Shah.

Further thanks are due to the following: Shree Ratilal Chandaria, who provided me with the software necessary to produce the manuscript; Dr Emma Tarlo, who lent materials for the artwork; Susan Madigan, for helping to make copies; my husband, Michael Dwyer, as ever.

For my mother, Vivian Jackson.

Introduction

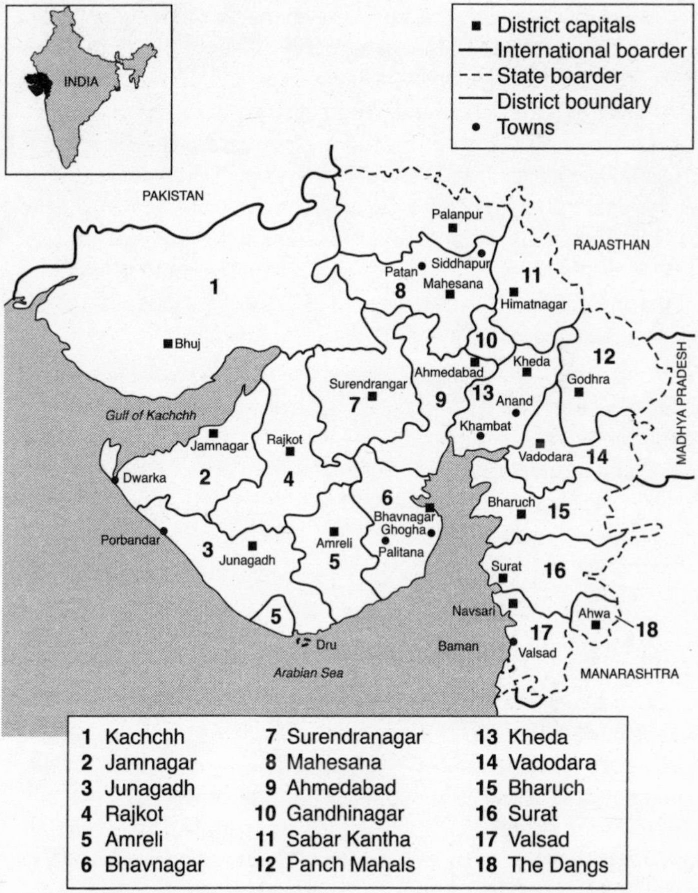

The geography of Gujarat

The modern state of Gujarat, which includes the desert region of Kachchh and the peninsula of Saurashtra (also known as Kathiawar), is situated on the north-west coast of India. This region of plains and low hills is approximately the same size as the United Kingdom. Its boundaries are formed by the states of Rajasthan to the north, Madhya Pradesh in the east, Maharashtra in the south and the national border with Pakistan in the north-west. The coastal border with the Arabian Sea is nearly 1,600 kilometres long, and nowhere in Gujarat is more than 160 kilometres from the sea. The climate of Gujarat is extreme, with temperatures varying from sub-zero in the winter to 48°C in the summer. The rainfall, most of which falls during the monsoon season (June to September), varies from 1,500 mm in the south to under 25 mm in Kachchh. The main rivers of Gujarat - the Narmada, the Tapti and the Sabarmati - all flow into the Gulf of Khambhat.

Even on contemporary maps of Gujarat one may find multiple spellings (in both Gujarati and roman scripts) for the names of geographical regions and cities. Throughout this text we have tried to use standard transliterated spellings, which might differ from what is used elsewhere. For example Saurashtra (for the Kathiawar peninsula), Ahmedabad (Amadabad or Amdavad), Kheda (Kaira), Vadodara (Baroda), Bharuch (Broach), Khambhat (Cambay) and Kachchh (Kutch).

The history of Gujarat

Prehistoric remains have been found in Gujarat, notably those at the Harappan port of Lothal in Ahmedabad district. At the turn of the millennium, the region was ruled by two empires - the Mauryas (about third century BCE) and the Guptas (about fifth century CE). In the fifth and sixth centuries CE the region was controlled by invaders from north-western India, including the Gurjara tribes (from which the name Gujarat may have come). The region went on to prosper under the Solanki, or Chalukyan, dynasty, founded in CE 942, and under the following Vaghela dynasty. Around this time, the Parsis (Zoroastrians) came as refugees from Iran and later settled as agriculturalists in areas including the Valsad district.

During the seventh and eighth centuries Arab communities took control of many coastal areas. From the ninth century onwards the chief cities of Gujarat increasingly saw the settlement of Muslim communities, many of whom had migrated from the Persian Gulf. Raids from the north began in 1026 when Muhammad of Ghazni sacked the prominent temple at Somnath, and petty raids continued until the area was brought under the rule of the Turkish sultans of Delhi (referred to as the Delhi Sultanate). Gujarat became independent under the Sultanate of Ahmedabad (1407–1573) but was brought under the rule of the north once again when the great Mughal Akbar annexed the area, which was ruled as a province of the Mughal empire (1573–1758) until the Marathas took Ahmedabad.

The first Europeans to arrive were the Portuguese, who came in the sixteenth century, followed soon after by the English who set up a factory in Surat in 1613 and soon installed themselves in Mumbai (previously Bombay). They came to power after defeating the last Maratha Peshwa in 1818, and consolidated their position in 1858 when the area was brought under the rule of what was then called the Bombay Presidency (whose capital was Bombay, now Mumbai), with residents in the many princely states.

The social unrest and political upheavals that occurred in the late eighteenth century led certain communities to migrate to Mumbai, which was perceived as an asylum for merchants from Gujarat and elsewhere. Gujarati traders soon came to economic and social prominence in association with the East India Company.

After independence from Britain in 1947, the region now known as Gujarat became part of the Bombay Presidency. In 1960 the Bombay Presidency split along linguistic lines and become two separate states: Gujarat (capital: Ahmedabad; since 1970 called Gandhinagar) and Maharashtra (capital: Bombay, now Mumbai). According to the 2011 census, the population of Gujarat is over 60 million. Today Gujaratis live in most regions of South Asia, but remain in largest numbers in the state of Gujarat, in the city of Mumbai and increasingly in the overseas diaspora, namely in East Africa, the United Kingdom and North America.

Religion in Gujarat

Despite centuries of Muslim rule, Muslims have remained a minority community in Gujarat (accounting for roughly 9 per cent of the state's population, according to the 2011 census). A majority of Gujaratis identify as Hindu, including those who identify as Vaishnav (those who worship Vishnu in his incarnations of Ram or Krishna), as Shaiva (worshippers of Shiva), or as worshippers of one or more forms of the Goddess. In contemporary Gujarat, there are two major Vaishnav communities who worship manifestations of the deity Krishna: the Vallabh Sampraday (also known as the Pushtimarg) and the Swaminarayan Sampraday. Since it was introduced to the region in the sixteenth century, the Pushtimarg has been the most culturally dominant Vaishnavaite presence in Gujarat – so much so, in fact, that sometimes people simply call themselves Vaishnav when they are actually referring specifically to the Pushtimarg. Today, however, the Swarninarayan Sampraday (established in the early nineteenth century) is growing rapidly and is an equally, if not more, visible presence in Gujarat than the Pushtimarg.

The Jain community, which has several distinct branches, has played a significant role in Indian cultural life, largely through spreading their doctrine of અહિંસા **ahiṃsā** (non-violence and strict vegetarianism). As a majority of Jains are traditionally merchants, they have also played an active role in India's commercial and political life. Jain merchants, particularly those belonging to the Svetambara branch, have migrated all over India and the rest of the world, but still maintain strong ties to Gujarat and Rajasthan. The branch of the Jain community known as Digambaras also have strong roots in and around the Maharashtra and Karnataka border.

The Parsi community (Zoroastrians who migrated from Iran some time between the eighth and tenth centuries) were among the wealthiest groups in Mumbai in the nineteenth century, and although they comprised only 6 per cent of the population, they owned an enormous part of its wealth. They have always been a distinctive community, playing important roles in India's intelligentsia, in law, publishing, social reform, real estate and development. Parsis continue to play a prominent role in independent India in spite of constant worries within the community about their declining influence and numbers. Many Parsis have migrated from Navsari, Gujarat to Mumbai since the late eighteenth century.

Prominent Muslim communities of Gujarat include the Shi'a Bohras and Khojas (who comprise both Aga Khani and Isna Ashari Khojas), and the Memons (Hanafite Sunni). Shi'a Muslims believe that Muhammad passed on his spiritual and temporal authority to his descendants, and the various Shi'a sects dispute the succession of imams. Many of these Muslims went to Pakistan at the time of Partition in 1947 and, like other Gujaratis, a large number have migrated around the world. Many Ismailis (the term is used here in its popular usage to refer to followers of the Aga Khan) and Borhas migrated to East Africa and then to the United Kingdom and to North America, while many Memons migrated to South Africa where there is still a significant community.

As elsewhere in India, politicized tensions between religious communities, including between Muslims and Hindus, have occasionally led to serious episodes of violence. Gujarat's most serious episode of violence erupted in 2002 in and around Ahmedabad, when thousands of civilians were systematically killed, the majority of whom were Muslims.

The Gujarati language

Gujarati is an Indo-Aryan language that shares many similarities in vocabulary, script and lexicography with other modern north Indian languages, such as Hindi and Marathi. While Gujarati is the official state language of Gujarat, there are many varieties of Gujarati as well as distinct regional languages spoken across the state. In the region of Kachchh, for instance, Kachchhi (which is related to another language called Sindhi) is the primary language.

As well as being the mother tongue of over 60 million speakers in Gujarat itself, the language is spoken by the many thousands of Gujaratis who have migrated to other parts of India and abroad, notably to Pakistan, East Africa, the United Kingdom and North America.

GUJARATI DIALECTS

In Gujarat there is a proverb બાર ગાઉએ બોલી બદલાય **bar gāue bolī badlāy** which means *the dialect is changed every 12 leagues*. Power in modern Gujarat has never been centralized enough for it to evolve a widely accepted standard form of the language. Some speakers claim that the Nāgar Brahmins speak the best Gujarati, others that it is spoken in Rajkot or Ahmedabad. In *Get started in Gujarati*, an attempt has been made to use what is called શુદ્ધ ગુજરાતી **śuddh gujarātī** (*pure Gujarati*), which most closely corresponds to the form of the language that one would be taught in university courses in India or abroad.

Many Gujaratis claim that there are Parsi and Muslim 'dialects' of Gujarati which are distinct from other forms of the language. While this may be true of some of the vocabulary, it would be more accurate to say that the varieties that occur are due rather to other factors, such as education and region. There are traditionally four main dialects of notable geographical locations: Surati or southern Gujarati (a variety of

which is used by many Parsis); Charotari Gujarati (from Kheda district); Pattani or northern Gujarati; and Kathiawadi or peninsular Gujarati (from the Saurashtran peninsula). Further dialects of Gujarati have developed among Gujarati migrants, notably those who went to East Africa (who incorporate many Swahili words); and English continues to influence the language, both locally
and abroad.

How this book works

Welcome to *Get started in Gujarati*. This course has been written for the absolute beginner who may not have studied any language before. There are many reasons to learn Gujarati: you may want to learn Gujarati to speak to your Gujarati friends, to study aspects of Gujarati culture, for business purposes, or simply to visit Gujarat, Mumbai or another area where Gujarati is widely spoken. This course is also suitable for those who already speak some Gujarati or who may feel that they lack the speaking confidence except with their families. During the course, you will encounter many situations and learn how to give and to ask for information, to express your feelings, and so on. Each unit includes some background information about Gujarat and Gujaratis.

This course covers basic Gujarati grammar and vocabulary and teaches you how to use the dictionary. *Get started in Gujarati* will give you all the tools you need to become proficient at speaking, reading and writing Gujarati at a basic level.

How to use this course

If you have not yet read the introduction to Gujarat, it is advisable to do so before proceeding with the course. Next, you should work your way through the section on the Gujarati script and sound system. Even if you do not intend to learn the script, you should still read this section carefully and practise reading the activities out loud.

Each unit in *Get started in Gujarati* is structured in the following way:

- **What you will learn** identifies what you will be able to do in Gujarati by the end of the unit.
- **Culture point** presents an interesting cultural aspect related to the unit theme and introduces some key words and phrases.
- **Vocabulary builder** introduces key unit vocabulary grouped by theme and conversations, and is accompanied by audio. Learn these words and you will be on your way to speaking Gujarati proficiently.
- **Dialogues** are recorded so that you can listen to them and read them; they each begin with a narrative that helps you understand what you will hear, a focusing question and follow-up activities.

- **Language discovery** draws your attention to key language points in the conversations, whether it is a grammar rule or a way of saying something. Read the notes and look at the conversations to see how the language is used in practice and to aid quicker learning.
- **Practice** offers a variety of exercises to give you a chance to 'pull it all together' and make active use of the language.
- The last four structures are then repeated: that is, each unit has two sets of **Dialogues** and **Vocabulary builders**, corresponding questions, **Language discovery** and **Practice**.
- સમજ્યા/સમજ્યાં? **samjyā/samjyaṃ?** *Do you understand?* This section asks you to read an extended narrative that further reviews the grammar and vocabulary presented in the unit and has some questions to test your understanding.
- **Test yourself** helps you assess what you have learned. Do the tests without looking at the text.
- **Self check** lets you see what you can do in Gujarati after mastering each unit. When you feel confident that you can use the language correctly, move on to the next unit.

Study the units at your own pace, and remember to make frequent and repeated use of the audio.

To help you through the course, a system of icons indicates the actions you should take.

Listen to audio

Figure something out

Culture tip

New words and phrases

Exercises coming up!

Read something

Write something

Check your Gujarati ability

The audio recording

Although this book is self-contained, you will find the accompanying audio recordings of great help in improving your speaking and listening skills. The recordings contain all the content of the dialogue sections as well as material relating to several of the exercises.

For each unit you should start by listening to the recording of the dialogue at the same time as you read it. Pay special attention to the pronunciation and intonation of the speakers, and try to imitate them out loud sentence by sentence.

ABBREVIATIONS USED IN THIS BOOK

f.	feminine	n.	neuter
intr.	intransitive	pl.	plural
lit.	literally	sing.	singular
m.	masculine	tr.	transitive

Learn to learn

The Discovery method

There are lots of philosophies and approaches to language learning, some practical, some quite unconventional, and far too many to list here. Perhaps you know of a few, or even have some techniques of your own. In this book we have incorporated the **Discovery method** of learning, a sort of DIY approach to language learning. What this means is that you will be encouraged throughout the course to engage your mind and figure out the language for yourself, through identifying patterns, understanding grammar concepts, noticing words that are similar to English, and more. This method promotes language awareness, a critical skill in acquiring a new language. As a result of your own efforts, you will be able to better retain what you have learned, use it with confidence, and, even better, apply those same skills to continuing to learn the language (or, indeed, another one) on your own after you've finished this book.

Everyone can succeed in learning a language – the key is to know how to learn it. Learning is more than just reading or memorizing grammar and vocabulary. It's about being an active learner, learning in real contexts, and, most importantly, using what you've learned in different situations. Simply put, if you figure something out for yourself, you're more likely to understand it. And when you use what you've learned, you're more likely to remember it.

And because many of the essential but (let's admit it!) dull details, such as grammar rules, are introduced through the **Discovery method**, you'll have more fun while learning. Soon, the language will start to make sense and you'll be relying on your own intuition to construct original sentences independently, not just listening and repeating.

Enjoy yourself!

Tips for success

1 MAKE A HABIT OUT OF LEARNING

Study a little every day, between 20 and 30 minutes if possible, rather than two to three hours in one session. Give yourself short-term goals, e.g. work out how long you'll spend on a particular unit and work within the time limit. This will help you to create a study habit, much in the same way you would a sport or music. You will need to concentrate, so try to create an environment conducive to learning which is calm and quiet and free from distractions. As you study, do not worry about your mistakes or the things you can't remember or understand. Languages settle differently in our brains, but gradually the language will become clearer as your brain starts to make new connections. Just give yourself enough time and you will succeed.

2 EXPAND YOUR CONTACT WITH THE LANGUAGE

As part of your study habit, try to take other opportunities to expose yourself to the language. As well as using this book you could try listening to radio, watching television or reading articles and blogs. Perhaps you could find information in Gujarati about a personal passion or hobby or even a news story that interests you. In time you'll find that your vocabulary and language recognition deepen and you'll become used to a range of writing and speaking styles.

3 VOCABULARY

- To organize your study of vocabulary, group new words under (a) **generic** categories, e.g. food, furniture, (b) **situations in which they occur**, e.g. under restaurant you can write waiter, table, menu, bill, (c) **functions**, e.g. greetings, departing, thanks, apologizing.
- Say the words out loud as you read them.
- Write the words over and over again. Remember that if you want to keep lists on your smartphone or tablet you can usually switch the keyboard language to make sure you are able to include all accents and special characters.
- Listen to the audio several times.
- Cover up the English side of the vocabulary list and see if you remember the meaning of the word.
- Create flash cards, drawings and mind maps.

- Write words for objects that can be found around your house and stick them to those objects so that you see them every time you walk past.
- Pay attention to patterns in words.
- Experiment with words: use the words that you learn in new contexts and find out if they are correct. Check the new phrases either in this book, a dictionary or with Gujarati speakers.

4 GRAMMAR

- To organize the study of grammar write your own grammar glossary and add new information and examples as you go along.
- Sit back and reflect on the rules you learn. See how they compare with your own language or other languages you may already speak. Try to find out some rules on your own and be ready to spot the exceptions. By doing this you'll remember the rules better and get a feel for the language.
- Try to find examples of grammar in conversations or other articles.
- Keep a 'pattern bank' that organizes examples that can be listed under the structures you've learned.
- Use old vocabulary to practise new grammar structures.
- When you learn a new verb form, write the conjugation of several different verbs you know that follow the same form.

5 PRONUNCIATION

- When organizing the study of pronunciation keep a section of your notebook for pronunciation rules and practise those that you find especially difficult.
- Repeat all of the conversations, line by line. Listen to yourself and try to mimic what you hear.
- Record yourself and compare yourself to a native speaker.
- Make a list of words that you find hard to pronounce and practise them.
- Study individual sounds, then full words.
- Don't forget, it's not just about pronouncing letters and words correctly, but using the right intonation. So, when practising words and sentences, mimic the rising and falling intonation of native speakers.

6 LISTENING AND READING

The conversations in this book include questions to help guide you in your understanding. But you can go further by following some of these tips.

- Imagine the situation. When listening to or reading the conversations, try to imagine where the scene is taking place and who the main characters are. Let your experience of the world help you guess the meaning of the conversation, e.g. if a conversation takes place in a snack bar you can predict the kind of vocabulary that is being used.
- Concentrate on understanding the main gist of the conversation. When watching a foreign film you usually get the meaning of the whole story from a few individual shots. Understanding a foreign conversation or article is similar. Concentrate on the main parts to get the message and don't worry about individual words.
- Guess the key words; if you are unable to, ask someone or look them up.
- When there are key words you don't understand, try to guess what they mean from the context. If you're listening to a Gujarati speaker and cannot get the gist of a whole passage because of one word or phrase, try to repeat that word with a questioning tone; the speaker will probably paraphrase it, giving you the chance to understand it.

7 SPEAKING

Practise the foreign language. As all language teachers will assure you, the successful learners are those students who overcome their inhibitions and get into situations where they must speak, write and listen to the foreign language. Here are some useful tips to help you practise speaking Gujarati:

- Hold a conversation with yourself, using the conversations of the units as models and the structures you have learnt previously.
- After you have conducted a transaction with a sales assistant, waiter, etc. in your own language, pretend that you have to do it in Gujarati, e.g. buying groceries, ordering food and drinks, and so on.
- Look at objects around you and try to name them in Gujarati.
- Look at people around you and try to describe them in detail.
- Try to answer all of the questions in the book out loud.
- Say the dialogues out loud then try to replace sentences with ones that are true for you.
- Try to role-play different situations in the book.

8 LEARN FROM YOUR ERRORS

Don't let errors interfere with getting your message across. Making errors is part of any normal learning process, but some people get so worried that they won't say anything unless they are sure it is correct. This leads to a vicious circle as the less they say, the less practice they get and the more mistakes they make.

Note the seriousness of errors. Many errors are not serious as they do not affect the meaning, for example if you use the wrong article or the wrong pronouns. So concentrate on getting your message across and learn from your mistakes.

9 LEARN TO COPE WITH UNCERTAINTY

- Don't over-use your dictionary. When reading a text in the foreign language, don't be tempted to look up every word you don't know. Underline the words you do not understand and read the passage several times, concentrating on trying to get the gist of the passage. If, after the third time, there are still words that prevent you from getting the general meaning of the passage, look them up in the dictionary.
- Don't panic if you don't understand. If at some point you feel you don't understand what you are told, don't panic or give up listening. Either try and guess what is being said and keep following the conversation or, if you cannot, isolate the expression or words you haven't understood and ask the speaker to explain them to you. The speaker might paraphrase them and the conversation will carry on.
- Keep talking. The best way to improve your fluency in the foreign language is to talk every time you have the opportunity to do so: keep the conversations flowing and don't worry about the mistakes. If you get stuck for a particular word, don't let the conversation stop; paraphrase or replace the unknown word with one you do know, even if you have to simplify what you want to say. As a last resort use the word from your own language and pronounce it in the foreign accent.

The Gujarati script and sound system

The Gujarati script is related to the Devanagari script, which is commonly used for many Indian languages including Hindi, Marathi, Nepali and Sanskrit. Gujarati has no capital letters, although in older texts a bold character is printed where English would use a capital letter. The script is quasi-phonetic (words are pronounced more or less as they are written), so there are almost none of the huge spelling difficulties presented by English. As words are pronounced as they are written, the pronunciation and script will be covered together in this section.

It is more accurate to call the Gujarati writing system a syllabary, rather than an alphabet, because each sign represents a syllable. Vowels are syllables by definition, but it is the representation of consonants which is different. Each consonant has an inherent 'a' sound which makes it a syllable, unless it occurs in an unstressed position, usually at the end of a word. If another vowel sound follows, the consonant is modified (see below).

Two phonetic features of all North Indian languages are the system of contrasts between aspirated and unaspirated consonants, and the contrast between retroflex and dental consonants. These are important in pronouncing Gujarati correctly.

Aspirated consonants are accompanied by audible breath, whereas unaspirated consonants have minimal breath. In English, initial voiceless consonants are always lightly aspirated (e.g. *kin, tin, pin*), whereas in other positions in a word they are not (e.g. *skin, sting, spin*). (Test for aspiration by putting your hand in front of your mouth when you say these. You will feel a puff of air for the aspirated consonants.) So if these English initial voiceless consonants are pronounced with extra aspiration in all positions in a word, they will be close to the Gujarati aspirated consonants. The aspirated Gujarati consonants will require more effort to pronounce than their unaspirated counterparts. At first, when you hear these two types of consonants pronounced by a Gujarati speaker they will all sound more like their voiced counterparts (for example, *g, d, b*) which are unaspirated in all positions in English. The voiced aspirates, which are accompanied by extra breath, are difficult for a native English speaker, and care should be taken to avoid making them disyllabic (e.g. you might say *baha* instead of *bha*).

The English so-called dental consonants (*t*, *d*, *n*) are articulated in a position in between the Gujarati dentals and retroflexes. The Gujarati dentals are pronounced like the Italian dentals, with the tongue in a position to pronounce English *thin*. The retroflex consonants, which are found in all Indian languages, are the sounds that characterize Indian English to foreigners. To an English speaker, the Indian dentals sound closer to the English dentals, but to a speaker of Gujarati, the English dentals sound more like the retroflexes. The retroflexes are articulated with the back of the tip of the tongue touching the upper palate. It is usually the dentals that the English speaker finds harder to pronounce, and the feature of aspiration makes these even more difficult! Gujarati native speakers will, of course, encounter a different set of problems. Many of them will be speakers of a dialect of Gujarati and will find some differences between their variety of the language and the written form. The standard spelling (and pronunciation) of a word may be very different from that expected, and care must be taken to learn the standard spellings and grammatical forms.

The Gujarati syllabary

The standard modern system of transliteration (the writing of Gujarati in the roman alphabet) has been used with the traditional use of **ṃ** to indicate nasalization. In the written form, Gujarati syllables are named by adding the ending કાર **kār** to a given character (e.g. ક **ka** + કાર **kār** is કકાર **kakār**, the character **ka**). The only exception is ર **ra**, which is known as રેફ **reph**.

The consonants below have been divided into groups according to standard phonetic classifications.

CONSONANTS

ક	**ka**	The *k* sound as in *sky*, but with less release of breath.
ખ	**kha**	The *k* sound as in *cot*, but with more release of breath.
ગ	**ga**	The *g* sound as in *go*, but with less release of breath.
ઘ	**gha**	The strongly aspirated counterpart of the above – like *dog-house* said quickly.
ચ	**ca**	The *ch* sound as in *cheese*, but with less release of breath, and with the tongue in the same position as for the English *t* and then released slowly and with no lip-rounding, somewhat similar to *tube*.
છ	**cha**	The strongly aspirated counterpart of the above.
જ	**ja**	The tongue should be in the same position as for the English *t* sound and then should be released slowly as in *jeer*, but with less breath and with no lip-rounding, somewhat similar to *duty*. In some borrowed words, the English *z* sound may be found, but most Gujarati speakers write and say *j* in this position.
ઝ	**jha**	The strongly aspirated counterpart of the above, somewhat like English *bridge*. This sign is used for writing English *z* which is pronounced as *jh* by many Gujarati speakers.
ટ	**ṭa**	This is the first of the retroflex consonants described above. It is pronounced somewhat similarly to *train*, but with the tongue curled further back and with less aspiration.
ઠ	**ṭha**	The strongly aspirated counterpart of the above.
ડ	**ḍa**	This voiced counterpart of **ṭa**, when pronounced in between vowels, has a less tense contact and is 'flapped', that is, the tongue makes only light contact with the roof of the mouth and then falls forward.
ઢ	**ḍha**	The strongly aspirated counterpart of the above.
ત	**ta**	As mentioned above, the relaxed tip of the tongue should be touching the back of the upper front teeth, in a similar position as for English *thin*, but pronounced as *stay*.
થ	**tha**	The strongly aspirated counterpart of the above.
દ	**da**	The voiced counterpart of **ta**, as in *breadth*.
ધ	**dha**	The strongly aspirated counterpart of the above.
પ	**pa**	Unaspirated as in *spade*.
ફ	**pha**	This is the aspirated form of **pa**, but most Gujaratis pronounce it like the *f* in *for*.

બ	**ba**	The *b* sound as in *be*.
ભ	**bha**	The strongly aspirated counterpart of the above.
ઙ	**ṅa**	The velar nasal as in *sing*.
ઞ	**ña**	The palatal nasal as in *onion*.
ણ	**ṇa**	This is a retroflex nasal, pronounced with the tongue in a similar position as for the retroflex stops, but less tense and with some flap. It rarely comes at the beginning of words.
ન	**na**	The *n* sound as in *no*.
મ	**ma**	The *m* sound as in *me*.
શ	**śa**	This is pronounced further forward in the mouth than English *ship* and with less lip-rounding.
ષ	**ṣa**	This was originally a retroflex, but it is usually pronounced as X **śa**.
સ	**sa**	This is similar to the *s* in the English word *sat*, although the tip of the tongue should be further forward in the mouth.

You should note that in many dialects of Gujarati there is no contrast between the three s sounds, and that **શ śa** is pronounced in most instances except before or after **i**. In colloquial (non-standard) speech **s** is pronounced as an aspirate (**ha**).

ર	**ra**	The tip of the tongue should actually touch the teeth ridge, as for English *t*, but pronounced like a Scottish rolled *r* although shorter. It is never lost like the English *r* in *motor* or *farm*.
લ	**la**	This is similar to the *l* in *leaf* or *feeling*, but not as in the southern English *feel* or *well*. The tongue should be in a similar position as for English *t*.
ળ	**ḷa**	This is a retroflex lateral, with the tongue in similar position as for a retroflex stop, but less tense, and with some flap.
ય	**ya**	This palatal semi-vowel is pronounced as in *yes* before a vowel and as in *egg* before a consonant.
વ	**va**	This labial semi-vowel is pronounced somewhere between English *v* and w, although without lip-rounding and with only a slight contact between the lower lip and the upper teeth.
હ	**ha**	Similar to the English *h* except that it has some voicing, as in *ahead*.

00.01 Activity A

It is easiest to learn to write Gujarati on lined paper, with each character hanging from the line. The characters are not difficult to learn and with regular practice can be learned in a couple of weeks.

1 **The following Gujarati words are arranged in alphabetical order. Practise pronouncing them. You may find it easiest to copy them out, then to copy out each character separately. For example:**

કમળ = ક + મ + ળ = **ka** + **ma** + **ḷ** **(a)**

ખબર	ધન	ટપક	યમ
ગરજ	નજર	ઠગ	રસ
ઘર	પદ	ડર	વખત
ચકમક	ફળ	ઢગ	શમ
છ	બચત	તક	સહન
જઠર	ભરત	થર	હવન
ઝટપટ	મઠ	દળ	

2 **The diagram on page xxxvi shows how the consonantal characters are formed. Practise writing them out, moving your pen in the direction of the arrows.**

3 **Now try writing out the following transliterated words in the Gujarati script. You may find it helpful to begin by segmenting them as in the first example:**

kamaḷ = **ka** + **ma** + **ḷa** = ક + મ + ળ = કમળ

phaḷ	**naḷ**	**naram**	**maḍh**
harap	**mat**	**bhay**	**batak**
kaḍak	**kam**	**saras**	**nakh**
hak	**maphat**	**taras**	**pal**
saḍak	**ṭak**	**baraph**	**vatan**
maraṇ	**man**	**ṭak**	**baḷ**
bhagat	**pag**	**nat**	**lasaṇ**
pharaj	**yam**	**paṭ**	**nar**
haṭh	**pad**	**kapaṭ**	**par**

VOWELS

The vowels of Gujarati are also different from English vowels. There are pure vowels (those where only one sound is made, for example, the English word *ago*) and diphthongs (where two vowels are combined and the sound changes, for example, English *bake*, where the a combines *a* and *i* sounds).

You saw in the introduction to the script that unless vowels precede syllables, they are written as part of the consonant with which they form syllables. The following examples are all shown with ક **ka**, but the same rule applies with most consonants.

અ	**a**	ક	**ka**	as in *ago*
આ	**ā**	કા	**kā**	as in *part*
ઇ	**i**	કિ	**ki**	as in *bit* (see below).
ઈ	**ī**	કી	**kī**	as in *beat* (see below).
ઉ	**u**	કુ	**ku**	as in *foot* (**ru** is written રુ) (see below).
ઊ	**ū**	કૂ	**kū**	as in *food* (**rū** is written રૂ)

As mentioned above, many Gujarati speakers do not distinguish between long and short i and u sounds.

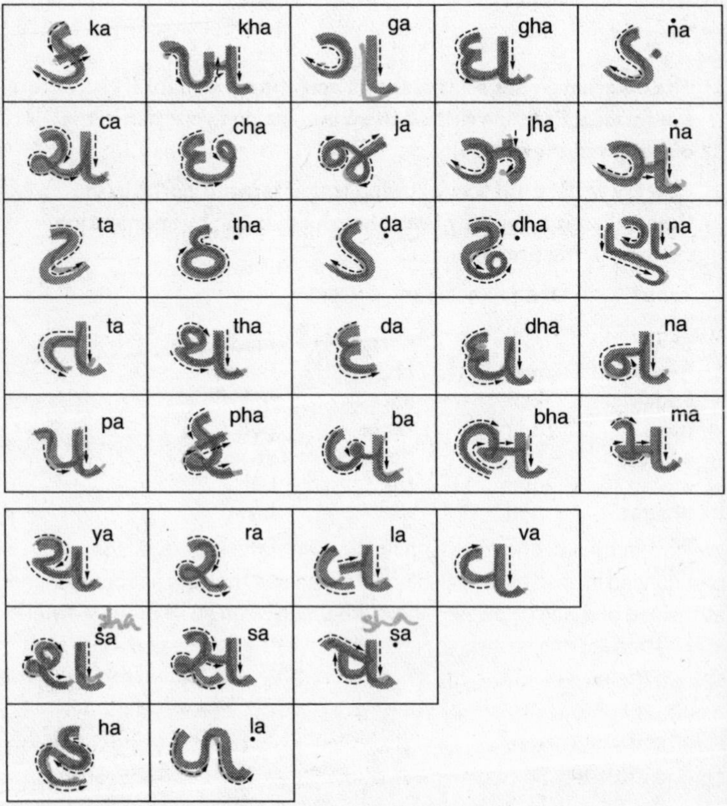

ઋ	**ṛ**	કૃ	**kṛu**	as in southern English *rook*. This sound is found only in Sanskrit loan words.
એ	**e**	કે	**ke**	as in the first part of English *day*. This is a pure vowel, not a diphthong as in English. There are two variants (which you will hear in the recording).
ઐ	**ai**	કૈ	**kai**	as in English *mice*
ઓ	**o**	કો	**ko**	as in the first part of English *hotel*

This is a pure vowel, not a diphthong as in English. There are two variants (which you will hear in the recording).

ઔ	**au**	કૌ	**kau**	as in English *house*

Nasalization

Most of the vowels above may occur with nasalization, that is, a large amount of breath that passes through the nose as the vowel is being pronunced. This is indicated in the script by an **anusvāra**, a dot that is placed above the vowel or consonant, and in transliteration with **ṃ**. Care must be taken not to pronounce this as a full English *m*, but rather as a nasalized vowel.

The **anusvāra** is also used to indicate any of the five nasal consonants of the syllabary when they occur as the first member of a conjunct (see page xxix), where the dot is written above the preceding character, for example, દુઃખ **Iṃdra** (the name of a god).

Visarga

This sign looks somewhat like a colon and may occur in the middle or at the end of a word. It occurs rarely and is not usually pronounced in Gujarati. It is transliterated as **ḥ**, for example દુઃખ **duḥkh**. It is found most frequently in Sanskrit loan words.

Inherent a

We saw in the introduction to this section that inherent **a** is not pronounced in unstressed positions. This means that **a** is not pronounced at the end of a word. However, there are times when an inherent **a** vowel is not stressed and so also not pronounced in the middle of a word, even though the spelling is not with a conjunct. The general rule is that when a word has three or more script syllables (or ends in a vowel other than the inherent **a**), the penultimate inherent vowel is not pronounced. Thus, સમજ **samaj**, but સમજણ **samjaṇ**; રચન **racan**, but રચના **racnā**.

This general rule does not always hold, but one soon becomes aware of how a word is pronounced. If the infinitive ending વું **vuṃ** is final, it is an exception to this rule; thus, સમજવું **samajvuṃ**.

00.02 Activity B

1 The following Gujarati words are arranged in alphabetical order. Practise writing them out. You may find it easiest to copy them out, then to separate each character, for example:

અધિકમાસ = અ + ધિ + ક + મા + સ = **a** + **dhi** + **ka** + **mā** + **s(a)** = (by the rule on inherent **a**) **adhikmās.**

અધિકાર	ઔષધ	એક	જમીન
આડણી	કારેલું	ઔડ	તિલક
ઈકોતેર	ખુશ	ઓછું	દલિત
ઈમાન	ગેંડો	નિવાસ	બોલાવવું
ઉપર	ઘેર	પેટી	લીધું
ઊનું	ચોપન	પાકવું	સંધિ
ઋણ	છોકરી		

2 Practise writing the vowels according to the following diagram.

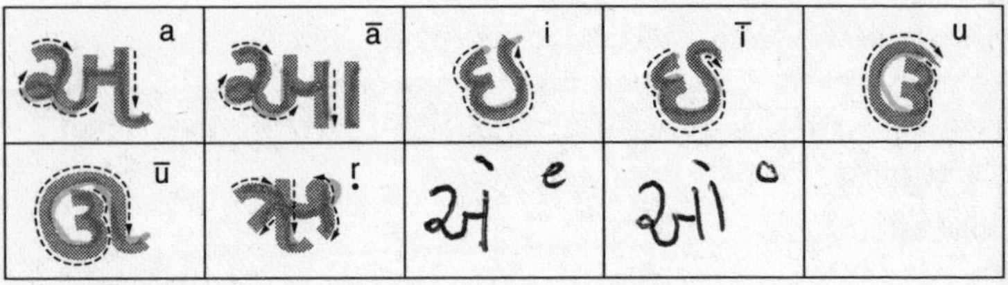

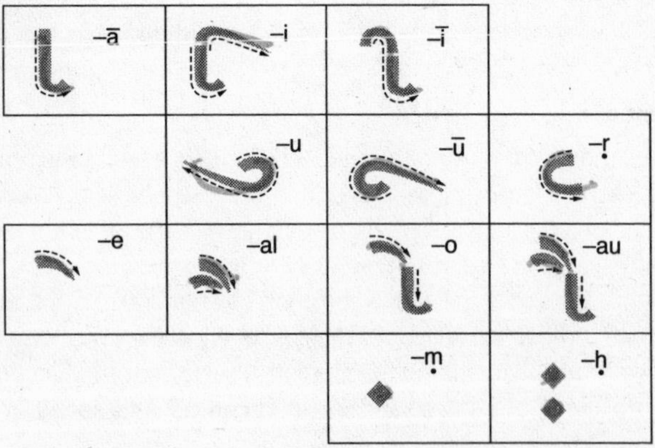

3 Write out the following transliterated words in Gujarati script, rereading the note on inherent a before beginning the second column. For example:

vahāṇ = **va** + **hā** + **ṇ(a)** = વ + હા + ણ = વહાણ

aṃg	**auṣadhī**	**uṭhāvvuṃ**	**ṣaṭkoṇ**
āṃgaḷiyāt	**utāvaḷ**	**ūtarvuṃ**	**oḷkhīto**
iśu	**ūn**	**orḍo**	**khurśī**
āśā	**jāuṃ**	**oṭlī**	**keṭluṃ**
uṃdar	**ṭhaḷiyo**	**talvār**	**āvjo**
ūṃṭ	**dayārām**	**amdāvād**	**garmī**
eśiyā	**gujarātī**	**jāmphaḷ**	**āṃgaṇ**
aitihāsik	**īḍlīpiḍlī**	**sapharjan**	**gamtuṃ**
audīc		**baḍbaḍ**	

CONJUNCT CHARACTERS

These are characters that form special combinations with vowels.

જ	ja	
	જા	**jā**
	જી	**jī**
	જુ	**ju**
	જૂ	**jū**
ર	ra	
	રુ	**ru**
	રૂ	**rū**
દ	da	
	દૃ	**dṛ**
હ	ha	
	હૃ	**hṛ**

Special conjunct characters are used when two characters are combined with no inherent **a** between them. The list in Appendix 1 shows almost all of the possible combinations. Most conjunct characters use simply a half-form (the first stroke) of the first consonant, and the others are quickly recognizable. The sign (called **virām**) under the first character shows that the inherent vowel is missing. For example:

ન્ **n** + ય **ya** = ન્ય **nya**

કન્યા **kanyā**

Conjunct characters combine with vowels in the same way as single consonants. For example:

સ્ **s** + મ **ma** = સ્મ **sma**

સ્મિતા **smitā**

ર **ra** needs some extra attention. If it is the first member of a consonant cluster, it is written as " at the very end of the syllable. For example:

સ્વર્ગ **svarg** વર્ગો **vargo**

If it is the second member of a consonant cluster, it is written below the first consonant in a number of ways. For example:

પ્ર **pra**, ત્ર **tra**, ટ્ર **ṭra**, ડ્ર **ḍra**

Do not worry about learning all of these immediately, but have a careful look through them so that you will be able to recognize them when you first meet them. In the third of the script activities below you will also practise writing them.

Here are some frequently occurring conjunct characters which are not immediately recognizable:

ક્ **k** + ર **ra** = ક્ર **kra**

ક્ **k** + ષ **śa** = ક્ષ **kṣa**

જ્ **j** + ઞ **ña** = જ્ઞ **jña**

દ્ **d** + મ **ma** = દ્મ **dma**

દ્ **d** + ય **ya** = દ્ય **dya**

દ્ **d** + ર **ra** = દ્ર **dra**

દ્ **d** + વ **va** = દ્વ **dva**

પ્ **p** + ર **ra** = પ્ર **pra**

બ્ **b** + ર **ra** = બ્ર **bra**

ત્ **t** + ત **ta** = ત્ત **tta**

ત્ **t** + ર **ra** = ત્ર **tra**

દ્ **d** + દ **da** = દ્દ **dda**

ભ્ **bh** + ર **ra** = ભ્ર **bhra**

શ્ **ś** + ચ **sa** = શ્ચ **śca**

શ્ **ś** + ન **na** = શ્ન **śna**

શ્ **ś** + ર **ra** = શ્ર **śra**

શ્ **ś** + વ **va** = શ્વ **śva**

00.03 Activity C

1 The following Gujarati words are arranged in alphabetical order. Practise writing them out. You may find it easiest to copy them out, then to write out each character separately, for example:

નિ + શ્ચ (શ+ચ) + ય = **ni** + **śca** + **y** = **niścay**

અક્ષર	નિષ્કલંક	જિલ્લો	રજોગુણ
આજ્ઞા	નિઃસ્પંદ	ટ્રેન	રાજીવ
ઉદ્ભવ	પદ્મા	દક્ષિણ	શુદ્ધાદ્વૈત
ઉદ્યોગ	પર્યષક	દૃઢ	શ્રીજી
કાર્યક્રમ	પિત્રાઈ	દ્રાવિડ	શ્વાસ
ચશ્મા	પ્રતિપત્તિ	દ્વાર	હૃદય
જાનુ	ફારુક	ધર્મપતિ	

2 Practise writing the conjunct characters in the following diagram.

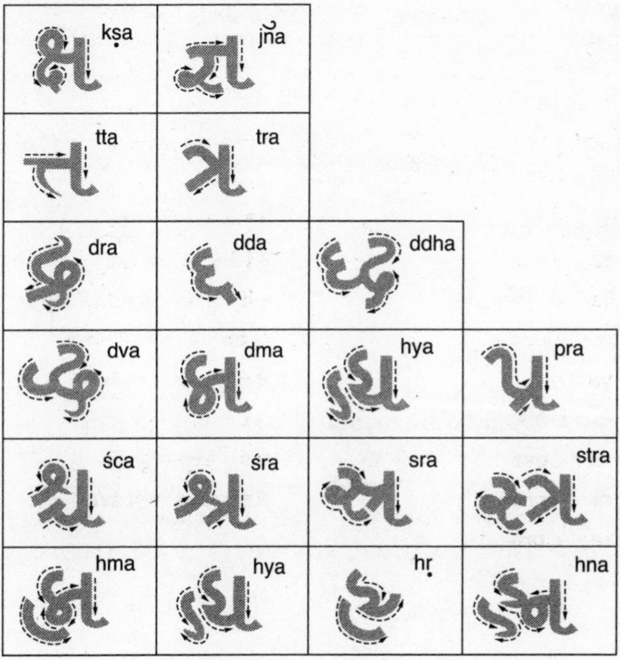

3 Write the following words out in Gujarati script. For example:

kṣetra = ક્ષેત્ર

Do this transliteration carefully and piece by piece:

(i) **kṣ** + **e** = **kṣe** (ii) **kṣe** + **tra** = **kṣetra** → (i) ક્ષ + એ = ક્ષે (ii) ક્ષે + ત્ર = ક્ષેત્ર

iṃdra	**maṇikarṇikā**	**drākṣa**	**bhāī**
iśk	**rakṣābandhan**	**viṣṇu**	**svīkār**
īrṣyā	**ṛgved**	**kṛṣṇa**	
ektā	**buddha**	**prakṛti**	
sāhitya	**dveṣ**	**śabda**	
yunivarsiṭī	**dhyān**	**utsav**	
jñān	**pyār**	**patra**	
aṃgreji	**ḍabbo**	**viśvās**	
pātra	**jvar**	**sthiti**	
joḍī	**iṣṭa**	**snān**	
joban	**caitra**	**rāṣṭra**	
netra	**khinna**	**śrī**	
pṛthvī	**āścarya**	**sṭeśan**	
najīk	**iṭhṭhoter**	**vidyārthī**	

PRONUNCIATION

It is helpful if you can find a native speaker of Gujarati to check your pronunciation. You will also find the recordings that accompany this course useful.

It is important to note the following:

- Doubled consonants must be pronounced with lengthening, or lingering briefly on the repeated sound. For example: પક્કું **pakkuṃ**.
- The inherent vowel **a** is not pronounced at the end of a word. However, when a word ends in a conjunct of two or more consonants, an 'echo' of the a vowel may be heard at the end of the consonant cluster. For example: યોગ્ય **yogy(a)**, રાષ્ટ્ર **raṣṭr(a)**.
- There are times when an inherent **a** vowel is not pronounced in the middle of a word, even though the spelling is not with a conjunct.
- No attempt has been made here to reproduce stress or intonation patterns in writing. You should learn these by listening to the recording and to native speakers.

PUNCTUATION

Modern Gujarati has adopted the same punctuation as English. For abbreviations, Gujarati uses a small circle (°) after the first syllable of the word abbreviated: thus, રૂ° **ru-** stands for રૂપિયા **rūpiyā**. With the initials of proper names, a Gujarati transliteration of the English form may be used, for example, બી°જે°પી° **bī.je.pī**. or ભા°જ°પા° **bhā.ja.pa.** may stand for *BJP* (*Bharatiya Janata Party*).

Sometimes ઓ is written ઑ to represent the English sound *o* in words like ચોકલેટ **cokleṭ** *chocolate*.

ALTERNATIVE SPELLINGS

Spelling was standardized in Gujarati only in the early twentieth century. Although it is mostly fixed, older texts (and dictionaries!) may fluctuate in spelling between long and short **i** and **u** (this is in part due to the fact that some Gujaratis do not distinguish these sounds in speech). It is important to learn the correct dictionary spelling.

NUMERALS

Numerals will be explained in more detail in Unit 7.

૧	૨	૩	૪	૫	૬	૭	૮	૯	૧૦
1	2	3	4	5	6	7	8	9	10

Practise writing the numerals out using the following diagram below as a model.

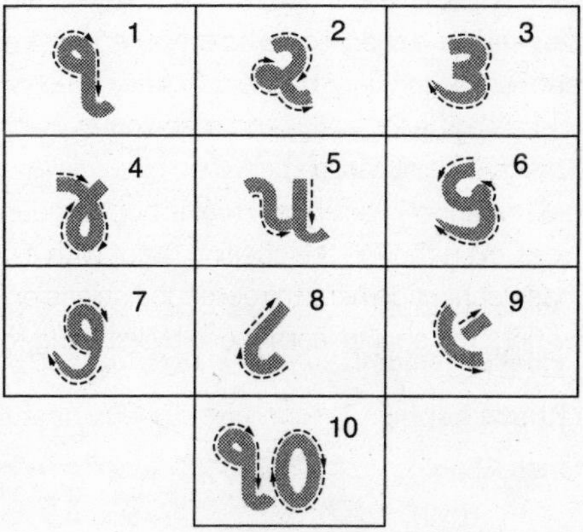

1 તમે કેમ છો? tame kem cho? *How are you?*

In this unit, you will learn how to:

- ***give information about yourself.***
- ***ask other people questions about themselves.***
- ***describe things and people.***
- ***exchange greetings.***

ગુજરાત અને ગુજરાતીઓ gujarāt ane gujarātīo *Gujarat and Gujaratis*

Members of the Daudi Bohra community, a well-known sect of Shi'a Islam, live primarily in the city of Mumbai and in regions of southern Gujarat (see Introduction). During the partition of 1947 some Daudi Bohras, as well as other Gujarati Muslims, migrated from today's India to Pakistan, where they settled mainly in Karachi and the region of Sindh. Today these communities are often multilingual (as are many South Asian communities), speaking not only Gujarati, but also Urdu and other local languages such as Sindhi. All of these languages share certain similarities, including words and expressions that derive from Arabic and Persian. While different accents and colloquialisms in spoken Gujarati might reveal which region a speaker hails from, the only notable differences in Gujarati spoken by members of different religious communities in the same region arise when discussing religious issues or when exchanging greetings. Some of the most commonly used Muslim greetings are:

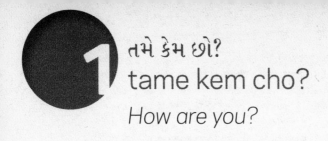

સલામ અલેકુમ!	**salām alekum!**	*hello!* (lit. *peace be on you!*)
વાલેકુમ સલામ!	**vālekum salām!**	*hello!* (in reply) (lit. *and peace on you!*)
ખુદા હાફિઝ!	**Khudā haphij!**	*goodbye!* (lit. *God be with you!*)
ઇન્શા અલ્લાહ!	**inśā Allah!**	*God willing!* (used by many Muslims when talking about any future event)

માશા અલ્લાહ!	**māśā Allāh!**	*may God save us!* (lit. *whatever God wills!*) This phrase may be used to counteract the effects of the evil eye (નજર **najar**). In this context, Hindus, Jains and Parsis may say ઓવાયું! **ovāryuṃ!** *blessings!*

In many communities across South Asia it is believed that the malignant effect of the evil eye arises when envy occurs. Children are thought to be highly susceptible to the evil eye, and so care should be taken when praising them, especially their beauty. Applying a black circle of *kajal* (કાજલ **kājaḷ**), a cosmetic used on the eyes, on children's faces makes their beauty imperfect, and is thus thought to protect them from the evil eye. Lemons and chillies are also believed to be effective in warding off the evil eye and can often be seen hanging over doorways and on motor vehicles for this purpose. A passage in Rohinton Mistry's book *Such a long journey* describes a woman's attempts to remove the evil eye from her son.

Vocabulary builder

નમસ્તે!	namaste!	*greetings!* (a respectful salutation common to many South Asian languages, which is used especially among Hindu communities)
તમે કેમ છો?	tame kem cho?	*how are you?* (formal use; can also mean *hello* informally)
હું મજામાં છું	huṃ majāmāṃ chuṃ	*I am fine*
કેમ છે?	kem che?	*how are you?* (informal)
મજામાં	majāmāṃ	*fine*
હું દીપક છું	huṃ Dīpak chuṃ	*I am Deepak*
તમે નીલાબેન છો?	tame Nīlāben cho?	*are you Neelaben?*
ના	nā	*no*
નથી	nathi	*(am/is/are) not*
આ નીલા છે	ā Nīlā che	*this is Neela*
તું ભારતીય છે?	tuṃ bhāratīy che?	*are you Indian?*
જી હા	jī hā	*yes* (formal)
આપણે ગુજરાતી છીએ	āpṇe gujarātī chīe	*we are Gujarati*
એ લોકો ભારતીય છે?	e loko bhāratīy che?	*are those people Indian?*
ના, તેઓ ભારતીય નથી	nā, teo bhāratīy nathī	*no, they are not Indian*
તેઓ પાકિસ્તાની છે	teo pākistānī che	*they are Pakistani*

તમે કેમ છો? TAME KEM CHO? HOW ARE YOU?

01.01 *Mr Deepak Mehta, who has just come to the United Kingdom from Mumbai, is being met at the airport by Leela Patel and her daughter Neela.*

1 How do Deepak, Leela and Neela introduce and describe themselves to each other? Has Deepak met Leela and Neela before coming to the United Kingdom?

Dialogue 1

દીપક	**નમસ્તે! તમે કેમ છો?**
Dīpak	namaste! tame kem cho?
લીલા	**હું મજામાં છું. કેમ છે?**
Līlā	huṃ majāmāṃ chuṃ. kem che?
દીપક	**મજામાં. હું દીપક છું. તમે નીલાબેન છો?**
Dīpak	majāmāṃ. huṃ Dipak chuṃ. Tame Nīlāben cho?
લીલા	**ના, હું નીલા નથી. આ નીલા છે. હું લીલા છું.**
Līlā	na, huṃ Nīlā nathī. ā Nīlā che. huṃ Līlā chuṃ
દીપક	**કેમ છે, નીલા? તું ભારતીય છે?**
Dīpak	kem che, Nīlā? tuṃ bhāratīy che?
નીલા	**જી હા, હું ભારતીય છું.**
Nīlā	jī, hā, huṃ bhāratīy chuṃ.
લીલા	**આપણે ગુજરાતી છીએ.**
Līlā	āpṇe gujarātī chīe.
(Neela sees a group of people; she wonders whether they are Indian.)	
નીલા	**દીપકભાઈ, એ લોકો ભારતીય છે?**
Nīlā	Dīpakbhāī, e loko bhāratīy che?
દીપક	**ના, તેઓ ભારતીય નથી, તેઓ પાકિસ્તાની છે.**
Dīpak	nā, teo bhāratīy nathī, teo pākistānī che.

2 True or false? Correct and rewrite the following sentences. Here's an example to start you off:

નીલા અંગ્રેજ છે. Nīlā aṃgrej che.

ના, નીલા અંગ્રેજ નથી. nā, Nīlā aṃgrej nathī.

નીલા ભારતીય છે. Nīlā bhāratīy che.

a **લીલાબેન ગુજરાતી છે.**
Līlāben gujarātī che.

b **એ લોકો ગુજરાતી નથી.**
e loko gujarātī nathī.

NEW VOCABULARY

અંગ્રેજ	**aṃgrej**	*English, British*
અમેરિકન	**amerikan**	*American*

3 Answer the following questions.

a દીપકભાઈ ગુજરાતી છે?
Dīpakbhāī gujarātī che?

b નીલા અમેરિકન છે?
Nīlā amerikan che?

Language discovery

Read and listen to the dialogue again.

Pay special attention to the underlined words, all of which are different forms of the same verb: હોવું **hovuṃ**, which you will be learning more about in this unit. Can you try to guess what the meaning of this verb is from reading and listening to the dialogue and from hints in the Vocabulary builder?

1 PERSONAL PRONOUNS, DEMONSTRATIVE PRONOUNS AND THE SIMPLE PRESENT TENSE OF હોવું **HOVUṂ** *TO BE*

When you study the following verbs you will notice that, just as in English, the verb is conjugated so that it matches the pronoun it is used with. For example, in the simple present tense, હોવું **hovuṃ** becomes છું **chuṃ** *am* to agree with હું **huṃ** *I*. So હું છું **huṃ chuṃ** = *I am*. Look at the dialogue again – can you find all the pronouns (and proper names) that correspond to the underlined forms of હોવું **hovuṃ**?

Singular			
First person	હું છું	**huṃ chuṃ**	*I am*
Second person	તું છે	**tuṃ che**	*you are* (informal)
Third person	તે છે (and આ, એ છે)	**te che** (and **ā**, **e che**)	*he, she, it is* (and *he, she, it* or *this, that is*)
Plural			
First person	અમે છીએ આપણે છીએ	**ame chīe** **āpṇe chīe**	*we are* (exclusive) *we are* (inclusive)
Second person	તમે છો આપ છો	**tame cho** **āp cho**	*you are* (formal) *you are* (formal)
Third person	તેઓ, તે છે (and આ, એ છે)	**teo, te che** (and **ā**, **e che**)	*they are* (and *they* or *these, those are*)

First person pronoun (*I*, *we*)

The first person plural pronoun (*we*) makes a distinction between inclusive and exclusive forms: **આપણે āpṇe** *we* is used when both the speaker and the person(s) addressed are referred to by the pronoun. When the person addressed is not included, **અમે ame** *we* is used. For example:

- ▶ **અમે ભારતીય છીએ ame bhāratīy chīe** *we are Indian*. In this sentence *we* (**અમે ame**) indicates that the speaker and others are Indian, but that the person addressed by the speaker is not (exclusive).
- ▶ **આપણે ભારતીય છીએ apṇe bhāratīy chīe** *we are Indian*. In this sentence, however, *we* (**આપણે apṇe**) includes the person being addressed by the speaker – he or she is also Indian (inclusive).

Second person pronoun (*you*)

In addition to the distinction between singular and plural forms, there is also a distinction between informal and formal forms with the second person pronoun.

a The informal (sometimes called the familiar) second person pronoun (**તું tuṃ**) is used when the speaker is addressing a person much younger than him or herself, a person of lower status (e.g. as a teacher to a student), a close friend, or an intimate family member (often younger than the speaker). Some speakers, notably speakers of Parsi Gujarati, use **તું tuṃ** more readily than others when talking to contemporaries. Beginners in Gujarati, however, should exercise caution and use the formal second person pronoun (**તમે tame**) when there is any doubt.

b The formal second person pronoun (**તમે tame**) is used when the speaker is addressing older relatives, any older person, or a person of higher status (e.g. as a student to a teacher). Gujarati speakers may occasionally use **આપ āp** (which is also the formal second person pronoun in Hindi and other related languages) when addressing someone of markedly higher status, or when wishing to imply such status.

c The second person plural form of the informal **તું tuṃ** is **તમે tame** (e.g. **તમે લોકો tame loko** *you people*), whereas the plural form of the formal **તમે tame** remains **તમે tame**. That is, **તમે tame** and **આપ āp** are grammatically plural, even when used as logical singulars (e.g. **તમે દીપકભાઈ છો, tame Dīpakbhāī cho** *you are Deepakbhai*).

Third person pronoun (*he, she, they, it* **and** *this, that, these, those***)**

While Gujarati nouns and adjectives are modified according to gender, there is no marking of gender in the third person pronoun as there is in English. The third person pronouns તે te, **આ ā** and **એ e** are all used when referring to a singular male or female person (*he* or *she*) who would be addressed informally as **તું tuṃ**. These pronouns are also used to refer to inanimate (non-living) objects (*it* and *this* or *that*). As in other South Asian languages, Gujarati differentiates between objects and persons according to their distance from the speaker: **આ ā** is the pronoun used when an object (*it* or *this*) or person (*he* or *she*) is near to the speaker, and **એ e** is used when something (*it* or *that* or *those*) or someone (*he* or *she*) is at a distance from the speaker. **તે te** is sometimes considered to be a more formal form of **એ e**, but can also be used to refer to singular objects or to a singular person who a speaker refers to informally. Here are some examples:

આ/તે પાકિસ્તાની છે	**ā/te pākistānī che**	*he/she/it/this* (near to speaker) *is Pakistani*
એ/તે પાકિસ્તાની છે	**e/te pākistānī che**	*he/she/this* (far from speaker) *is Pakistani*

The plural form of the third person pronoun **તેઓ teo** is used to refer to more than one person. **તેઓ teo** is also used formally to refer to a person addressed by the second person formal pronouns **તમે tame** or **આપ āp** (e.g. હા, તેઓ છે, દીપકભાઈ **hā, teo che, Dīpakbhāī** *Yes, it is him, Deepakbhai*). **તેઓ teo** is used to refer to people both near and far from the speaker, but is never used to refer to inanimate objects: when referring to plural objects **તે te**, **આ ā**, or **એ e** should be used as shown above. Here are some examples:

તેઓ પાકિસ્તાની છે	**teo pākistānī che**	*he, she* (formal) *is Pakistani; they are Pakistani*
તે/આ/એ પાકિસ્તાની છે	**te/ā/e pākistānī che**	*these, those are Pakistani* (also: *he, she* (informal) and *this, that is Pakistani*)

As you might have guessed, the third person pronouns that we have just learned can also be used demonstratively, or as noun markers. Just as in English we can say *this person* or *those people*, Gujarati demonstrative pronouns can be used to 'point' towards nouns. For example:

આ વ્યક્તિ પાકિસ્તાની છે	ā vyaktī pākistānī che	*this person is Pakistani*
એ લોકો પાકિસ્તાની છે	e loko pākistānī che	*those people are Pakistani*

Note that એ લોકો **e loko** (lit. *those people*) is used frequently to mean simply *they*, just as તમે લોકો **tame loko** (lit. *you people*) means *you* (plural).

1 Now you have learned all the basics of how pronouns work with verbs in the simple present tense. Test your knowledge by matching the following pronouns with the correct verb ending of the verb હોવું hovuṃ *to be* **(છું chuṃ, છીએ chīe, છો cho, or છે che). After you complete each sentence with the correct form of the verb say the sentence out loud in Gujarati and then translate it into English.**

a હું ગુજરાતી hum̩ gujarātī ____________________
b તમે લોકો પંજાબી tame loko paṃjābī ____________________
c તું ભારતીય tuṃ bhāratīy ____________________
d તે પાકિસ્તાની te pākistānī ____________________
e અમે અંગ્રેજ ame aṃgrej ____________________
f તેઓ બંગાળી teo baṃgāḷī ____________________

2 NEGATION IN THE SIMPLE PRESENT TENSE

In the simple present tense the negative of the verb હોવું **hovuṃ** *to be* for all pronouns (*I*, *we*, *you*, *they*, *he*, *she*, *it*, *these*, *those*, etc.) is નથી **nathī**. નથી **nathī** is never followed by an auxiliary, so the use of નથી છે **nathī che** to mean *is not* is always incorrect! Here are some examples of how નથી **nathī** is used to negate simple present tense statements:

તમે પંજાબી નથી	**tame paṃjābī nathī**	*you are not Punjabi*
હું અંગ્રેજ નથી	**huṃ aṃgrej nathī**	*I am not English*
તેઓ ગુજરાતી નથી	**teo gujarātī nathī**	*they are not Gujarati*

You could replace any of the verb endings that you used for the above exercise with નથી **nathī** and your answers would also be correct!

3 SIMPLE QUESTIONS AND ANSWERS

In English we can form simple questions by changing the word order of a sentence. For example, *you are Gujarati* can be made into a question by changing the word order to *are you Gujarati?* We can also make the sentence a question by simply changing our intonation (*you are Gujarati?*, with our voice rising at the end of the sentence). Gujarati questions can be formed in similar ways. For example:

તમે ગુજરાતી છો	**tame gujarātī cho**	*you are Gujarati*
તમે ગુજરાતી છો?	**tame gujarātī cho?**	*you are Gujarati?*

When you listen to the dialogues, you will notice the difference between the statements and the questions because the questions have a rising tone.

In English, the reply to a question usually has the following pattern: *Are you Gujarati? Yes, I am.* However, in Gujarati, it is common that most of the words in a question sentence are repeated in the reply. For example:

તમે ગુજરાતી છો?	**tame gujarātī cho?**	*you are Gujarati?*
હા, હું ગુજરાતી છું	**hā, huṃ gujarātī chuṃ**	*yes, I am Gujarati*
ના, હું ગુજરાતી નથી	**nā, huṃ gujarātī nathī**	*no, I am not Gujarati*

2 Turn the following statements into questions. Then answer the questions as if they were being addressed to you.

a તમે ભારતીય છો tame bhāratīy cho
b તમે અંગ્રેજ નથી tame aṃgrej nathī
c તમે અમેરિકન છો? tame amerikan cho?

4 GOOD MANNERS

When addressing someone whom you would call તમે **tame**, respectful terms such as ભાઈ **bhāī** (*brother*) or બેન **ben** (*sister*) are added to the name, as in લીલાબેન **Līlāben** and દીપકભાઈ **Dīpakbhāī**. Note that the word for sister is actually બહેન **bahen**, but in spoken Gujarati it sounds as though it is pronounced બેન **ben**. When used as this polite feminine suffix it is almost always written in this shortened manner. In Gujarati these terms are just are as polite as *Mr*, *Mrs*, or *Ms* in English. Even married couples will refer to one another by these terms when speaking to a third party. For example, if Mr Deepak Sharma introduced his wife, Mrs Lila Sharma, to a third party he might say આ લીલાબેન છે **ā Līlāben che** *This is Leelaben.*

Although હા **hā** and ના **nā** (*yes* and *no* respectively) are used on most occasions, some speakers use the more formal હા જી **hā jī** or જી હા **jī hā** (or simply જી **jī**) for *yes*, and ના જી **nā jī** for *no*. જી **jī** is a common expression of honour or respect and is much more commonly used in Gujarati's sister languages Hindi and Urdu. Therefore, જી **jī** is often used in Gujarati when referring to an individual who would be addressed as આપ **āp** *you* – also a common Hindi and Urdu pronoun.

નમસ્તે **namaste** *hello* or *goodbye* (lit. *homage to you*) is a formal greeting used by some Hindus and Jains. It is usually sufficient to say કેમ છો? **kem cho?** *how are you?* as a standard greeting. Likewise, આવજો **āvjo!** *goodbye!* (lit. *please come again*) is a standard way to bid farewell.

3 Test your understanding of negation in the simple present, simple questions and answers, and good manners by translating the following sentences from Gujarati into English.

a આ દીપકભાઈ છે — ā Dīpakbhāī che
b આ દીપકભાઈ છે? — ā Dīpakbhāī che?
c આ દીપકભાઈ નથી — ā Dīpakbhāī nathī
d નમસ્તે! કેમ છો, લીલાબેન? તમે ભારતીય છો? — namaste! kem cho, Līlāben? tame bhāratīy cho?
e હા જી, હું ગુજરાતી છું. આપ ભારતીય છો? — hā jī, huṃ gujarātī chuṃ. āp bhāratīy cho?
f ના, હું ભારતીય નથી – આવજો! — nā, huṃ bhāratīy nathī – āvjo!

Vocabulary builder

સારું છે	sāruṃ che	*(I'm) fine* (lit. *it is good*)
મોટા ભાઈ	moṭā bhāī	*older brother*
અને	ane	*and*
નાનો ભાઈ	nāno bhāī	*younger brother*
મોટી બહેન	moṭī bahen	*older sister*
અહીં	ahīṃ	*here*
નાનો	nāno	*young, small*
પણ	paṇ	*but, also*
હોશિયાર	hośiyār	*clever*
આળસુ	āḷsu	*lazy*
પેલી લાંબી છોકરી	pelī lāṃbī chokrī	*that tall girl*
ભલે	bhale	*well then, OK, so be it*
આવજો!	āvjo!	*goodbye!* (lit. *please come again!*)

1 01.02 **To whom does Neela introduce Deepak in the following dialogue? How does Neela describe the people she introduces to Deepak?**

Dialogue 2

નીલા	**કેમ છો, દીપકભાઈ?**
Nīlā	kem cho, Dīpakbhāī?
દીપક	**મજામાં. કેમ છે, નીલા?**
Dīpak	majāmāṃ. kem che, Nīlā?
નીલા	**સારું છે. આ મોટા ભાઈ, સેતુ, અને આ નાનો ભાઈ, સમીર. મોટી બહેન અહીં નથી.**
Nīlā	sāruṃ che. ā moṭā bhāī Setu, ane ā nāno bhāī Samīr. moṭī bahen ahīṃ nathī.
દીપક	**કેમ છો? સમીર, તું નાનો છે?**
Dīpak	kem cho? Samīr tuṃ nāno che?
સેતુ	**હા, એ નાનો છે, અને એ પણ હોશિયાર છે.**
Setu	hā, e nāno che, ane e paṇ hośiyār che.
દીપક	**તું પણ હોશિયાર છે, સેતુ?**
Dīpak	tuṃ paṇ hośiyār che, Setu?
નીલા	**તેઓ પણ હોશીયાર છે, પણ આળસુ છે!**
Nīlā	teo paṇ hośiyār che, paṇ āḷsu che!
દીપક	**પેલી લાંબી છોકરી શ્રુતિ છે!**
Dīpak	pelī lāṃbī chokrī Śruti che?
સમીર	**હા, મોટી બહેન છે!**
Samīr	ha, moṭī bahen che!
નીલા	**મોટી બહેન છે? ભલે. આવજો, દીપકભાઈ!**
Nīlā	moṭī bahen che? bhale. āvjo, Dīpakbhāī!
દીપક	**આવજો!**
Dīpak	āvjo!

2 True or false? Based on what you have just learned from the dialogue, correct the following sentences and translate your corrected sentences into English. Here is an example to start you off:

સેતુ નાનો ભાઈ છે.	**Setu nāno bhāī che.**	*Setu is the younger brother.*
ના, સેતુ નાનો નથી, એ મોટો ભાઈ છે.	**nā, Setu nāno nathī, e moṭo bhāī che.**	*No, Setu is not the younger brother, he is the older brother.*

a સેતુ હોશિયાર છે.
Setu hośiyār che.

b શ્રુતિ મોટી ભાઈ છે.
Śruti moṭī bhāī che.

3 Now answer the following questions about the dialogue.

a મોટી બહેન સેતુ છે?
moṭī bahen Setu che?

b શ્રુતિ લાંબી છે?
Śruti lāṃbī che?

Language discovery

Listen to the dialogue again.

a Pay special attention to the underlined words and use the Vocabulary builder to help you determine how these words work in the sentence. What do these underlined words do to the pronouns and nouns that they are paired with?

b If you look at the Vocabulary builder and dialogue again you will notice that one of the underlined words appears to have different endings in various places in the dialogue but means the same thing throughout. Can you find this word? Can you guess why this word changes its ending? (Here is a hint: the meaning of this word is *older* in English.)

5 NOUNS

You have already been introduced to a few nouns, for example ભાઈ **bhāī** *brother*. As in English, Gujarati nouns are either singular or plural (e.g. *chair* and *chairs*). Unlike English, however, all Gujarati nouns have a gender and are classified as either masculine, feminine, or neuter. These genders are called grammatical genders because there is no logical reason why, for example, ખુરશી **khurśī** *chair* should be feminine, rather than neuter or masculine. While you will have to learn the gender of each noun as you meet it, the following rules will help:

a Sometimes grammatical gender is the same as natural gender. That is, names or nouns that indicate male people are masculine, while names or nouns that indicate female people are feminine. For example, the noun બહેન **bahen** *sister* is feminine and the noun ભાઈ **bhāī** *brother* is masculine.

b Nearly all nouns ending in ઓ **-o** are masculine, nearly all nouns ending in ઉં **-uṃ** are neuter and most nouns ending in આ **ā**, ઈ **i**, ઈ **ī** or ઉ **u** are feminine.

c Rule **a** has precedence over rule **b** so that although a noun may end in ઈ **ī**, ભાઈ **bhāī** *brother*, as a naturally male gendered noun, is still masculine.

In Gujarati there is no definite article (*the*) or indefinite article (*a, an*), although એક **ek** *one* is sometimes used to mean *a*. Accordingly, ખુરશી **khurśī** can mean *chair*, *a chair*, or *the chair* (Remember that *this chair* or *that chair* would be તે/આ or તે/એ ખુરશી **te/ā** or **te/e khurśī**).

Many adjectives change their endings to agree with the nouns that they describe. For example, the adjective નાનું **nānuṃ** *young* or *small* becomes નાની **nānī** when it is used to describe a female noun, like ખુરશી **khurśī** *chair*, but નાનો **nāno** when it is used to describe a masculine noun, like ભાઈ **bhāī** *brother*. Because of this, you may find it helpful to learn Gujarati genders along with an adjective that changes according to its gender. For example, memorizing નાની ખુરશી **nānī khurśī** *small chair* may help you recall that ખુરશી **khurśī** *chair* is a feminine noun more easily than simply memorizing ખુરશી **khurśī** *chair* on its own.

The plural of all nouns (except masculine nouns ending in ઓ **-o** and neuter nouns ending in ઉં **-uṃ**) is formed by adding ઓ **-o** to the end of the word. However, when plurality is indicated by another word, such as a number like the adjective ચાર **cār** *four*, the ઓ **-o** ending is often omitted. For example:

બહેન	**bahen** (sing.)	*sister*	બહેનો	**baheno** (pl.)	*sisters*
ભાઈ	**bhāī** (sing.)	*brother*	ભાઈઓ	**bhāīo** (pl.)	*brothers*

But:

ચાર બહેન	**cār bahen** (pl.)	*four sisters*
ચાર ભાઈ	**cār bhāī** (pl.)	*four brothers*

The plural marker ઓ **-o** is not deleted if leaving it out would make the number of the noun unclear. For example:

બહેનો હોશિયાર છે	**baheno hośiyār che**	*the sisters are clever*
બહેન હોશિયાર છે	**bahen hośiyār che**	*the sister is clever*

But:

ચાર બહેન હોશિયાર છે	**cār bahen hośiyār che**	*the four sisters are clever*

An exception to this rule is that the final ઓ **-o** can never be omitted in the word લોકો **loko** (m. pl.) *people* because the noun is inherently plural.

Masculine nouns that already end in ઓ **-o**, such as છોકરો **chokro** *boy*, are pluralized by adding આઓ **-āo** to the end of the word. It is also possible simply to use આ **-ā** (without the ઓ **-o**) in all circumstances. For example:

છોકરો **chokro** (sing.) boy

છોકરાઓ, છોકરા	**chokrāo, chokrā** (pl.)	*boys*
છોકરો હોશિયાર છે	**chokro hośiyār che**	*the boy is clever*
છોકરા હાશિયાર છે	**chokrā hośiyār che**	*the boys are clever*

Or:

છોકરાઓ હોશિયાર છે	**chokrāo hośiyār che**	*the boys are clever*

Some nouns, such as the word છોકરું **chokruṃ** *child*, can assume any of the three genders. છોકરું **chokruṃ** *child* is neuter (that is, neither female nor masculine gender is specified), but may become છોકરો **chokro** *boy* (lit. *male child*), or છોકરી **chokrī** *girl* (lit. *female child*). All neuter nouns ending in ઉં **-uṃ** take the આં **-āṃ** ending when they become plural. The extended plural ending આંઓ **-āṃo** can also be used, although it is uncommon. For example:

છોકરું	**chokruṃ** (sing.)	*child*
છોકરાં, છોકરાંઓ	**chokrāṃ, chokrāṃo** (pl.)	*children*
છોકરું હોશિયાર છે	**chokruṃ hośiyār che**	*the child is clever*
છોકરાં હોશિયાર છે	**chokrāṃ hośiyār che**	*the children are clever*

Or:

છોકરાંઓ હોશિયાર છે	**chokrāṃo hośiyār che**	*the children are clever*

4 You have just learned a lot about Gujarati nouns and how they change depending on gender and number. Test your knowledge by completing the following activities.

a Just like the neuter noun છોકરું **chokruṃ** *child*, there are other variable nouns that can become masculine or feminine by replacing the ઉં **-uṃ** ending with આ **-ā** or ઈ **-ī** accordingly. Change the following two variable nouns into both their masculine and feminine forms.

વાંદરું vāṃdruṃ *monkey*
કૂતરું kūtruṃ *dog*

b Make the following singular nouns plural.

લાકડું	lākḍuṃ *wood* (n.)
જીવડું	jīvḍuṃ *insect* (n.)
બારી	bārī *window* (f.)
બગીચો	bagīcho *garden* (m.)

6 ADJECTIVES

In the previous dialogue you were asked to identify how the underlined words operated in the sentence: if you said that they were descriptive – that is, that they were adjectives – then you were correct. Gujarati has two types of adjectives: variable and invariable. Invariable adjectives (for example હોશિયાર **hośiyār** *clever*) do not change their endings even when they are used with nouns of different genders or numbers. For example:

છોકરી હોશિયાર છે	**chokrī hośiyār che**	*the girl is clever*
છોકરાં હોશિયાર છે	**chokrāṃ hośiyār che**	*the children are clever*

Variable adjectives change their form according to the gender and number of the nouns they describe. In dictionaries, as well as in the Vocabulary section at the end of this book, variable adjectives are displayed with the ending ઉં **-uṃ**, the neuter singular form (this is often the same for nouns that can be modified according to gender, like છોકરું **chokruṃ** *child*). You should note that only adjectives ending in ઉં **-uṃ** are variable; all others are invariable. From now on, all variable adjectives will appear in the Vocabulary builder sections with their neuter ઉં **-uṃ** endings.

Variable adjectives that describe singular masculine or feminine nouns will always end in ઓ **-o** or ઈ **-ī** respectively. So નાનું **nānuṃ** *small, young(er)*, which is used to describe a neuter noun, becomes નાની **nānī** when it describes a feminine noun and નાનો **nāno** when it describes a masculine noun.

Plural endings for adjectives that describe male nouns behave similarly to male nouns ending in **ઓ -o**, that is they take **આ -ā**. Likewise, plural adjectives that describe neuter nouns behave similarly to neuter nouns ending in **ઉં -uṃ**, that is, they take **આં -āṃ**. Feminine adjective endings always take **ઈ -ī** in both singular and plural forms. Unlike the nouns that modify them, plural adjectives (of any gender) do not end in **ઓ -o**. For example:

છોકરો મોટો છે	**chokro moṭo che**	*the boy is big*
છોકરા મોટા છે	**chokrā moṭā che**	*the boys are big*
છોકરી મોટી છે	**chokrī moṭī che**	*the girl is big*
છોકરીઓ મોટી છે	**chokrīo moṭī che**	*the girls are big*
છોકરું મોટું છે	**chokruṃ moṭuṃ che**	*the child is big*
છોકરાં મોટાં છે	**chokrāṃ moṭāṃ che**	*the children are big*

Adjectives that agree with nouns for which you would use the formal pronouns તમે **tame** or આપ **āp** in the first person or તેઓ **teo** in the third person will take the corresponding plural ending. When showing respect to women, the neuter plural form આમે **-āṃ** may be used. For example:

સમીર નાનો છે	**Samīr nāno che**	*Sameer is small*

But:

દીપકભાઈ મોટા છે	**Dīpakbhāī moṭā che**	*Deepakbhai is big*
આ છોકરીઓ લાંબી છે	**ā chokrīo lāṃbī che**	*these girls are tall*
તે ખુરશીઓ નાની છે	**te khurśīo nānī che**	*those chairs are small*
બહેનો માંદી છે	**baheno māṃdī che**	*the sisters are ill*

But:

લીલાબેન લાંબાં છે અને તે પાકિસ્તાની સ્ત્રીઓ મોટાં છે

Līlāben lāṃbāṃ che ane te pākistānī strīo moṭāṃ che

Leelaben is tall and those Pakistani women are old

Adjectives that describe two or more nouns of different genders at once usually use the neuter plural. For example:

ભાઈઓ અને બહેનો મોટાં છે

bhāīo ane baheno moṭāṃ che

the brothers and sisters are big

5 Now you have learned how Gujarati adjectives change according to the gender and number of the nouns that they describe. Test your knowledge by finding the error in each of the following sentences and correcting them so that adjectives and nouns agree correctly.

a આ ખુરશી નવો છે ā khurśī navo che

b ના, આ ખુરશી જૂનું છે nā, ā khurśī jūnuṃ che

c એ છોકરા ચોકખી છે e cokrā cokkhī che

d આ બગીચો મેલું છે ā bagīcho meluṃ che

NEW VOCABULARY

નવું	**navuṃ**	*new*
જૂનું	**jūnuṃ**	*old*
ચોકખું	**cokkhuṃ**	*clean*
મેલું	**meluṃ**	*dirty*

7 SENTENCE PATTERNS

In Gujarati the subject usually comes at the beginning of the sentence and the verb at the end. However, note the important distinction between the following two sentences, showing how adjectives and nouns can trade places in the same way as in English:

આ છોકરી નાની છે	**ā chokrī nānī che**	*this girl is small*
આ નાની છોકરી છે	**ā nānī chokrī che**	*this is a small girl*

Even though there is no possessive pronoun, the following expressions can imply that the speaker is referring to his or her own brother or sister:

આ નાનો ભાઈ છે	**ā nāno bhāī che**	*this is (a/the or my) younger brother*
આ મોટી બહેન છે	**ā moṭī bahen che**	*this is (an/the or my) older sister*

Although you would call your younger brother and sister by their first names, in some families you would always refer to or address your older brother and sister as મોટા ભાઈ **moṭā bhāī** *older brother* or મોટી બહેન **moṭī bahen** *older sister.*

6 Go back to the previous activity and switch around the noun and adjectives from your corrected sentences so that the meaning of the sentence changes. For example, if we take exercise a from the previous activity we would make the following sentences:

આ ખુરશી નવી છે **ā khurśī navī che** *this chair is new* becomes આ નવી ખુરશી છે **ā navī khurśī che** *this is a new chair*

a ____________________

b ____________________

c ____________________

8 પણ PAṆ BUT, HOWEVER, ALSO

The word **પણ paṇ** means *but* or *however* when it is contrasting two things. It can occur at the beginning of a sentence or it can appear as the second idea (not necessarily the second word). For example:

આ છોકરી લાંબી છે, પણ એ છોકરી ટૂંકી

ā chokrī lāṃbī che, paṇ e chokrī ṭūṃkī

this girl is tall, but that girl is short

In cases where no contrast is implied, **પણ paṇ** means *also* or *even*. For example:

આ છોકરી લાંબી છે, અને એ છોકરી પણ લાંબી છે

ā chokrī lāṃbī che, ane e chokrī paṇ lāṃbī che

this girl is tall, and that girl is also tall

7 Use the word પણ paṇ to make statement a and statement b into one sentence c that means *this chair is new, but that chair is old.*

a આ ખુરશી નવી છે ā khurśī navī che

b એ ખુરશી જૂની છે e khurśī jūnī che

c ____________________

Now insert the word પણ paṇ and the word અને ane into statements d and statement e to make one sentence f that means *this chair is new and also clean.*

d આ ખુરશી નવી છે ā khurśī navī che

e આ ખુરશી ચોખ્ખી છે ā khurśī cokhkhī che

f ____________________

Practice

1 Choose the correct response to each of the following questions and greetings.

a કેમ છો? kem cho?

હું મજામાં છું huṃ majāmā chuṃ

હું ગુજરાતી છું huṃ gujarātī chuṃ

આવજો! āvjo!

b આવજો! āvjo!

મજામાં majāmāṃ

હું ગુજરાતી છું huṃ gujarātī chuṃ

આવજો! āvjo!

c તમે ગુજરાતી છો? tame gujarātī cho?
હા, હું ગુજરાતી છું hā huṃ gujarātī chuṃ
તમે ભારતીય છો tame bhāratīy cho
હા, એ ગુજરાતી છે hā, e gujarātī che

d નીલા અંગ્રેજ છે? Nīlā aṃgrej che?
ના, એ લાંબો નથી nā, e lāṃbo nathī
ના, એ ગુજરાતી છે nā, e gujarātī che
સારું છે sāruṃ che

e તું અંગ્રેજ છે? tuṃ aṃgrej che?
ના, આપણે જૈન છીએ nā, āpne jain chīe
હા, અમે અંગ્રેજ છીએ hā, ame aṃgrej chīe
હા, હું અંગ્રેજ છું hā, huṃ aṃgrej chuṃ

PRONUNCIATION TIP

જૈન	**jain**	*Jain*, member of the Jain religious community (see the Religion in Gujarat section)

2 Choose the correct form of the verb હોવું hovuṃ *to be*.

a નીલાબેન ગુજરાતી છે/છો.
Nīlāben gujarātī che/cho.

b તેઓ કેમ છે/છો? તેઓ મજામાં છે/છો.
teo kem che/cho? teo majāmāṃ che/cho.

c નીલાબેન, તમે કેમ છે/છો?
Nīlāben, tame kem che/cho?

d હું મજામાં છું/છો.
huṃ majāmāṃ chuṃ/cho.

e નીલાબેન, તમે ગુજરાતી છે/છો? હા, હું ગુજરાતી છીએ/છું.
Nīlāben, tame gujarātī che/cho? hā huṃ gujarātī chīe/chuṃ.

3 Read the following dialogue carefully. Then make three sentences about the character Sonal.

વીરેન	**કેમ છો, સોનલ?**
Vīren	kem cho, Sonal?
સોનલ	**હું મજામાં છું. તું કેમ છે, વીરેન?**
Sonal	huṃ majāmāṃ chuṃ. tuṃ kem che, Viren?
વીરેન	**મજામાં. તમે ગુજરાતી છો?**
Vīren	majāmāṃ. tame gujarātī cho?
સોનલ	**હા, હું ગુજરાતી છું. હું ભારતીય છું.**
Sonal	hā, huṃ gujarātī chuṃ. huṃ bhāratīy chuṃ.

4 Next, imagine that Viren has a similar conversation with Maher, Neela, Javed and Steve. Create and write out dialogues based on the model of the one above using the information given below. Finally, create a similar dialogue as if Viren were talking to you.

મહેર **Maher**	પારસી **pārsī**	ગુજરાતી **gujarātī**	ભારતીય **bhāratīy**
નીલા **Nīlā**	જૈન **jain**	ગુજરાતી **gujarātī**	અંગ્રેજ **aṃgrej**
જાવેદ **Jāved**	મુસલમાન **musalmān**	ગુજરાતી **gujarātī**	ભારતીય **bhāratīy**
સ્ટીવ **Sṭīv**	ખ્રિસ્તી **khristī**	ગુજરાતી નથી **gujarātī nathī**	અમેરિકન **amerikan**

As your dialogues will be unique, there is no model answer in the key to the exercises. If you can, check your fluency by asking a Gujarati speaker to read your answer with you.

NEW VOCABULARY

પારસી	**pārsī**	*Parsi* (member of the Parsi religious community)
મુસલમાન	**musalmān**	*Muslim*
ખ્રિસ્તી	**khristī**	*Christian*

5 Choose the correct form of the pronoun: તેઓ teo (formal *he/she* **or** *they***) or એ -e (informal** *he/she***).**

a દીપકભાઈ ગુજરાતી છે. એ/તેઓ લાંબા છે.
Dīpakbhāī gujarātī che. e/teo lāṃbā che.

b નાનો ભાઈ હોશિયાર છે. એ/તેઓ આળસુ નથી.
nāno bhāī hośīyār che. e/teo āḷsu nathī.

c નીલાબેન અહીં છે. એ/તેઓ માંદાં નથી.
Nīlāben ahīṃ che. e/teo māṃdāṃ nathī.

d મહેર પાતળી છે. એ/તેઓ જાડી નથી.
Maher pātḷī che. e/teo jāḍī nathī.

e આ સ્ત્રીઓ બંગાળી છે? ના, એ/તેઓ પંજાબી છે.
ā strīo baṃgāḷī che? nā, e/teo paṃjābī che.

NEW VOCABULARY

માંદું	**māṃduṃ**	*ill*	પાતળું	**pātḷuṃ**	*thin, slim*
જાડું	**jāḍuṃ**	*fat*	સ્ત્રી (f.)	**strī**	*woman*
બંગાળી	**baṃgāḷī**	*Bengali*	પંજાબી	**paṃjābī**	*Panjabi*

6 Choose the correct forms of the given adjectives, paying attention to the gender and number of the nouns that they describe.

આ મકાન (મોટું) છે. ઓરડાઓ (સારું) અને (મોટું) છે. એક (સફેદ) મેજ છે અને ત્રણ (લાલ) ખુરશી છે. મેજ અને ખુરશીઓ (સાફ) છે.

ā makān (moṭuṃ) che. orḍāo (sāruṃ) ane (moṭuṃ) che. ek (saphed) mej che ane traṇ (lāl) khurśī che. mej ane khurśīo (sāph) che.

7 Using the information in a, answer the following questions.

a ચાર ખુરશી છે?
cār khurśī che?

b ખુરશીઓ સફેદ છે?
khurśīo saphed che?

c મેજ ગંદું છે?
mej gaṃduṃ che?

d ખુરશીઓ સાફ છે?
khurśīo sāph che?

NEW VOCABULARY

મકાન (n.)	**makān**	*house*	લાલ	**lāl**	*red*
ઓરડો (m.)	**orḍo**	*room*	સાફ	**sāph**	*clean*
સફેદ	**saphed**	*white*	ગંદું	**gaṃduṃ**	*dirty*
મેજ (n.)	**mej**	*table*	ચાર	**cār**	*four*
ત્રણ	**traṇ**	*three*			

સમજયા/સમજયાં? SAMJYĀ/SAMJYAṂ? DO YOU UNDERSTAND?

The forms સમજયા/સમજયાં? **samjyā/samjyāṃ?** *Do you understand?* (lit. *did you understand?*), which come from the verb સમજવું **samjvuṃ** *to understand*, agree with the subject in the same way as variable adjectives. For example:

સમજયા, દીપકભાઈ? **samjyā, Dipakbhāi?** *Do you understand, Deepakbhai?*

સમજી, નીલા? **samjī, Nīlā?** *Do you understand, Neela?*

સમજયાં, લીલાબેન? **samjyaṃ, Līlāben?** *Do you understand, Leelaben?*

Read the following passage that describes a family group.

આ ડોકટર ફિરોઝ નસીર અને બેગમ નસીર છે. તેઓ ગુજરાતી છે. તેઓ પણ મુસલમાન છે. તેઓ ભારતીય નથી, પણ તેઓ પાકિસ્તાની છે. બે છોકરા છે. અદનાન અને અમ્મર. અદનાન મોટો છે અને અમ્મર નાનો છે. ઓ છોકરા સાજા અને હોશિયાર છે. તેઓ આળસુ નથી. તે લોકો ખુશ છે, માશા અલ્લાહ!

ā ḍokṭar Phirojh Nasīr ane Begam Nasīr che. teo gujarātī che. teo paṇ musalmān che. teo bhāratīy nathī, paṇ teo pākistānī che. be chokrā che, Adnān ane Ammar. Adnān moṭo che ane Ammar nāno che. ā chokrā sājā ane hośīyār che, teo āḷsu nathī. te loko khuś che, māśā Allāh!

NEW VOCABULARY

ડોક્ટર (m.)	**ḍoktār**	*doctor*
સાજું	**sajuṃ**	*well, in good health*
ખુશ	**khuś**	*happy*
માશા અલ્લાહ!	**māsā Allāh!**	*May God save us!*

True or false? Give the correct answer. Then give the English translation of each question and of each answer that you give in Gujarati. Use the following model as a guide.

ફિરોઝ મુસલમાન છે?	**Phirojh musalmān che?**	*Is Phiroz Muslim?*
હા, તેઓ મુસલમાન છે.	**hā, teo musalmān che.**	*Yes, he is Muslim.*

1 તે લોકો ગુજરાતી નથી.
te loko gujarātī nathī.

2 એકે છોકરી અને એક છોકરો છે.
ek chokrī ane ek chokro che.

3 ફિરોઝ ડોક્ટર છે.
Phirojh ḍokṭar che.

4 મોટો છોકરો અમ્મર છે.
moṭo chokro Ammar che.

Test yourself

How would you do the following in Gujarati?

1 Say hello to somebody (in two different ways).

2 Bid farewell to somebody.

3 Ask if Deepakbhai is Indian.

4 Say that you are American, but Neelaben is Pakistani.

5 Ask if these little children are American?

6 Say that this is a small chair, but that is a big chair.

SELF CHECK

	I CAN...
○	... give information about myself.
○	... ask other people questions about themselves.
○	... describe things and people.
○	... exchange greetings.

2 તમે રોજ અહીં આવો છો? tame roj ahīṃ āvo cho? *Do you come here every day?*

In this unit you will learn how to:

- ***talk about your daily activities.***
- ***ask complex questions.***
- ***use the simple present and past tenses.***

ગુજરાત અને ગુજરાતીઓ gujarat ane gujarātio *Gujarat and Gujaratis*

Although many younger Gujaratis speak Gujarati at home, many of them do not know how to read or write in Gujarati and are not confident about using it in formal situations. Gujarati is available as a GCSE subject in the UK, usually outside mainstream teaching, but there is no provision for A-level Gujarati. Only a small handful of universities in the UK and the US offer courses in Gujarati language and literature. The School of Oriental and African Studies (SOAS), part of the University of London, is one of the few places where it can be studied from beginner's level to an advanced level, at which it is possible to study both modern and medieval literature. In 2013 the University of Florida's Center for the Study of Hindu Traditions launched its 'Gujarat Program,' which has resources for undergraduate and graduate students to become familiar with Gujarati culture and literature. When there is adequate student interest, both the University of Pennsylvania's South Asia Studies department and the South Asia Language Institute (SASLI) at the University of Wisconsin Madison offer courses in Gujarati language (all levels). The American Institute of Indian Studies (AIIS) also offers Gujarati language courses for all levels at their centre in Ahmedabad, Gujarat.

Vocabulary builder

બસ	bas	*enough* (see Point 5 below)
ખૂબ	khūb	*very*
ગઈ કાલે	gaī kāle	*yesterday*

બાપુજી	bāpujī	*daddy*
હતા	hatā	*(he) was* (formal)
તેથી	tethī	*therefore, and so*
હું ઘેર હતો	huṃ gher hato	*I was at home*
આજે	āje	*today*
સાજું	sājuṃ	*well, in good health*
કાલે	kāle	*yesterday* (= ગઈ કાલે **gaī kāle**)
ન હતું	na hatāṃ	*was not*
અહીં જ	ahīṃ j	*right here* (As you can hear in the audio for this dialogue જ **j** is pronounced together with the word that it follows, in order to show emphasis. There is no inherent *a* vowel attached to જ **j**, which is why in transliteration we write **j** rather than **ja**.)
સવારે	savāre	*in the morning*
તું કયાં હતો?	tuṃ kyāṃ hato?	*where were you?*
બજારમાં	bajārmāṃ	*in the bazaar, in the market*
સારું!	sāru!	*good!*
ચા (f.)	cā	*tea*
કેવું ?	kevuṃ?	*what sort of?, how?*
ગરમ	garam	*hot*
ઠંડું	ṭhaṃḍuṃ	*cold*
બહુ	bahu	*very, many*
ખરાબ	kharāb	*bad*
પાણી (n.)	pāṇī	*water*
મેજ પર	mej par	*on the table*
આ શું છે?	ā śuṃ che?	*what's this?*
નવું	navuṃ	*new*
ચોપડી (f.)	copḍī	*book*
આ કોણ છે?	ā koṇ che?	*who's this?*
મિત્ર	mitra	*friend*
વિદ્યાર્થી (m.)	vidyārthī	*student* (male)
વિદ્યાર્થિની (f.)	vidyārthinī	*student* (female)
કેટલું ?	keṭluṃ?	*how much?, how many?*
વર્ગ (m.)	varg	*class*
ચાલો!	cālo!	*let's go!*

યુનિવર્સિટીમા YUNIVARSITIMĀṂ *IN THE UNIVERSITY*

02.01 *Firdaus Desai and Bhavna Patel meet in the students' coffee bar at the university where they are studying Gujarati. Akshar Patel is a new student who is about to start learning Gujarati.*

1 What is the main topic of Firdaus and Bhavna's conversation? Which other people do Firdaus and Bhavna refer to in their conversation?

Dialogue 1

ફિરદોસ	**કેમ છો, ભાવનાબેન?**
Phirdos	kem cho, Bhāvnāben?
ભાવના	**બસ, ખૂબ મજામાં. કેમ છે?**
Bhāvnā	bas, khūb majāmāṃ. kem che?
ફિરદોસ	**મજામાં. ગઈ કાલે બાપુજી માંદા હતા, તેથી હું ઘેર હતો.**
Phirdos	majāmāṃ. gaī kāle bāpujī māṃdā hatā, tethī huṃ gher hato.
ભાવના	**આજે તેઓ કેમ છે?**
Bhāvnā	āje teo kem che?
ફિરદોસ	**આજે તેઓ સાજા છે. તમે કાલે અહીં ન હતાં?**
Phirdos	āje teo sājā che. tame kāle ahīṃ na hatāṃ?
ભાવના	**હા, હું અહીં જ હતી. તું સવારે કયાં હતો? અહીં ન હતો?**
Bhāvnā	ha, huṃ ahīṃ j hatī. tuṃ savāre kyāṃ hato? ahiṃ na hato?
ફિરદોસ	**ના, હું અહીં ન હતો. હું બજારમાં હતો.**
Phirdos	nā, huṃ ahīṃ na hato. huṃ bajārmāṃ hato.
ભાવના	**સારું. ચા કેવી છે? ગરમ છે?**
Bhāvnā	sāru. cā kevī che? garam che?
ફિરદોસ	**ના, ગરમ નથી, ઠંડી છે. બહુ ખરાબ છે. પાણી છે?**
Phirdos	nā, garam nathī, ṭhaṃḍī che. bahu kharāb che. pāṇī che?
ભાવના	**હા, પેલી મેજ પર પાણી છે. આ શું છે?**
Bhāvna	hā, pelī mej par pāṇī che. ā śuṃ che?
ફિરદોસ	**એક નવી ચોપડી છે.**
Phirdos	ek navī copḍī che.
ભાવના	**ફિરદોસ, આ કોણ છે?**
Bhāvnā	Phirdos, ā koṇ che?
ફિરદોસ	**એક મિત્ર છે. એ પણ વિદ્યાર્થી છે. અક્ષર, કેમ છે?**
Phirdos	ek mitra che. e paṇ vidyārthī che. Akṣar, kem che?

અક્ષર	ફિરદોસ, કેમ <u>છે</u>? આ કોણ <u>છે</u>?
Akṣar	Phirdos, kem <u>che</u>? ā koṇ <u>che</u>?
ફિરદોસ	આ ભાવનાબેન <u>છે</u>.
Phirdos	ā Bhāvnāben <u>che</u>.
અક્ષર	કેમ <u>છો</u>, ભાવનાબેન? તમે વિદ્યાર્થિની <u>છો</u>?
Akṣar	kem <u>cho</u>, Bhāvnāben? tame vidyārthinī <u>cho</u>?
ભાવનિા	હા, <u>હું</u> વિદ્યાર્થિની <u>છું</u>.
Bhāvnā	hā, huṃ vidyārthinī <u>chuṃ</u>.
અક્ષર	ફિરદોસ, આજે કેટલા વર્ગો <u>છે</u>?
Akṣar	Phirdos, āje keṭlā vargo <u>che</u>?
ફિરદોસ	આજે એક જ છે – ગુજરાતી. ચાલો, આવજો.
Phirdos	āje ek j che – gujarātī. cālo, āvjo!

2 True or false? Read and correct the following sentences based on the information given in the dialogue. Here's an example to start you off:

ફિરદોસ વિદ્યાર્થિની છે. **Phirdos vidyārthinī che.**

ના, ફિરદોસ વિદ્યાર્થિની નથી, એ વિદ્યાર્થી છે. **na, Phirdos vidyārthinī nathi, e vidyārthī che.**

a કાલે ભાવનાબેન અહીં ન હતાં.
kāle Bhāvnāben ahīṃ na hatāṃ.

b સવારે ફિરદોસ ઘેરજ હતા.
savāre Phirdos gher j hatā.

3 Answer the following questions based on what you learned in the above dialogue.

a ચોપડી કેવી છે?
copḍī kevī che?

b કાલે ભાવનાબેન બજારમાં હતાં?
kāle Bhāvnāben bajārmāṃ hatāṃ?

Language discovery

Read and listen to the dialogue again.

a Pay special attention to the <u>underlined</u> words, all of which are different forms of the same verb: હોવું **hovuṃ**, which you have already learned a bit about in Unit 1 and will learn more about in this unit. From reading and listening to the dialogue and from hints in the Vocabulary builder try to guess how the verb is being used in a different way from how you saw it behave in Unit 1.

b Most questions begin with interrogative (question) words such as *who, what, when, where, why* and *how*. Before reading on, return to the previous dialogue and find all the question words in Gujarati. Here is a tip that will help you: all question words in Gujarati begin with the same letter, ક **ka**.

c In the above dialogue there is only one noun that appears in both its feminine and masculine forms – can you find it?

1 THE SIMPLE PAST TENSE OF THE VERB હોવું **HOVUṂ** *TO BE*

The simple past tense of the verb હોવું **hovuṃ** *to be* (i.e. *I was, you were, he was*, etc.) is હતું **hatuṃ** *was*. The stem of this form (હત **hat**) will change according to number (singular or plural) and gender (masculine, feminine, or neuter).

As you read through the following grammar table pay special attention to the endings of the verb. Can you see, for example, how all feminine singular pronouns end with the sound ઈ **ī**? All of the endings for the simple past tense follow a similar pattern as that of variable adjectives, which you were introduced to in Unit 1, and which we will learn more about below.

Singular			
Feminine			
First person	હું હતી	**huṃ hatī**	*I was*
Second person	તું હતી	**tuṃ hatī**	*you were*
Third person	તે (and આ, એ) હતી	**te** (and **ā, e**) **hatī**	*she* (and *it, this, that*) *was*
Masculine			
First person	હું હતો	**huṃ hato**	*I was*
Second person	તું હતો	**tuṃ hato**	*you were*
Third person	તે (and આ, એ) હતો	**te** (and **ā, e**) **hato**	*he* (and *it, this, that*) *was*
Neuter			
Third person	તે, આ, એ હતું	**te, ā, e hatuṃ**	*it, this, that was*
Plural			
Feminine			
First person	અમે હતાં આપણે હતાં	**ame hatāṃ** **āpṃe hatāṃ**	*we were* (exclusive) *we were* (inclusive)
Second person	તમે હતાં	**tame hatāṃ**	*you were*
Third person	તેઓ (and તે, આ, એ હતાં) હતાં	**teo** (and **te, ā, e**) **hatāṃ** (when referring to inanimate objects, use હતી **hatī**)	*they* (and *these, those*) *were*

Masculine			
First person	અમે હતા આપણે હતા	**ame hatā** **āpṇe hatā**	*we were* (exclusive) *we were* (inclusive)
Second person	તમે હતા	**tame hatā**	*you were*
Third person	તેઓ (and તે, આ, એ) હતા	**teo** (and **te**, **ā**, **e**) **hatā**	*they* (and *these, those*) *were*
Neuter			
Third person	તે, આ, એ હતાં	**te, ā, e hatāṃ**	*they, these, those were*

The negative of the simple past is formed by using ન **na** before the verb. So ન + હતું **na** + **hatuṃ** = *was not*. This can also be written as નહોતું **nahotuṃ** *was not*, but it is usually written and pronounced as નોહતું **nohtuṃ**. Here are some further examples:

ગઈ કાલે હું ઘેર જ હતો	**gaī kāle huṃ gher j hato**	*yesterday I* (masculine) *was just at home*

But:

સવારે હું અહીં નહોતી	**savāre huṃ ahīṃs nahoti**	*this morning I* (feminine) *was not here*
કાલે તેઓ બજારમાં નહોતા	**kāle teo bajārmāṃ nahotā**	*yesterday they* (masculine) *were not in the market*

2 INTERROGATIVE (QUESTION) WORDS

Most questions begin with interrogative (question) words such as *who, what, when, where, why* and *how*. In Gujarati, many of these interrogative words begin with the letter ક **k-**. The following are among the most frequently used:

કોણ	**koṇ**	*who?*
ક્યાં	**kyāṃ**	*where?*
ક્યારે	**kyāre**	*when?*
કેમ	**kem**	*why?*
કેવું	**kevuṃ**	*what sort of?, how?*
કેટલું	**ketluṃ**	*how much?, how many?*
શું	**śuṃ**	*what?*

The first four of these question words are invariable, while the last three decline like variable adjectives according to gender and number. For example, કેવું **kevuṃ** becomes કેવી **kevī** when referring to a feminine noun: આ સાડી કેવી છે? **ā sāḍī kevī che?** *what is this sari like?*

When the gender of the person is not known કોણ **koṇ** *who* is declined as if it refers to a neuter noun. For example:

કોણ હતું?	**koṇ hatuṃ?**	*who was it?*
કોણ છે?	**koṇ che?**	*who is this?* or *who is it?* (when answering the phone)

Question words are usually placed just before the verb. For example:

એ કોણ છે?	**e koṇ che?**	*who is that?*
એ લોકો કયાં હતા?	**e loko kyāṃ hatā?**	*where were they?* (lit. those people)
ઘર કેવું છે?	**ghar kevuṃ che?**	*what's the house like?*
શું છે?	**śuṃ che?**	*what is it?, what's the matter?*

But:

કેટલા લોકો ત્યાં હતા?	**ketlā loko tyāṃ hatā?**	*how many people were there?*

1 Now you have learned how the endings of verbs and adjectives/ question words change based on the gender and number of the nouns/pronouns that they modify in similar ways. Test your knowledge by matching the following nouns/pronouns with the correct form of (A) the adjectives/question words and (B) the verbs provided below.

a ચા (f.) cā **A**____ **B**____
b ઘર (n.) ghar **A**____ **B**____
c આપણે āpṇe **A**____ **B**____
d વિદ્યાર્થી (m.) vidyārthī **A**____ **B**____

	A	B
	Adjectives/Question words	Verbs
a	સારું **sāru**	હતાં **hatāṃ**
b	કેવી **kevī**	છે **che**
c	કેટલાં **keṭlāṃ**	હતી **hatī**
d	સાજો **sājo**	હતો **hato**

3 CLITICS

In English and other European languages, words such as *in*, *from*, etc. precede the words to which they relate and are thus called *prepositions*. In Gujarati, such words follow the words that they govern and are thus called *postpositions*. However, it is more accurate to call these words *clitics* because they form compounds with the words to which they relate (*clitic* comes from the Greek for *leaning*). The exception is પર **par** *on*, which is usually written separately from the word that it governs. In this unit, the following simple clitics are introduced: માં **mām** *in*; થી **thī** *from*; પર **par** *on*; and એ **e** *in, at, on*. Here are some simple sentences in which these words appear:

કાલે હું બજારમાં હતી	**kāle huṃ bajārmāṃ hatī**	*yesterday I (f.) was in the market*
પાણી મેજ પર છે	**pāṇī mej par che**	*the water is on the table*

The clitics પર **par** *on* and માં **mām** *in* can be combined with થી **thī** *from*, as in the example below:

મેજ પરથી	**mej parthī**	*from on top of the table*

2 Test your knowledge of clitics by translating the following phrases from Gujarati into English.

a ગઈ કાલે હું ક્યાં હતો? gaī kāle huṃ kyāṃ hato?
b ચોપડી અલમારી માં છે. chopḍī almārī māṃ che.
c ચા બજારમાં છે. cā bajārmāṃ che.
d ગઈ કાલે વિદ્યાર્થિની બજારમાં નહોતી. gaī kale vidyārthinī bajārmāṃ nahotī.

NEW VOCABULARY

અલમારી (f.) **almārī** *cupboard*

The clitic એ **-e** is used with certain words in order to give a locative meaning (*in, at, on*, etc.). For example, adding એ **-e** *to* નિશાળ **niśaḷ** *school* produces નિશાળે **niśāḷe**, which means *at* or *in school*. Likewise, adding એ **-e** *to* આજ **āj** *today* produces આજે **āje**, the literal meaning of which is *on today*. In English we cannot say *on today*, of course, but in Gujarati this is common. Here are some further examples:

આજે તે નિશાળે નથી	**āje te niśaḷe nathī**	*today he is not at school*
સાંજે ભાવનાબેન બજારમાં હતાં	**sāṃje Bhāvnāben bajārmāṃ hatāṃ**	*in the evening Bhavnaben was in the market*
આજે તે માંદો છે	**āje te māṃdo che**	*(on) today he/she is ill*

The word ઘર **ghar** *home* has a special form ઘેર **gher** *at home*, as well as the following forms which are less frequently written, but often used in spoken Gujarati: ઘરે **ghare** and ઘેરે **ghere** *at home*. For example:

આજે તે ઘેર છે	**āje te gher che**	*today he/she is at home*

Note that the word ગામ **gām** *town, village* does not take એ **-e**; it can indicate the locative sense (e.g. *in the village, to the village*) without the need for a clitic. For example:

ગઈ કાલે હું ગામ હતી	**gaī kāle huṃ gām hatī**	*yesterday I was in the village*

Adding clitics to variable nouns and adjectives

You have already seen that nouns vary based on gender and number. For example:

છોકરી	**chokrī**	*girl*
છોકરીઓ	**chokrīo**	*girls*
છોકરો	**chokro**	*boy*
છોકરા	**chokrā**	*boys*

Remember that the form of variable nouns listed in the Vocabulary section and in dictionaries will appear in their neuter forms (e.g. છોકરું **chokruṃ** *child*). This is called the independent form.

When a clitic is added to a single noun that ends in a vowel (e.g. છોકરું **chokruṃ** *child*) the noun will change just as if it were becoming a form of a plural noun. For example:

ઓરડો **orḍo** *room* + માં **-māṃ** *in* → ઓરડામાં **orḍāmāṃ** *in the room*
રસ્તો **rasto** *road* + પર **par** *on* → રસ્તા પર **rastā par** *on the road*
છોકરું **chokruṃ** *child* + થી **thī** *from* → છોકરાથી **chokrāthī** *from the child*

When a clitic is added to plural nouns of any variety, the noun ending does not change. For example:

બજારો **bajāro** *markets* + માં **-māṃ** *in* → બજારોમાં **bajāromāṃ** *in the markets*
રસ્તાઓ **rastāo** *roads* + પર **par** *on* → રસ્તાઓ પર **rastāo par** *on the roads*
છોકરાં **chokrāṃ** *children* + થી **thī** *from* → છોકરાંથી **chokrāṃthī** *from the children*

Variable adjectives will also change according to the noun that they modify. For example:

મોટો ઓરડો **moṭo orḍo** *a big room* + માં **-māṃ** *in* → મોટા ઓરડામાં **mota orḍāmāṃ** *in the big room*

લાંબો રસ્તો **lāṃbo rasto** *the long road* + પર **par** *on* → લાંબા રસ્તા પર **lāṃbā rastā par** *on the long road*

નાનું છોકરું **nānuṃ chokruṃ** *the small child* + થી **thī** *from* → નાના છોકરાથી **nānā chokrāthī** *from the small child*

Note that variable adjectives will decline in response to the added clitic even if the noun they modify does not end in a vowel. For example:

ગામ **gām** *town, village* + માં **-māṃ** *in* મોટા ગામમાં **moṭā gāmmāṃ** *in the big town/village*

3 You have just learned some complex grammar points! If you practise what you have learned, you will quickly feel comfortable with recognizing and using clitics. Each of the following

sentences contains an error with respect to the correct use and meaning of the clitic. Find the errors and correct them according to what the English translation tells you:

a	આજ માં તે માંદો છે	āj māṃ te māṃdo che	*today he is sick*
b	છોકરું રસ્તો પર છે	chokruṃ rasto par che	*the child is on the road*
c	મોટો ઓરડામાં	moṭo orḍāmāṃ	*in the big room*

4 WORD ORDER

When a time word (e.g. આજે **āje** *today*) and a place word (e.g. અહીં **ahīṃ** *here*) occur in the same sentence, the time word is placed first. For example:

તેઓ આજે અહીં નથી	**teo āje ahīṃ nathī**	*they are not here today*
આજે તેઓ ઘેર છે	**āje teo gher che**	*today they are at home*

5 બસ! BAS! *ENOUGH!*

The word બસ **bas** *enough* is used idiomatically in many situations. It can be used as an exclamation to indicate that the speaker has said all that he or she wants to say about a topic. The word can also be used to end a list of items or to say that's all or that's it. For example:

બે છોકરા છે, બસ	**be chokrā che, bas**	*there are two children, that's all*

It can also be used in questions. For example:

આજે બે વર્ગો છે.	**āje be vargo che**	*today there are two classes*
બસ?	**bas?**	*is that all?*

It may be useful to know that બસ! **bas!** *enough!* is also used when you do not want any more to eat. Gujaratis have a very strong tradition of hospitality, so your hosts may continue to offer you food until you say clearly that you have had enough!

Vocabulary builder

શું ખબર છે?	śuṃ khabar che?	*what's new?* (lit. *what is the news?*)
ખબર (f.)	khabar	*news*
ખાસ કંઈ નહિ	khās kaṃī nahi	*nothing special*
આજે બહુ ઠંડી છે, ને?	āje bahu ṭhaṃḍī che, ne?	*it's very cold today, isn't it?*
હા, છે	hā, che	*yes it is* (note that Gujarati does not need the pronoun *it* here)

કેટલા બધા લોકો અહીં છે!	keṭlā badhā loko ahīṃ che!	*what a lot of people are here!*
તેઓ શું કરે છે?	teo śuṃ kare che?	*what are they doing?*
ખબર નથી	khabar nathī	*no idea, I don't know*
ઘણું	ghaṇuṃ	*much, many*
તું રોજ અહીં આવે છે?	tuṃ roj ahīṃ āve che?	*do you come here daily?*
હું રોજ નથી આવતો	huṃ roj nathī āvto	*I don't come daily*
દર અઠવાડિયે	dar aṭhvāḍiye	*every week*
બે-ત્રણ વાર	be-traṇ vār	*two or three times*
કયારે?	kyāre?	*when?*
બપોરે	bapore	*in the afternoon*
હું ઘેર જાઉં છું	huṃ gher jauṃ chuṃ	*I am going home*
તું હવે કયાં જાય છે?	tuṃ have kyāṃ jāy che?	*where are you going now?*
એ દુકાનો કેટલી સારી છે!	e dukāno keṭlī sārī che!	*how great are those shops!* (rhetorical question)

યુનિવર્સિટીમાં YUNIVARSIṬĪMĀṂ *IN THE UNIVERSITY 2*

02.02 *Shailesh Patel and Jui Barot are also students.*

1 What is Shailesh and Jui's conversation about? They are talking to each other in one location, but they mention other places in their conversation. Which other places do they refer to?

Dialogue 2

શૈલેશ	**કેમ છે, જૂઈ?**
Śaileś	kem che, Jūī?
જૂઈ	**સારું છે. શું ખબર છે, શૈલેષ?**
Jūī	sāruṃ che. śuṃ khabar che, Śaileś?
શૈલેશ	**ખાસ કંઈ નહિ. <u>આજે</u> બહુ ઠંડી છે ને?**
Śaileś	khās kaṃī nahi. <u>āje</u> bahu ṭhaṃḍī che ne?
જૂઈ	**હા, છે. કેટલા બધા લોકો <u>અહીં</u> છે! એ લોકો કોણ છે? તેઓ શું કરે છે?**
Jūī	hā, che. keṭlā badhā loko <u>ahīṃ</u> che! e loko koṇ che? teo śuṃ kare che?
શૈલેશ	**ખબર નથી. ઘણા લોકો છે, ને?**
Śaileś	khabar nathī. ghaṇā loko che, ne?

જૂઈ	તું રોજ <u>અહીં</u> આવે છે?
Jūī	tuṃ roj <u>ahīṃ</u> āve che?
શૈલેશ	હું <u>રોજ</u> નથી આવતો. દર અઠવાડિએ હું બે-ત્રણ વાર આવું છું.
Śaileś	huṃ <u>roj</u> nathī āvto. dar aṭhvāḍive hum be-traṇ vār avuṃ chuṃ.
જૂઈ	તું કયારે આવે છે – <u>બપોરે</u>?
Jūī	tuṃ kyāre āve che – <u>bapore</u>?
શૈલેશ	ના, હું સવારે આવું છું અને સાંજે હું ઘેર જાઉં છું. તું હવે કયાં જાય છે?
Śaileś	nā, huṃ savāre āvum chuṃ ane sāṃje huṃ gher jāuṃ chuṃ, tuṃ have kyāṃ jāy che?
જૂઈ	હું અહીંથી બજારે જાઉં છું. એ દુકાનો કેટલી સારી છે! આવજો, શૈલેશ!
Jūī	hūṃ ahīṃthī bajāre jāuṃ chuṃ, e dukāno keṭlī sārī che! āvjo, Śaileś!
શૈલેશ	આવજો!
Śaileś	avjo!

2 True or false? Read and correct the following sentences based on the information in the dialogue. Here's an example to start you off:

આજે બહુ ગરમી છે.	**āje bahu garmī che**	*today is very hot*
ના, આજે બહુ ગરમી નથી. આજે બહુ ઠંડી છે.	**nā, āje bahu garmī nathī. āje bahu ṭhaṃḍī che**	*no, today is not very hot. Today is very cold*

a આજે ઓછા લોકો અહીં છે.
āje ochā loko ahīṃ che.

b શૈલેશ રોજ અહીં આવે છે.
Śaileś roj ahīṃ āve che.

3 Answer the following questions.

a જૂઈ કયાં જાય છે?
Jūī kyāṃ jāy che?

b બજાર કેવી છે?
bajār kevī che?

NEW VOCABULARY

ઓછું	**ochuṃ**	*few, insufficient*

2 તમે રોજ અહીં આવો છો? tame roj ahīṃ āvo cho? *Do you come here every day?*

Language discovery

Listen to the dialogue again.

a Pay special attention to the underlined words, which indicate place and time. Seven of these underlined words appear with one of the clitics that you learned about earlier in this unit – can you find them?

b There are only two plural nouns in the dialogue – can you find them?

6 STEM AND BASE FORMS OF NOUNS AND ADJECTIVES

You have already seen that nouns vary in singular and plural forms. For example:

છોકરી	**chokrī**	*girl*
છોકરીઓ	**chokrīo**	*girls*
છોકરો	**chokro**	*boy*
છોકરા	**chokrā**	*boys*

The singular form, which is the one you will find in the Vocabulary section, is called the independent form.

Stem forms

a In the singular, clitics must be added after another form of the noun, which is called the stem form. Sometimes this is the same as the independent form. For example:

independent form: બજાર **bajār** *market*
stem form with the clitic માં **-māṃ** *in* → બજારમાં **bajārmāṃ** *in the market*

However, independent and stem forms may be different, as in the case of masculine nouns ending in ઓ **-o** and neuter nouns ending in ઉં **-uṃ**, where these endings are replaced with એ **-a**. For example:

independent form: ઓરડો **orḍo** *room*
stem form with the clitic માં **-māṃ** *in* → ઓરડામાં **orḍāmāṃ** *in the room*

independent form: રસ્તો **rasto** *road*
stem form with the clitic પર **par** *on* → રસ્તા પર **rastā par** *on the road*

independent form: છોકરું **chokruṃ** *child*
stem form with the clitic થી -**thī** *from* → છોકરાથી **chokrāthī** *from the child*

The stem form is also used when addressing someone directly. This form is known as the vocative. For example:

એ છોકરા **e chokrā!** *that boy!*

b Plural nouns do not require a special stem form; they use the same form with or without clitics. For example:
plural: બજારો **bajāro** *markets*
with the clitic માં **-māṃ** *in* → બજારોમાં **bajāromāṃ** *in the markets*

plural: રસ્તાઓ **rastāo** *roads*
with the clitic પર **par** *on* → રસ્તાઓ પર **rastāo par** *on the roads*

plural: છોકરાં **chokrāṃ** *children*
with the clitic થી **-thī** *from* → છોકરાંથી **chokrāṃthī** *from the children*

c A variable adjective that agrees with a stem form noun will also appear in the stem form. For example:
independent form: મોટો ઓરડો **moṭo orḍo** *a big room*
stem form with the clitic માં **-māṃ** *in* → મોટા ઓરડામાં **mota orḍāmāṃ** *in the big room*
independent form: લાંબો રસ્તો **lāṃbo rasto** *the long road*
stem form with the clitic પર **par** *on* → લાંબા રસ્તા **lāṃbā rastā** par *on the long road*
independent form: નાનું છોકરું **nānuṃ chokruṃ** *the small child*
stem form with the clitic થી **-thī** *from* → નાના છોકરાથી **nānā chokrāthī** *from the small child*

An adjective will appear in its stem form even if the noun with which it agrees has the same form in its independent and stem forms. For example:
independent form: ગામ **gām** *town, village*
stem form with the clitic માં -**māṃ** *in* → મોટા ગામમાં **moṭā gāmmāṃ** *in the big village*

Base forms

a Base forms are a special form of stem forms that are used only before the clitic એ **-e**. Nouns which have no special stem form add એ **-e** to the independent form. For example:

independent form: સાંજ **sāṃj** *evening*
base form: સાંજે **sāṃje** *in the evening*

This means that only singular forms of masculine nouns ending in ઓ **-o** and neuter nouns ending in ઉં **-uṃ** have base forms. This form is created by replacing ઓ **-o** or યું **-uṃ** with the clitic એ **-e**. For example:

independent form: દહાડો **dahāḍo** *day*

stem form with the clitic થી **thī** *from* → એ દહાડાથી **e dahāḍāthī** *from that day*
base form: તે દહાડે **te dahāḍe** *on that day*

independent form: અઠવાડિયું **aṭhvāḍiyuṃ** *week*
stem form with the clitic સુધી **sudhī** *for, until* → એક અઠવાડિયા સુધી **ek aṭhvāḍiyā sudhī** *for a week*
base form: ગયે અઠવાડિયે **gaye aṭhvāḍiye** *last week*

b A variable adjective agreeing with the base form of a noun is also in the base form. For example:

ગયે અઠવાડિયે	**gaye aṭhvāḍiye**	*last week*

Since it is invariable, the feminine adjective does not have a base form and does not add એ **-e**. For example:

ગઈ કાલે	**gaī kāle**	*yesterday*

7 THE PRESENT CONTINUOUS

Formation and use

The forms of verbs given in the dictionary and in the Vocabulary section in this book are known as the infinitive forms and always end in વું **-vuṃ**. When the વું **-vuṃ** suffix of the infinitive is removed, what is left is called the root or stem of the verb. For example: આવવું **āvvuṃ** *to come* (infinitive form) à આવ **āv** (verb stem).

From the verb stem various tenses (present, past and future) can be formed. The tense endings of all verbs will decline according to person (*I*, *you*, etc.), number (singular or plural) and sometimes gender (masculine, feminine, or neuter). For example:
છું **chuṃ** *am* indicates the first person singular ending and thus agrees with the pronoun હું **huṃ** *I* (masculine or feminine). છું chuṃ *am* + હું **huṃ** *I* = *I am*

છીએ **chīe** *are* indicates the first person plural ending and thus agrees with the pronoun અમે **ame** *we* (masculine and/or feminine). છીએ **chīe** *are* + અમે **ame** *we* = *we are*

Other sets of endings indicates gender and number, but not person. For example, હતી **hatī** was agrees with feminine singular nouns or pronouns in the first, second, or third person forms. For example:

હું હતી	**huṃ hatī**	*I* (feminine) *was*
તું હતી	**tuṃ hatī**	*you* (feminine) *were*
એ હતી	**e hatī**	*she was*

The present continuous tense of verbs (other than the irregular verb હોવું **hovuṃ** *to be*) in Gujarati is formed by first adding the personal endings to the verb stem and then adding the present tense of the verb હોવું **hovuṃ** *to be* as an auxiliary verb.

Let's conjugate the verb આવવું **āvvuṃ** *to come*. Can you identify what the stem of this verb is?

Singular			
First person	હું આવું છું	**huṃ āvum chuṃ**	*I am coming*
Second person	તું આવે છે	**tuṃ āve che**	*you are coming*
Third person	તે, આ, એ આવે છે	**te, ā, e āve che**	*he, she, it is coming*
Plural			
First person	અમે આવીએ છીએ	**ame āvīe chīe**	*we are coming* (exclusive)
	આપણે આવીએ છીઅ	**āpṇe avīe chīe**	*we are coming* (inclusive)
Second person	તમે આવો છો	**tame āvo cho**	*you are coming*
Third person	તેઓ, તે આવે છે	**teo, te āve che**	*they are coming*

English has several present tenses, whose meanings are all covered in Gujarati by the present continuous tense. This present tense is used in Gujarati for expressing an action that:

a takes place at a particular time in the present. For example:

હું આવું છું **huṃ āvuṃ chum** *I'm coming* (now)

b occurs habitually. For example:

હું રોજ આવું છું **huṃ roj āvuṃ chum** *I come every day*

c takes place in the immediate future. For example:

હું હવે જાઉં છું **huṃ have jāuṃ chuṃ** *I'm going now*

The negative of the present continuous tense is formed by adding the suffix તું **-tuṃ** to the present stem and adding નથી **nathī**, the negative of the present tense of the verb હોવું **hovuṃ** *to be*. For example:

આવવું **āvvuṃ** *to come* (infinitive)

આવ **āv** (verb stem) + તું **-tuṃ** = આવતું **āvtuṃ** *coming*

આવતું **āvtuṃ** *coming* + નથી **nathī** *is not* (negative of auxiliary verb) = આવતું નથી **āvtuṃ nathī** *not coming*

The તું **-tuṃ** suffix will modify to agree with the gender and number of the noun or pronoun to which it is attached. For example:

Singular			
Feminine			
First person	હું આવતી નથી	**huṃ āvtī nathī**	*I am not coming*
Second person	તું આવતી નથી	**tuṃ āvtī nathī**	*you are not coming*
Third person	તે (and આ, એ) આવતી નથી	**te** (and **ā, e**) **āvtī nathī**	*she* (and *it, this, that*) *is not coming*
Masculine			
First person	હું આવતો નથી	**huṃ āvto nathī**	*I am not coming*
Second person	તું આવતો નથી	**tuṃ āvto nathī**	*you are not coming*
Third person	તે (and આ, એ) આવતો નથી	**te** (and **ā, e**) **āvto nathī**	*he* (and *it, this, that*) *is not coming*
Neuter			
Third person	તે (and આ, એ) આવતું નથી	**te** (and **ā, e**) **āvtuṃ nathī**	*it (and this, that) is not coming*
Plural			
Feminine			
First person	અમે આવતાં નથી આપણે આવતાં નથી	**ame āvtāṃ nathī** **āpne āvtāṃ nathī**	*we are not coming* (exclusive) *we are not coming* (inclusive)
Second person (formal)	તમે આવતાં નથી	**tame āvtāṃ nathī**	*you are not coming*
Third person	તેઓ (and તે, આ, એ) આવતાં નથી	**teo** (and **te, ā, e**) **āvtāṃ nathī** (when referring to inanimate objects, use આવતી **āvtī**)	*they* (and *these, those*) *are not coming*
Masculine			
First person	અમે આવતા નથી આપણે આવતા નથી	**ame āvtā nathī** **āpṉe āvtā nathī**	*we are not coming* (exclusive) *we are not coming* (inclusive)
Second person	તમે આવતા નથી	**tame āvtā nathī**	*you are not coming*
Third person	તેઓ (and તેલ આ, એ) આવતા નથી	**teo** (and **te, ā, e**) **āvtā nathī**	*they* (and *these, those*) *are not coming*
Neuter			
Third person	તે,આ,એ આવતાં નથી	**te, ā, e āvtaṃ nathī**	*they* (and *these, those*) *are not coming*

4 In the present continuous tense the following verbs behave regularly and in the same way as આવવું āvvuṃ *to come*: **પીવું pīvuṃ** *to drink*; **નાખવું nākhvuṃ** *to throw*; **and વાપરવું vāparvuṃ** *to spend*. **Test your understanding of how to use the present continuous tense by filling in the missing auxiliaries or negation.**

a તું પાણી પીએ ___ છે ___
tuṃ pāṇī pīe ___ che ___
you drink/are drinking water

b તમે પાણી પીતા ___
tame pāṇī pītā ___
you do not drink/are not drinking water

c તે કચરો રસ્તો પર નાખે ___
te kacro rasto par nākhe ___
he/she throws rubbish/is throwing rubbish onto the street

d તેઓ પૈસા વાપરે___
teo paisā vāpare ___
they spend/are spending money

NEW VOCABULARY

કચરો (m.)	**kacro**	*trash*
પૈસા (m.)	**paisā**	*money*

8 IRREGULAR PRESENT VERB FORMS

Gujarati has several irregular verbs. These are verbs that behave differently from regular verbs such as **આવવું āvvuṃ** *to come* in that the verb stem may vary, or certain tense endings may follow distinct patterns. You will be able to learn irregular present tense verbs quickly. Note that the negative form of irregular verbs will always behave in the same way as their regular counterparts (i.e. just as **આવતું āvtuṃ** given above).

રહેવું **rahevum** *to remain, to stay* and કહેવું **kahevuṃ** *to say* are irregular verbs because they have two verb stems:

a રહ **rah** and કહ **kah** which are used before tenses that end in a vowel; and

b રહે **rahe** and કહે **kahe** which are used before endings that end in a consonant. For example:

હું કહું છું	**hu kahuṃ chuṃ**	*I am saying*
હું કહેતી નથી	**huṃ kahetī nathī**	*I am not saying*

જવું **javuṃ** *to go* is also irregular because it has two different stems (જા **jā-** and જ **ja-**). Look at the table to see how these two endings are used differently when applied to second and third person singular and third person plural nouns.

Singular			
First person	હું જાઉં છું	**huṃ jāuṃ chuṃ**	*I am going/go*
Second person	તું જાય છે	**tuṃ jāy che**	*you are going/go*
Third person	તે (and આ, એ) જાય છે	**te** (and **ā**, **e**) **jāy che**	*he, she* (and *it, this, that*) *goes/is going*
Plural			
First person	અમે જઈએ છીએ	**ame jaīe chīe**	*we go/are going* (exclusive)
	આપણે જઈએ છીએ	**āpṇe jaīe chīe**	*we go/are going* (inclusive)
Second person	તમે જાઓ છો	**tame jāo cho**	*you go/are going*
Third person	તેઓ, તે જાય છે	**teo, te jāy che**	*they go/are going*
Negative			
	જતું નથી	**jatuṃ nathī**	*not going*

9 TO GO TO

When going to somewhere, but not into somewhere, a clitic is not required. For example:

હું ભારત જાઉં છું **huṃ bhārat jāuṃ chuṃ** *I am going to India*

But:

હું દુકાને જાઉં છું **huṃ dukāne jāuṃ chuṃ** *I am going to the shops* (here there is the notion of going *into* the shops)

This means that for countries or cities, no clitic is needed when expressing going *to* them. For example:

હું મુંબઈ જાઉં છું **huṃ Mumbaī jāuṃ chuṃ** *I am going to Mumbai*

But in order to express staying *in* them, માં -māṃ is used. For example:

હું ભારતમાં હતી **huṃ Bhāratmāṃ hatī** *I was in India*

In order to express going up to a person પાસે **pāse** *near* is used. For example:

છોકરો દીપક પાસે જાય છે **chokro Dīpak pāse jāy che** *the boy goes up to Deepak*

10 THE INDEFINITE

When the present form is used without the auxiliary (that is, without છું **chuṃ**, છો **cho**, છીએ **chīe**, etc.), it is called the indefinite present. While this is sometimes used to express general truths and things that should be, its main use is to ask for permission and to make suggestions such as *Let's…* For example:

શું કરું?	**śuṃ karuṃ?**	*what should I do?*
હું જાઉં ?	**huṃ jāuṃ?**	*may/should I go?*
આપણે આવીએ?	**āpṇe āvīe?**	*may/should we come?*
આપણે આવીએ!	**āpṇe āvīe!**	*let's come!*

The negative used in these cases is ન **na** instead of નથી **nathī**. For example:

હું ન જાઉં ?	**hu na jāuṃ?**	*shall/should I not go?*

5 Did you spot the pattern in the above examples? Test your understanding of the indefinite present by translating the following sentences from Gujarati to English.

a આપણે જઈએ! āpṇe jaīe!
b હું અંદર આવું? huṃ aṃdar āvuṃ?
c અમે જઈએ? ame jaīe?
d તે ઘેર આવે? te gher āve?

11 IDIOMS AND COMMON EXPRESSIONS

Idioms in another language can be difficult to learn because they do not always correspond exactly to similar idioms in English. It is, however, important to learn a variety of idioms if you wish to express yourself with any degree of fluency. The following are simple idioms that are frequently used by Gujarati speakers and can easily be included in everyday speech.

a કેટલું **keṭluṃ** *how much?, how many?* can be used to qualify an adjective. For example:

કેટલી સારી છે!	**keṭlī sāri che!**	*how good!* (i.e. very good!)

When used to qualify a noun, કેટલું **keṭluṃ** must be followed by બધું **badhuṃ** (lit. *all*). For example:

કેટલા બધા લોકો હતા!	**keṭlā badhā loko hatā!**	*what a lot of people were there!*

b ખબર **khabar** *news* is also used idiomatically. For example:

શું ખબર છે? **śuṃ khabar che?** *what's new?* (lit. *what is the news?*) is a question frequently asked when meeting an acquaintance.

ખાસ કંઈ ખબર નથી **khās kaṃī khabar nathī** *nothing much* (lit. *there is no special news*) can be used in reply when the speaker has nothing specific to report.

ખબર નથી **khabar nathī** (lit. *there is no news*) is a standard way of saying *I don't know*.

c Gujarati speakers often add the word ને **ne** at the end of questions, invitations, or commands. ને **ne** can mean different things depending on the context, but it most closely corresponds to the English phrase *isn't it?* Accordingly, it can also be added to simple statements or exclamations to create a question or rhetorical question, for example: **આજ બહુ ગરમી છે ને? āj bahu garmī che, ne?** *It's really hot today, isn't it?* Here are some further examples, which show the most common ways in which the word can be used in conversation:

બસ, જાઓ, ને?	**bas, jāo, ne?**	*just go, won't you?*
તે તમારી બહેન છે, ને?	**te tamārī bahen che, ne?**	*she's your sister, isn't she?*
આવો, ને?	**āvo, ne?**	*come in, won't you?*
સારું, ને?	**sāruṃ, ne?**	*it's good, isn't it?*

When the speaker is more doubtful about the reply to the question, કે **ke** is used instead. Here are three ways of expressing the same thing with the use of કે **ke**:

તું આવે, કે?	**tuṃ āve, ke?**	*you are coming, aren't you?*
તું આવે કે, નહિ?	**tuṃ āve ke, nahi?**	*you are coming, aren't you?*
તું આવે કે, કેમ?	**tuṃ āve ke, kem?**	*you are coming, aren't you?*

Practice

1 Take the following statements below and turn them into interrogative (question) statements.

a આજે બહુ ગરમી છે.
āje bahu garmī che.

b ગઈ કાલે ઠંડી હતી.
gaī kāle ṭhaṃḍī hatī.

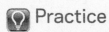

c ફિરદોસ વિદ્યાર્થી છે.
Phirdos vidyārthī che.

d નીલા ગામ જાય છે.
Nīla gām jāy che.

e તમે નથી આવતાં.
tame nathī āvtāṃ.

2 Shaheena is asking Neena some questions. Use the interrogative (question) words given below to create the question that must have been asked in each case. Use the formal second person pronoun તમે tame *you*.

a	શહીના	(કેવું?)
	Śahīnā	(kevuṃ?)
	નીના	ચોપડી બહુ ખરાબ છે.
	Nīnā	Nīnā copḍi bahu kharāb che.
b	શહીના	(કયાં?)
	Śahīnā	(kyāṃ?)
	નીના	ગઈ કાલે હું ઘેર હતી.
	Nīnā	gaī kāle huṃ gher hatī.
c	શહીના	(કયારે?)
	Śahīnā	(kyāre?)
	નીના	હું રોજ સવારે દુકાને જાઉં છું.
	Nīnā	huṃ roj savāre dukāne jāuṃ chuṃ.
d	શહીના	(કોણ?)
	Śahīnā	(koṇ?)
	નીના	ખબર નથી.
	Nīnā	khabar nathī.

3 Neena is now angry and wants to contradict everything Shaheena says. Give her replies to Shaheena's remarks in the dialogue below. Look at this example first:

શહીના	આજે બહુ ઠંડી છે ને?
Śahīnā	āje bahu ṭhaṃḍī che ne?
નીના	ના, બહુ ગરમી છે.
Nīnā	nā, bahu garmī che.

a	શહીના	ગઈ કાલે શૈલેશભાઈ અહીં હતા ને?
	Śahīnā	gaī kāle Śaileśbhāī ahim hatā ne?
	નીના	ના...
	Nīnā	nā, ...

2 તમે રોજ અહીં આવો છો? tame roj ahīṃ āvo cho? *Do you come here every day?*

b શહીના — એ મોટી દુકાનો કેટલી સારી છે
Śahīnā — ā moṭī dukāno keṭlī sārī che!
નીના — ના...
Nīnā — nā, ...
c શહીના — તમે રોજ અહીં આવો છો ને?
Śahīnā — tame roj ahīṃ āvo cho ne?
નીના — ના...
Nīnā — nā, ...
d શહીના — તમારા મોટા ભાઈ મુંબઈમાં રહે છે ને?
Śahīnā — tamārā moṭā bhāī muṃbaīmāṃ rahe che ne?
નીના — ના...
Nīnā — nā, ...

4 Translate the following phrases. Then put all of the present tense forms of the verb હોવું **hovuṃ to be into the simple past and all of the past forms into the simple and continuous present forms.**

a તે માંદો છે.
te māṃdo che.

b તે લોકો અહીં છે.
te loko ahīṃ che.

c અમે ખુશ હતા.
ame khuś hatā.

d તમે મજામાં છો?
tame majāmāṃ cho?

5 02.03 **Imagine that you are in a students' coffee bar with your friend Priya. Use the English cues to say your part of the conversation.**

a પ્રિયા — કેમ છે? શું ખબર છે?
Priyā — kem che? śuṃ khabar che?
You — Greet her and say everything's OK.
b પ્રિયા — આજે હું બજારે જાઉં છું. તું શું કરે છે?
Priyā — āje huṃ bajāre jāuṃ chuṃ. tuṃ śuṃ kare che?
You — Say you are studying.
c પ્રિયા — આપણે જઈએ!
Priyā — āpṇe jaīe!
You — Refuse and tell her you have two Gujarati classes.

d પ્રિયા ચાલ, હું જાઉં. આવજો!
Priyā cāl, huṃ jāuṃ. āvjo!
You Say goodbye.

NEW VOCABULARY

અભ્યાસ (m.)	**abhyās**	*study*
અભ્યાસ કરવો	**abhyās karvo**	*to study*

6 Choose the correct form from the two alternatives given in each of the following sentences.

a આજે ગરમ/ગરમી છે.
āje garam/garmī che.

b તું નથી આવતી/આવતાં.
tuṃ nathī āvtī/āvtāṃ.

c ગઈ કાલે દીપકભાઈ અહીં ન હતા/હતાં.
gaī kāle Dīpakbhāī ahīṃ na hatā/hatāṃ.

d હું મુંબઈમાં નથી રહતી/રહેતી
huṃ muṃbaīmāṃ nathī rahtī/rahetī.

e તેઓ ભારતમાં/ભારત જાય છે
teo bhāratmāṃ/bhārat jāy che.

7 In the following passage, the nouns and verbs are in their dictionary form with no endings. Using the English translation as a guide, write out the passage in script or transliteration, correcting the dictionary forms in brackets.

એક મિત્ર અહીં (હતું). પણ તે આ (ગામ)માં (નથી) (રહેવું) અને હવે તે અહીં (ન + છે). પણ હવે (પેલું) (મોટું) (મકાન)માં એક (નાનું) છોકરો (રહેવું). હું રોજ આ (ઘર) (જવું) અને અમે ખુશ (છે).

ek mitra ahīṃ (hatuṃ). paṇ te ā (gām)maṃ (nathī) (rahevuṃ) ane have te ahīṃ (na + che). paṇ have (peluṃ) (moṭuṃ) (makān)māṃ ek (nānuṃ) chokro (rahevuṃ). huṃ roj ā (ghar) (javuṃ) ane ame khuś (che).

One friend (of mine) was here. But he does not live in this town and now he is not here. But now a young boy lives in that big house. I go to this house every day and we are happy.

Read the following passage.

શૈલેશ: દર અઠવાડિયે હું લેસ્ટર જાઉં છું. હું ત્યાં નથી રહેતો–હું લંડનમાં રહું છું. બાપુજી શિક્ષક છે અને તેઓ લેસ્ટરમાં કામ કરે છે. હું લંડનમાં અભ્યાસ કરું છું. સવારે હું યુનિવર્સિટીમાં જાઉં છું અને બપોરે હું ઘેર આવું છું સાંજે હું ઘેર અભ્યાસ કરું છું.

Śaileś: dar aṭhvāḍiye huṃ Lesṭar jāuṃ chuṃ. huṃ tyāṃ nathī raheto–huṃ Laṃḍanmāṃ rahuṃ chuṃ. bāpujī śikṣak che ane teo Lesṭarmāṃ kām kare che. huṃ Laṃḍanmāṃ abhyās karuṃ chuṃ. savāre huṃ yunivarsiṭīmaṃ jāuṃ chuṃ ane bapore huṃ gher āvuṃ chuṃ sāṃje huṃ gher abhyās karuṃ chuṃ.

NEW VOCABULARY

શિક્ષક (m.) શિક્ષિકા (f.)	**śikṣak, śikṣikā**	*teacher*

Answer the following questions.

a શૈલેશ ક્યાં રહે છે?
Śaileś kyāṃ rahe che?

b શૈલેશ દુકાનમાં કામ કરે છે?
Śaileś dukānmāṃ kām kare che?

c એ ક્યારે યુનિવર્સિટીમાં જાય છે?
e kyāre yunivarsiṭīmāṃ jāy che?

d બપોરે એ ક્યાં જાય છે?
bapore e kyāṃ jāy che?

e સાંજે એ શું કરે છે?
sāṃje e śuṃ kare che?

A special note on pronunciation

The rule of syllabification that was given in the script section may have become evident in the course of this chapter and should be noted so that you are aware of pronunciation. For example, see the following ways in which the verb **સમજવું samajvuṃ** *to understand* has been transliterated:

સમજવું	**samajvuṃ**	*to understand*
તે સમજતો નથી	**te samajto nathī**	*he does not understand*

But:

તે સમજે છે	**te samje che**	*he understands*

Do not worry too much about this – you will soon pick it up by hearing the language spoken.

Test yourself

How would you do the following in Gujarati?

1 *Ask a person politely how they are.*
2 *Ask a woman politely where she was yesterday.*
3 *Tell someone that the water is on the table.*
4 *Tell someone that the good children are at school.*
5 *Ask Ramesh politely if he comes to university every day.*
6 *Ask someone if you may leave now.*

SELF CHECK

I CAN...
... talk about daily activities.
... ask complex questions.
... talk about when, where and how people and things are.
... make indefinite statements (such as asking for permission and making suggestions).
... use the simple present and past tenses to create complex sentences.

3 તમે ક્યાં રહો છો?
tame kyāṃ raho cho?
Where do you live?

In this unit you will learn how to:

- ***talk about where you live and ask others questions about where they live.***
- ***talk about your family.***
- ***express opinions.***
- ***give commands.***

ગુજરાત અને ગુજરાતીઓ *gujarat ane gujarātio*
Gujarat and Gujaratis

Some Gujaratis live in what are called joint family households – that is, households in which more than two generations of a family live together. Traditionally, after marriage a woman goes to live with her husband in his family's home. Sometimes this means that a woman moves in not only with her husband and his parents, but also her husband's paternal grandparents, brothers, brother's wives and children, and unmarried sisters! Since paternal cousins of joint family households are brought up together, they often call one another brothers and sisters (although sometimes cousins are distinguished by being called cousin-brothers and cousin-sisters). While traditional joint families are still common in both urban and rural communities across all of South Asia and throughout the world in the South Asian diaspora, it is becoming increasingly common for newly married couples to live separately from their parents in their own homes, especially in wealthy urban areas. It is also perfectly common for a woman to have her own parents live with her and her husband in the couple's own home. Just like everywhere else in the world, there are many different types of Gujarati families and households!

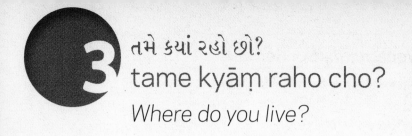

Vocabulary builder

ામારું	tāmāruṃ	*your*
ારું	māruṃ	*mine*
ંબલી	veṃblī	*Wembley*
ઈલિંગ રોડ	Īliṃg roḍ	*Ealing Road* (a street in Wembley inhabited by many Gujaratis)
ણું દૂર	ghaṇuṃ dūr	*a little way*
ને ગમે છે	mane game che	*I like*
ણું	ghaṇuṃ	*many, quite a few*
ને મળે છે	mane…maḷe che	*I get…, I receive…*
સ્તું	sastuṃ	*cheap, inexpensive*
ચીજ (f.)	cīj	*thing*
સ્તામાં	rastāmāṃ	*on the street, in the street*
મે અમારા મિત્રોને મળીએ છીએ	ame amārā mitrone maḷīe chīe	*we meet our friends*
મારું	amāruṃ	*our*
ળવું	maḷvuṃ	*to meet*
હેર (n.)	śaher	*city*
ને સારું લાગે છે	mane sāruṃ lāge che	*I think it's nice*
ાત	sāt	*seven*
ારી પત્નીને એ ઘર નથી ગમતું	mārī patnīne a ghar nathī gamtuṃ	*my wife doesn't like that house*
પત્ની (f.)	patnī	*wife*
ારણ કે	kāraṇ ke	*because*
જૂનું	jūnuṃ	*old*
મારું	tamāruṃ	*yours*
સામાન (m.)	sāmān	*luggage, furniture*
ારી (f.)	bārī	*window*
પ્રકાશ (m.)	prakāś	*light*
સુંદર (m.)	suṃdar	*beautiful*
લાગે છે (m.)	lāge che	*it seems*
દિવસ (m.)	divas	*day*
ભાડું (m.)	bhāḍuṃ	*rent*
મોંઘું (m.)	moṃghuṃ	*expensive*
મને બહુ પૈસા મળે છે?	tamne bahu paisā maḷe che?	*do you earn much money?*
હવે	have	*now*

તમારું ઘર કેવું છે? TAMĀRUṂ GHAR KEVUṂ CHE?

WHAT'S YOUR HOUSE LIKE?

03.01 *Jagdish Modi and Mohammad Thobani work together.*

1 What are the main topics of Jagdish and Mohammad's conversation? How do they describe the places and objects that they are discussing?

Dialogue 1

મોહમ્મદ — જગદીશભાઈ , તમે કયાં રહો છો?

Mohammad — Jagdīśbhāī, tame kyāṃ raho cho?

જગદીશ — મારું ઘર વેંબલીમાં છે. ઈલિંગ રોડથી ઘણું દૂર નથી. મને વેંબલી બહુજ ગમે છે.

Jagdīś — māruṃ ghar veṃblīmāṃ che. īliṃg roḍthī ghaṇuṃ dūr nathī. mane veṃblī bahu j game che.

મોહમ્મદ — વેંબલી કેવું છે?

Mohammad — veṃblī kevuṃ che?

જગદીશ — ઈલિંગ રોડ પર ઘણી ગુજરાતી દુકાનો છે અને ત્યાં મને સસ્તી ગુજરાતી ચીજો મળે છે અને રસ્તામાં અમે અમારા મિત્રોને મળીએ છીએ. તમે કયાં રહો છો?

Jagdīś — īliṃg roḍ par ghaṇī gujarātī dukāno che ane tyāṃ mane sastī gujarātī cījo maḷe che ane rastāmāṃ ame amārā mitrone maḷīe chīe. tame kyāṃ raho cho?

મોહમ્મદ — હું શહેરમાં રહું છું. મારું મકાન બહુ નાનું છે પણ એ મને બહુ સારું લાગે છે. એમાં ચાર જ ઓરડા છે. તમારા ઘરમાં કેટલા ઓરડા છે?

Mohammad — huṃ śahermāṃ rahuṃ chuṃ. māruṃ makāṇ bahu nānuṃ che paṇ e mane bahu sāruṃ lāge che. emāṃ cār j orḍā che. tamārā gharmāṃ keṭlā orḍā che?

જગદીશ — અમારા ઘરમાં સાત ઓરડા છે. મને એ ઘર બહુ ગમે છે. પણ મારી પત્નીને એ ઘર નથી ગમતું કારણ કે એ ઘણું જૂનું છે. તમારું મકાન કેવું છે?

Jagdīś — amārā gharmāṃ sāt orḍā che. mane e ghar bahu game che paṇ mārī patnīne e ghar nathī gamtuṃ kāraṇ ke e ghaṇuṃ jūnuṃ che. tamāruṃ makān kevuṃ che?

મોહમ્મદ — એ નવું છે અને દરેક ઓરડામાં નવો સામાન છે. દરેક ઓરડાની બારીઓ મોટી છે અને એમાંથી બહુ પ્રકાશ આવે છે. બહુ સુંદર લાગે છે. એક દિવસ અમારે ઘેર આવજો!

Mohammad — e navuṃ che ane darek orḍāmāṃ navo sāmān che. darek orḍānī bārīo moṭī che ane emāṃthī bahu prakāś āve che. bahu suṃdar lāge che. ek divas amāre gher āvjo!

જગદીશ	પણ ભાડું કેટલું છે? મોંઘું છે? તમને હવે બહુ પૈસા મળે છે?
Jagdīś	paṇ bhāḍuṃ keṭluṃ che? moṃghuṃ che? tamne have bahu paisā maḷe che?
મોહમ્મદ	ના, મને બહુ પૈસા નથી મળતા. બાપુજીના મિત્રનું મકાન છે.
Mohammad	nā, mane bahu paisā nathī maḷtā. bāpujīnā mitranuṃ makān che.

2 True or false? Read and correct the following sentences based on the information given in the dialogue.

a જગદીશ ભારતમાં રહે છે.
Jagdīś bhāratmāṃ rahe che.

b જગદીશ બહુ પૈસા મળે છે.
Jagdīś bahu paisā maḷe che.

c મોહમ્મદનું ઘર માં જૂનો સામાન છે.
Mohammadnuṃ māṃ jūno sāmān che.

3 Answer the following questions.

a મોહમ્મદનું ઘર કેવું છે?
Mohammadnuṃ ghar kevuṃ che?

b વેંબલી કેવું છે?
vembḷī kevuṃ che?

Language discovery

Read and listen to the dialogue again.

a Pay special attention to the underlined words in the dialogue. All these words are pronouns but look different from the pronoun forms you have been introduced to in previous units. Use the Vocabulary builder to try to figure out why these pronouns look different. What kind of pronouns are they?

b There are three instances in the dialogue where one of the speakers expresses how they or a third party feels about a particular object or place. Use the Vocabulary builder to find these three instances. Do you notice anything similar about the endings of the pronouns and nouns that appear in these three instances?

Direct and indirect objects: ને -ne

The direct object is the person or thing that receives the effect of a verb. So in the sentence *I see Deepak*, *Deepak* is the direct object of the verb *to see*. Verbs may have two objects, one being the direct object and the other the indirect object. For example, in the sentence *I give Deepak the book*, *the book* is the direct object (the thing that is being given) and *Deepak* is the indirect object (the person to whom the thing is being given). In English, this sentence could be written *I gave the book to Deepak*. In this sentence *to* marks the indirect object (*Deepak*) of the verb (*give*). Some sentences do not have direct objects. For example, in the sentence *I told Deepak*, *Deepak* is still the indirect object as the direct object (the thing said, the story, etc.) has been left unstated.

The clitic or ending **ને -ne** is used in Gujarati to mark both direct and indirect objects.

ને -ne is always used with the indirect object, and always with the direct object when it is a person. It is often used when the direct object is an animal, but is used less often when the direct object is an inanimate object. Here are some examples:

હું ભાઈને ચોપડી આપું છું

huṃ bhāīne copḍī āpuṃ chuṃ

I give the book (direct object) *to my brother* (indirect object)

હું જગદીશભાઈ ને સાંભળું છું

huṃ Jagdīśbhāīne saṃbhaḷuṃ chuṃ

I listen to Jagdishbhai (direct object – person)

But:

હું વાત સાંભળું છું

huṃ vāt sāṃbhaḷuṃ chuṃ

I listen to the speech (direct object – inanimate)

As with other clitics, **ને -ne** is added to the stem form of nouns. As you will see, pronouns take special forms when used with **ને -ne**. As with other clitics that you have seen (such as **પર par** *on*), adjectives that agree with a noun or pronoun that takes **ને -ne** are also declined from their stem forms.

For example:

હું નાના છોકરાને ચોપડી આપું છું

huṃ nānā chokrāne copḍī āpuṃ chuṃ

I give the book to the small boy

1 The following sentences are all grammatically correct except that ને -ne is missing from each one. Decide where ને -ne should be placed and give the corrected sentences.

a છોકરી ભાઈ ગીત ગાય છે cokrī bhāī gīt gāve che

b હું લીલા વાર્તા સંભળાવું છું huṃ Līlā vārtā saṃbhaḷāvūṃ chuṃ

c આ વાંદરો છોકરા કેળું ગાય છે ā vāndro cokrā keluṃ āpe che

NEW VOCABULARY

આપવું	**āpvuṃ**	*to give*
ગાવું	**gāvuṃ**	*to sing*
ગીત	**gīt**	*song*
સંભળાવવું	**saṃbhaḷāvvuṃ**	*to tell* (as in a story)
વાર્તા	**vārtā** (f.)	*story*
કેળું	**keḷuṃ** (n.)	*banana*

Possession: નું -nuṃ

The clitic **નું -nuṃ** *of* changes just like a variable adjective. When it is added to the stem form of a noun it usually indicates possession, like the English *'s* (in, for example, *Nila's brother = the brother of Nila*). Note that **નું -nuṃ** agrees with the object, idea, or person possessed, and not with the possessor. Here are some examples:

નીલાનો ભાઈ	**Nīlāno bhaī**	*Neela's brother* (where **નું -nuṃ** becomes **નો -no** to agree with the word *brother* (m.), not with *Neela* (f.))
એનો ભાઈ	**eno bhāī**	*his brother* or *her brother*

But:

એની બહેન	**enī bahen**	*his sister* or *her sister*

It is often unnecessary in Gujarati to use possessive pronouns, as you will have seen in the dialogues and examples. For instance, in the following sentence there is no need to specify whose sister is coming if it is the sister of the speaker. However, if it is someone else's sister then this must be made clear. For example:

બહેન આવે છે **bahen āve che** *(my) sister is coming*

But:

નીલાની બહેન આવે છે **Nīlānī bahen āve che** *Neela's sister is coming*

Pronouns with ને -n and નું -num

In the table you will notice that certain pronouns do not change their forms as much as others when used with ને **-ne** and નું **-nuṃ**. For instance, હું **huṃ** *I* changes quite considerably (to મારું **māruṃ** with નું **-nuṃ** and to મને **mane** with ને **-ne**), while તે **te** does not change its original form at all with the added નું **-nuṃ** or ને **-ne** – it simply becomes તેનું **tenuṃ** and તેને **tene**. Can you notice any other patterns?

	Independent form of pronoun		Possessive form of pronoun (નું -num form or equivalent)		Pronoun with ને -ne	
Singular						
First person	હું	**huṃ**	મારું	**māruṃ**	મને	**mane**
Second person	તું	**tuṃ**	તારું	**tāruṃ**	તને	**tane**
Third person	તે	**te**	તેનું	**tenuṃ**	તેને	**tene**
	એ	**e**	એનું	**enuṃ**	એને	**ene**
	આ	**ā**	આનું	**ānuṃ**	આને	**āne**
	કોણ	**koṇ**	કોનું	**konuṃ**	કોને	**kone**
Plural						
First person	અમે	**ame**	અમારું	**amāruṃ**	અમને	**amne**
Second person	આપણે	**āpṇe**	આપણું	**āpaṇuṃ**	આપણને	**āpaṇne**
Third person	તમે	**tame**	તમારું	**tamāruṃ**	તમને	**tamne**
	આપ	**āp**	આપનું	**āpnuṃ**	આપને	**āpne**
	તેઓ	**teo**	તેઓનું	**teonuṃ**	તેઓને	**teone**
			તેમનું	**temnuṃ**	તેમને	**temne**

You will have the opportunity to look at further uses of નું **-nuṃ** in Unit 5.

2 You have now learned how to use the endings નું -num̥ and ને -ne and how these endings change the pronouns or nouns that they modify. Test your knowledge by filling in the blanks according to the English translations in brackets.

a દીપક ભાઈ (*'s sister*) _____ આ ચોપડી (*to my brother*) _____ આપે છે
Dīpakbhāī (*'s sister*) _____ ā copḍī (*to my brother*) _____ āpe che

b (*my wife's*) _____ ભાઈ સુંદર ગીત ગાય છે
(*my wife's*) _____ bhāī sum̥dar gīt gāve che

c તે (*to me*) _____ જૂની ચીજ આપે છે
te (*to me*) _____ junī cīj āpe che

d (*our*) _____ ભાડું મોંઘું છે
(*our*) _____ bhāḍum̥ mom̥ghum̥ che

2 IMPERSONAL VERBS

Gujarati has a very small number of verbs of a type similar to the English *it seems (to me)*. For example, if you want to say that you like something or someone in Gujarati, you will literally have to say that *it pleases you* or *is pleasing to you*; if you want to say that you think something, you may say that *it seems to you*; if you want to say that you get or receive something, you have to literally say that *it comes to you*, and so on.

The construction of the English expression *it seems to me* is very similar to that of Gujarati expressions which use ને **-ne** and a verb such as લાગવું **lāgvum̥** *to seem* (lit. *to stick to*).

a The impersonal construction *it seems (to me)* does not need a grammatical subject in Gujarati (i.e., you do not need to say *it*). For example:

મને લાગે છે	**mane lāge che**	*I think* (lit. *it seems to me*)
મને થાય છે	**mane thāy che**	*I think* (lit. *it is to me*)
મને ગમે છે	**mane game che**	*I like* (lit. *it is pleasing to me*)
તેને સારું છે	**tene sārum̥ che**	*he is well* (lit. *it is good to him*)

In these types of expressions where there is no grammatical subject, both verbs and adjectives will appear to be agreeing with neuter nouns in both positive and negative statements. For example:

મને સારું લાગે છે	**mane sārum̥ lāge che**	*it seems good to me*
મને નથી લાગતું	**mane nathī lāgtum̥**	*it doesn't seem to me*

b However, some impersonal constructions do have a grammatical subject, as in the English sentence *this book is pleasing to me*, in which *the book* is the grammatical subject. When there is a grammatical subject in Gujarati, the verb must agree with it. For example:

આ છોકરા મને નથી ગમતા	**ā chokrā mane nathī gamtā**	*I don't like these boys*

Here the verb ending agrees with the grammatical subject, which is છોકરા **chokrā** (m.pl.) *boys*.

Or:

મને સમજ નથી પડતી	**mane samaj nathī padtī**	*I do not understand* (lit. *to me understanding does not fall*)

Again, in this sentence the verb agrees with સમજ **samaj** (f. sing.) *understanding*. The affirmative of the same sentence would be: મને સમજ પડે છે **mane samaj paḍe che** *I understand.*

The verb મળવું **maḷvuṃ** (lit. *to meet*) can be used as an impersonal verb to mean *to get* or *to obtain*. In the negative of the impersonal construction the verb agrees with the subject. For example:

મને પૈસા મળે છે	**mane paisā maḷe che**	*I earn money* (lit. *money gets to me*)
મને પૈસા નથી મળતા	**mane paisā nathī maḷtā**	*I don't earn money* (lit. *money does not get to me*)

In these sentences the verb agrees with પૈસા **paisā** *money*, which is the grammatical subject.
However, when મળવું **maḷvuṃ** is used to mean *to meet* when referring to another person or group, it behaves like a regular personal verb. For example:

આપણે ત્યાં તમને મળીએ છીએ	**āpṇe tyāṃ tamne maḷīe chīe**	*we* (inclusive) *meet you there*
અમે ત્યાં એને નથી મળતા	**ame tyāṃ ene nathī maḷtā**	*we don't meet him there*

In this sentence note that ને **-ne** appears after the pronoun એ **-e** *him*, which means that the sentence literally translates as *we don't meet to him there*. While there are other ways to express meeting or doing things with people, in this case ને **-ne** can also indicate *with* as in *we don't meet with him there*.

You will have another opportunity to look at impersonal verbs in Unit 4.

3 Test your understanding of how impersonal verbs work by translating the brief statements below from English into Gujarati:

a I do not like that girl, but I do like these girls.
b I do not meet Deepakbhai at home.
c Deepakbhai does not understand.
d It seems to Deepakbhai…
e She does not understand the story (lit. the meaning of the story does not fall to her).
f I don't feel well.

3 NEGATIVES

The forms નહિ **nahi** and નહીં **nahīṃ** *no* or *not* are interchangeable in most circumstances and can be placed before or after the verb to make a sentence negative. However, ન **na** is used only before the verb. While some verb forms may take any of these negatives, others are restricted to using only ન **na**, as with the simple past tense (e.g., ન હતું **na hatuṃ** *(it) was not*). Accordingly, each time a new verb tense is introduced we will also present the corresponding negatives.

નહીં **nahīṃ** and નહિ **nahi** can also mean *no* in reply to a question, just as you have seen with the use of ના **nā** *no*. The negative મા**-mā** is used only when telling someone what not to do (negative commands), but is rarely used in colloquial speech. As you have already learned, નથી **nathi** (*is not*, etc.) is the negative of all forms of the verb હોવું **hovuṃ** *to be*.

When નથી **nathi** is used as an auxiliary verb, it may appear before or after the main verb. For example:

તે રોજ નથી આવતો	**te roj nathi avto**	*he doesn't come every day*

Or:

તે રોજ આવતો નથી	**te roj avto nathi**	*he doesn't come every day*

4 Review your knowledge of how to use negatives by making the following sentences negative.

a હું ત્યાં હતો/હતી huṃ tyāṃ hato/hatī

b દીપક ઘરે રોજ આવે છે Dīpak ghare roj ave che

c આ ખુરશી છે ā khurśī che

d હા, આ છોકરી ભારતીય છે hā, ā cokrī bhāratīy che

4 COMMANDS AND REQUESTS

In Gujarati, as in English, there are special forms of verbs, called imperatives, which are used for giving commands. In written English there is often an exclamation mark (!) after imperative forms (e.g. *do it!*, *go away!*). As with English, Gujarati imperatives do not require the use of a pronoun (for example, in the command *do it!* the pronoun *you* is implied but not stated), and often use an exclamation mark in the written form. Direct imperative statements in the simple present tense are formed by taking the stem of a verb (e.g. કર **kar** from the verb કરવું **karvuṃ** *to do, to make*) and making it agree with the stated or implied pronoun *you* (either તું **tuṃ** *you* (formal and/or plural) or તમે **tame** *you* (informal)).

a To make a command that agrees with the second person તું **tuṃ** *you* (informal), only the stem of the verb is used. Remember that the pronoun need not be written or spoken. For example:

કરવું **karvuṃ** *to do, to make* → કર! **kar!** *do (it)!*

જવવું **javvuṃ** *to go* → જા! **jā!** *go!*

Or, making a more complex command:

ઘેર જા!	**gher jā!**	*go home!*

b To make a command that agrees with the formal/plural second person pronoun તમે **tame** *you* ઓ **-o** is added to the stem of the verb.
For example:

આવવું **avvuṃ** *to come* → આવો! **āvo!** *come!*

Or, making a more complex command:

અંદર આવો!	**aṃdar āvo!**	*come in!*

જવવું **javvuṃ** *to go* → જાએ! *go!*

Or, making a more complex command:

ઘેર જાઓ!	**gher jāo!**	*go home!*

c To make indirect commands, as in *let's go*, the verb should be conjugated just as it would be in the continuous present, but without the auxiliary form of હોવું **hovuṃ** *to be*. For example:

જવવું **javvuṃ** *to go* → **āpṇe jaīe!** *let's* (inclusive) *go!*

d When expressing a wish indirectly for a third person pronoun, such as *may he come*, the verb should be conjugated as if it were a command given to a second person pronoun. So, an indirect command or 'wish' verb that agrees with તેઓ **teo** *he/they* (formal and/or plural) would be conjugated just as a direct command for તું **tuṃ** *you* (informal and/or singular). For example:

આવવું **āvvuṃ** *to come* → આવો! **āvo!** *may he* (formal) *come!*

ભગવાન એનું ભલું કરો!	**Bhagvān enuṃ bahluṃ karo!**	*May God grant him* (formal) *good fortune!* (lit. *may his good fortune be granted*)

Asking someone to do something

Normally when asking someone to do something politely a special form of the imperative is used. The 'polite' imperative is formed by inserting the suffix જ **-j** after the verb stem and before the personal endings એ **-e** and ઓ **-o** (as in the sounds that appear in છે **che** *is* and છો **cho** *are*), which correspond to either તું **tuṃ** or તમે **tame**. For example:

આવવું **āvvuṃ** *to come* → આવજે! **āvje!** *please come!* (agrees with તું **tuṃ**)
→ અવાજો! **āvjo!** *please come!* (agrees with તમે **tame**)

આપવું **āpvuṃ** *to give* → આપજે! **āpje!** *please give!* (agrees with તું **tuṃ**)
→આપજો! **āpjo!** *please give!* (agrees with તમે **tame**)

Asking someone to do a favour

For very formal requests, or when asking for favours, a form of the future imperative is used. This form requires adding the future verb ending શો **śo** to the verb stem (note that the future tense will be introduced in Unit 4). Using the future imperative can have a future sense or can simply express especially polite requests. For example:

મારા ઘેર આવશો!	**mārā gher āvśo!**	*would/will you please come to my house?*

Can you detect the difference between the above sentence and this one:

મારા ઘેર આવજો!	**mārā gher āvjo!**	*please come to my house!*

Note that there is no equivalent of the separate English word *please* when making requests in Gujarati. Extra politeness can also be expressed by using the particle જરા **jarā** *just, a little*, which can have special idiomatic implications. For example:

જરા મને ચોપડી આપો/આપજો/આપશો!

jarā mane copḍī āpo/āpjo/āpśo!

just give me the book, won't you!

Asking someone not to do something

These negative imperatives or commands take ન **na**, નહિ **nahi** or નહીં **nahiṃ**. For example, if you want to make a negative command that agrees with તમે **tame** (*you* formal and/or plural) you can use the following:

ઘેર નહિ જાઓ!	**gher nahi jāo!**	*don't go home!*
ઘેર ન જાઓ!	**gher na jāo!**	*don't go home!*
ઘેર ન જશો!	**gher na jaśo!**	*please don't go home!*

The form of the 'polite' imperative, where જ **-j** is added to the verb stem, cannot be used in the negative.

The negation મા **mā** may be used in some common expressions. For example:

ચિંતા મા કરો!	**ciṃtā mā karo!**	*don't worry!*

It is also correct (and more common) to say:

ચિંતા ના કરો!	**ciṃtā na karo!**	*don't worry!*

Another type of prohibitive statement can be formed by using ન **na**, નહિ **nahi** or નહીં **nahīṃ** instead of નથી **nathī** with the present tense form of a verb that would otherwise agree with નથી **nathī**. For example:

ઘેર નહિ જતો!	**gher nahi jato!**	*don't go home!*

5 You have now learned how to make commands and requests. Test your knowledge by translating the following sentences from Gujarati to English or from English to Gujarati.

a Don't worry, Deepakbhai, Leelaben comes here daily.
b દીપક! મને પાણી આપજે! Dīpak! mane pānī āpje!
c Deepakbhai, you and Leelaben (will) please come to my home today!
d ઘેર ન જશો! અંદર આવો, ચિંતા ન કરો, હું પણ આવું છું gher na jaśo! aṃdar āvo, ciṃtā na karo, huṃ paṇ avuṃ cuṃ

Vocabulary builder

તમારે... છે	tamāre ... che	*you have...*
ભાઈ-બહેન (n.pl.)	bhāī-bahen	*brothers and sisters*
નામ (n.)	nām	*name*
મારે કોઈ બહેન નથી	māre koī bahen nathī	*I don't have a sister/ any sisters*
એકની એક દીકરી (f.)	eknī ek dīkrī	*only daughter* (lit. *one of one daughters*)
અમારી સાથે	amārī sāthe	*with us*
કાકા (m.pl.)	kākā	*uncle*
દીકરો (m.)	dīkro	*son*
સંયુકત કુટુંબ (n.)	saṃyukta kuṭumb	*joint family*
ઠીક	ṭhīk	*OK*
કોઈ આવે છે!	koī āve che!	*someone's coming!*
માણસ (m./n.)	māṇas	*person*
જુઓ!	juo!	*look!*
એની પાસે નવી ગાડી છે	eṇī pāse navī gāḍī che	*he has a new car*
ફાઈન	phāīn	*fine* (an English loan word)
તમારી સાથે	tamārī s āthe	*with you*
અમારે ત્યાં	amāre tyāṃ	*to/at our place*
તમારે ત્યાં	tāmāre tyāṃ	*to/at your place*
જરૂર	jarūr	*certainly*
કંઈ વાંધો નહિ	kamī vāṃdho nahi	*no problem*
મારી રાહ જોજો!	mārī rāh jojo!	*wait for me!*

તમારે કેટલાં ભાઈ-બહેન છે? TAMĀRE KETLĀṂ BHĀĪ-BAHEN CHE? HOW MANY BROTHERS AND SISTERS DO YOU HAVE?

03.02 *Nalini Patel and Gopi Parekh are having a discussion in a café on the Ealing Road.*

1 What is the main focus of Nalini and Gopi's conversation and to whom do they refer?

Dialogue 2

ગોપી	**તમારે કેટલાં ભાઈ-બહેન છે?**
Gopī	tamāre keṭlām bhāī-bahen che?
નલિની	**મારે એક મોટા ભાઈ અને એક નાનો ભાઈ છે.**
Nalinī	māre ek moṭā bhāī ane ek nāno bhāī che.

ગોપી	**એમનાં નામો શું છે?**
Gopī	emnāṃ nāmo śuṃ che?
નલિની	**મોટા ભાઈ નું નામ શૈલેશ છે અને નાના ભાઈનું નામ કમલેશ છે. મારે કોઈ બહેન નથી. તમારે એક જ બહેન છે, ને?**
Nalinī	moṭā bhāī num nām Śaileś che ane nānā bhāī nuṃ nām Kamleś che. māre koī bahen nathī. tamāre ek j bahen che, ne?
ગોપી	**ના, હું એકની એક દીકરી છું, પણ મારા કાકાનો દીકરો અમારી સાથે રહે છે. એનું નામ અનુજ છે.**
Gopī	nā, huṃ eknī ek dīkrī chuṃ, paṇ mārā kākā no dīkro amārī sāthe rahe che. enuṃ nām Anuj che.
નલિની	**તમે સંયુકત કુટુંબમાં રહો છો?**
Nalinī	tame saṃyukt kuṭuṃbmāṃ raho cho?
ગોપી	**હા, અમારું ઘર મોટું છે, તો ઠીક છે.**
Gopī	hā, amāruṃ ghar moṭum che, to ṭhīk che.
નલિની	**કોઈ આવે છે! આ માણસ કોણ છે?**
Nalinī	koī āve che! ā māṇas koṇ che?
ગોપી	**અનુજ છે. જુઓ, એની પાસે નવી ગાડી છે. ફાઈન છે, ને? ચાલો, હું ઘેર જાઉં.**
Gopī	Anuj che. juo, enī pāse navī gāḍī che. phāīn che, ne? cālo, huṃ gher jāuṃ.
નલિની	**હું તમારી સાથે આવું?**
Nalinī	huṃ tāmārī sāthe āvum?
ગોપી	**જરૂર. કંઈ વાંધો નહિ. અમારે ત્યાં આવો, ને?**
Gopī	jarūr. kaṃī vāṃdho nahi. amāre tyāṃ āvo, ne?
નલિની	**મારી રાહ જોજો. ચાલો, આપણે તમારે ત્યાં જઈએ!**
Nalini	mārī rāh jojo. cālo, āpṇe tamāre tyāṃ jaīe!

2 True or false? Read and correct the following sentences based on the information in the dialogue.

a **નલિનીને બે બહેનો છે.**
Nalinīne be baheno che.

b **ગોપીને બે ભાઈઓ છે.**
Gopīne be bhāīo che.

c **નલિનીના કાકાના દીકરાનું નામ અનુજ છે.**
Nalinīnā kākānā dikrānuṃ nāṃ Anuj che.

3 Answer the following questions.

a શૈલેશ અને કમલેશ કોણ છે?
Śaileś ane Kamaleś koṇ che?

b કોની પાસે નવી ગાડી છે?
konī pāse navī gāḍi che?

Note that **કોની પાસે konī pāse** literally means *near whom*, but suggests *with whom* when used with reference to an object.

Language discovery

Read and listen to the dialogue again.

a Pay special attention to the underlined words – what do all these words have in common?

b You will easily recognize some of the underlined words, but you are being introduced to some others for the first time. Which ones?

5 MORE IRREGULAR VERB FORMS IN THE SIMPLE PRESENT TENSE

જોવું jovuṃ *to see* is irregular in the present tense. You are already familiar with how verbs work in the simple present tense, but some verbs behave irregularly. Can you see how this verb is different from others you have been introduced to? (For the first explanation of this see Unit 2.)

Singular			
First person	હું જોઉં છું	**huṃ jouṃ chuṃ**	*I see/am seeing*
Second person	તું જુએ છે	**tuṃ jue che**	*you see/are seeing*
Third person	તે જુઓ છે (and આ, એ છે)	**te jue che** (and **ā**, **e che**)	*he, she, it sees/is seeing* (and *it, this, that sees/is seeing*)
Plural			
First person	અમે જોઈએ છીએ આપણે જોઈએ છીએ	**ame joīe chīe** **āpṇe joīe chīe**	*we see/are seeing* (exclusive) *we see/are seeing* (inclusive)
Second person	તમે જુઓ છો	**tame juo cho**	*you see/are seeing*
Third person	તેઓ, તે જુએ છે (and આ, એ છે)	**teo, te jue che** (and **ā**, **e che**)	*they see/are seeing* (and *they, these, those see/are seeing*)
Negative			
	જોતું નથી	**jotuṃ nathī**	*does not see/is not seeing*

6 PRONOUNS WITH ADVERBIALS

In Unit 2, you were introduced to several simple clitics, such as માં **-māṃ** *in*. While clitics are usually written as part of the word that they govern (for example, બજારમાં **bajārmāṃ** *in the market*), there is another group of clitics that function in a similar way, but which are written separately from the word that they govern. These are called adverbials (for example, પાસે **pāse** *near* and સાથે **sāthe** *with*). In most cases when such clitics are used the variable નું **-nuṃ** must be added to the word governed by the adverbial. Depending on which adverbial is being used, નું **-nuṃ** may appear as ન **-na**, ની **-ni** or ને **-ne**. Although some speakers use ના **-nā** with all adverbials, in written Gujarati it is best to memorize and use the various forms of નું **-nuṃ** as appropriate (see Appendix 2 for a full list of these adverbials). The corresponding possessive forms of pronouns are also used in the case of adverbials (e.g. મારા **mārā**, મારી **mārī**, મારે **māre**, etc.). Here are some examples:

ભાઈની સાથે આવો	**bhāīnī sāthe āvo**	*come with (your) brother*
એની સાથે આવો	**enī sāthe āvo**	*come with him/her*
મારી સાથે આવો	**mārī sāthe āvo**	*come with me*

While pronouns always take the appropriate form of નું **-nuṃ** (e.g. એને **ene**, એના **enā**, એની, **enī**, etc.), when adverbials are attached to nouns or proper names, the various forms of નું **-nuṃ** may be omitted. For example:

તે ભાઈ સાથે આવે છે	**te bhāī sāthe āve che**	*she is coming with (her) brother*

Or:

તે ભાઈની સાથે આવે છે	**te bhāīnī sāthe āve che**	*she is coming with her brother*

But:

તે એની સાથે આવે છે	**te enī sāthe āve che**	*she is coming with him*

And:

આપણે સાથે બજારે જઈએ છીએ	**āpṇe sāthe bajāre jaīe chīe**	*we are going to the market together* (lit. *with each other*)

6 Translate the following sentences from Gujarati to English.

a લીલાબેન દીપકભાઈ (ની) સાથે ઘરે આવે છે Līlāben Dīpakbhāī (nī) sāthe ghare āve che

b એ છોકરીઓ ભાઈઓ (ની) સાથે નથી આવતાં e cokrīo bhāīo (nī) sāthe nathi āvtāṃ

7 EXPRESSIONS FOR *TO HAVE*

Gujarati does not have an equivalent for the verb *to have* in English and thus expresses possession in a variety of ways. The main distinction is between having things that are movable and those that involve a more permanent relationship.

a In the case of movable objects ની પાસે **nī pāse** is used. For example:

મારી પાસે પૈસા છે	**mārī pāse paisā che**	*I have money*

b In the case of immovable objects (such as houses), relatives and parts of the body, a form of નું **-nuṃ** will be used which agrees with the thing possessed. Sometimes ને **-e**, which does not directly correspond to gender and number, can also be used. For example:

એનું એક મોટું ઘર છે	**enuṃ ek moṭuṃ ghar che**	*he/she has a big house*

But:

એને બે છોકરા છે	**ene be chokrā che**	*he/she has two boys*
મારે બે છોકરા છે	**māre be chokrā che**	*I have two boys*

As you have already seen in several dialogues, using ને **-ne** with a pronoun followed by ત્યાં **tyāṃ** *there* means *at x's place*. For example:

અમારે ત્યાં આવો!	**amāre tyāṃ āvo!**	*come to our place!*
હું એને ત્યાં રહું છું	**huṃ ene tyāṃ rahuṃ chuṃ**	*I am staying at her place*

8 EXPRESSIONS FOR *SOME* AND *ANY*

a In Gujarati there are three different adjectives that mean *some* or *any*: કોઈ **koī** *some, any*, કંઈ **kaṃī** *some, any*, કશું **kaśuṃ** *any (at all)*. કોઈ **koī** and કંઈ **kaṃī** are invariable, while કશું **kaśuṃ** is variable. Some speakers will use કોઈ **koī** and કંઈ **kaṃī** interchangeably; others will use કોઈ **koī** when referring to people and કંઈ **kaṃī** when referring to inanimate objects. કંઈ **kaṃī** is often used with neuter nouns. કશું **kaśuṃ** is used mainly in negative situations. For example:

હું કોઈ દિવસ બજારમાં નથી જતી	**huṃ koī divas bajārmāṃ nathī jatī**	*I never go to the market*
કોઈ સ્ત્રી તમારી રાહ જુએ છે	**koī strī tamārī rāh jue che**	*some woman is waiting for you*
તમારી પાસે કંઈ ચોપડી છે?	**tamārī pāse kaṃī copḍī che?**	*have you got a book with you?*
મારે કોઈ કામ નથી	**māre koī kām nathī**	*I don't have any work*
મારે કંઈ કામ નથી	**māre kaṃī kām nathī**	*I've not got any work or I don't have any work*
કંઈ કામ છે?	**kaṃī kām che?**	*is there any work? or may I help you?*
તે કશું કામ નથી કરતો	**te kaśuṃ kām nathī karto**	*he doesn't do any work*

b These three forms are also used as pronouns, meaning *someone, anyone, anything*. Here, કોઈ **koī** is used for people and કંઈ **kaṃī** for inanimate objects. For example:

કોઈ બારણા પાસે છે?	**koī bārṇā pāse che?**	*is there someone at the door?*
કંઈ નહિ	**kaṃī nahi**	*it's nothing, it's all right*
મેજ પર શું છે? – કંઈ નથી	**mej par śuṃ che? – kaṃī nathī**	*what's on the table? – nothing*
કોઈ છે?	**koī che?**	*is anyone there?*

c These forms are not used in the plural, although a reduplicated form કોઈ કોઈ **koī koī** is used with people and inanimate objects. For example:

કોઈ કોઈ માણસો અહીં છે	**koī koī māṇaso ahīṃ che**	*some people are here*
કોઈ કોઈ વાર તે આવે છે	**koī koī vār te āve che**	*he comes sometimes*

Otherwise, કેટલાંક **keṭlāṃk** *some, quite a few* and થોડાંક **thoḍāṃk** *some, not many* are used. These words behave like variable adjectives before their ક **-ka** endings. For example:

કેટલાક માણસો ત્યાં હતા	**keṭlāk māṇaso tyāṃ hatā**	*some people were there*
થોડાક માણસો ત્યાં હતા	**thoḍāk māṇaso tyāṃ hatā**	*a few people were there*

Practice

અભ્યાસ ABHYĀS

A traditional Gujarati house uses space quite differently from a modern house. In traditional houses the important division is between private and public space. In such homes, outside visitors are not admitted to the inner rooms, which are private family spaces. Amongst family members, however, there is no private space; people may not have their own bedrooms. Often the men of the house sleep in one area, and the women in another. In modern houses, space is used as it might be in most European homes, to a greater or lesser degree.

NEW VOCABULARY

ઓટલો (m.)	**oṭlo**	*verandah at the front of a house*
પડસાળ (f.)	**paḍsāḷ**	*room at the front of a house in front of the* ઓરડો **orḍo** *(usually with a swing)*
ઓરડો (m.)	**orḍo**	*room (traditionally a rear room)*
ચોક (m.)	**cok**	*internal courtyard*

Modern names for rooms include:

સૂવાનો ઓરડો (m.)	**sūvāno orḍo**	*bedroom*
બેઠક (f.)	**beṭhak**	*living room*
રહેવાનો ઓરડો (m.)	**rahevano orḍo**	*living room*
રસોડું (n.)	**rasodum**	*kitchen*
નાહવાનો ઓરડો (m.)	**nāhvāno orḍo**	*bathroom*

1 Answer the following questions in Gujarati about the house in this drawing.

a આ ઘર કેવું છે?
ā ghar kevuṃ che?

b એ મોટું છે?
e moṭuṃ che?

c કેટલા ઓરડા છે?
keṭlā orḍā che?

d ઓરડાઓનાં નામો શું છે?
orḍāonāṃ nāmo śuṃ che?

e તમને આ ઘર ગમે છે?
tamne ā ghar game che?

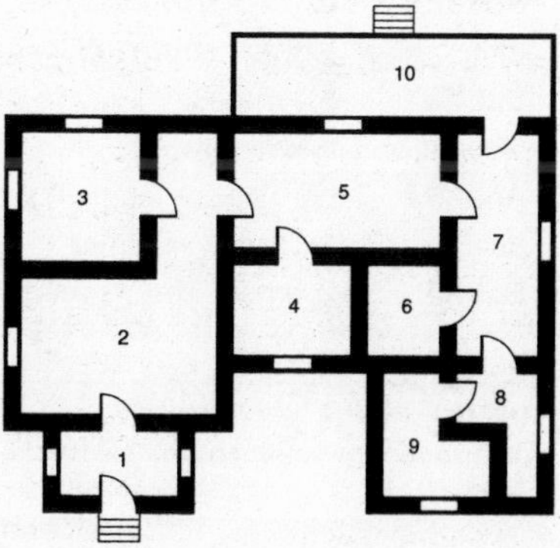

2 Based on what you have learned in this unit thus far, find one grammatical error in each sentence and correct it accordingly.

a હું તારો ભાઈને સાંભળું છું.
humṃ tāro bhāīne sāṃhaḷuṃ chuṃ.

b એ મારું સારું લાગે છે.
e māruṃ sāruṃ lāge che.

c આ ઘર મારી પત્નીને નથી ગમતી.
ā ghar mārī patnīne nathī gamtī.

d મારું ઘરમાં ચાર ઓરડા છે.
māruṃ gharmāṃ cār orḍā che.

NEW VOCABULARY

સાંભળવું	**sāṃbhaḷvuṃ**	*to hear, to listen*
ઓછું	**ochuṃ**	*few, less, insufficient*

3 The following dialogue between Anahita and Shobha has been mixed up. Find what has been put out of place and rearrange the sentences into a coherent order.

અનાહિતા	**મને ખબર છે. મારી પાસે થોડા પૈસા છે.**
Anāhitā	mane khabar che māri pāse thoḍā paisā che.
શોભા	**શહેરના બજારમાં વેપારીઓ સારો પણ મોંઘો માલ રાખે છે.**
Śobhā	śahernā bajārmāṃ vepārīo sāro paṇ moṃgho māl rākhe che.
અનાહિતા	**કેમ નહીં? ચાલો જઈએ!**
Anāhitā	kem nahīṃ? cālo jaīe!
શોભા	**આજે મારે કંઈ કામ નથી. હું તારી સાથે આવું?**
Śobhā	āje māre kaṃī kāṃ nathī. huṃ tārī sāthe āvuṃ?
અનાહિતા	**હું બજારે જાઉં છું.**
Anāhitā	huṃ bajāre jāuṃ chuṃ.
શોભા	**ક્યાં જાય છે, અનાહિતા?**
Śobhā	kyāṃ jāy che, Anāhitā?

વેપારીઓ સારો પણ મોંઘો માલ રાખે છે
vepārīo sāro paṇ moṃgho māl rākhe che
the merchants keep nice but expensive goods

4 03.03 **Your name is Steve and you have just started to learn Gujarati. You'd like to practise speaking with Viren. Complete your part of the dialogue.**

a	**You**	*Say hello to Viren.*
	વિરેન	**મજામાં. કેમ, સ્ટીવ, તમે ગુજરાતી શીખો છો?**
	Viren	majāmāṃ. kem che, Sṭiv, tame gujarātī śīkho cho?
b	**You**	*Say yes, you're learning Gujarati and that it's very difficult.*
	વિરેન	**ના, સહેલું છે! તમને ગુજરાતી ગમે છે?**
	Viren	nā, sahelum che! tamne gujarātī game che?
c	**You**	*Ask him what he's saying. Say you don't understand. Ask him to speak slowly.*
	વિરેન	**તમને ગુજરાતી ગમે છે?**
	Viren	tamne gujarātī game che?
d	**You**	*Say you like it very much indeed.*

NEW VOCABULARY

શીખવું	**sīkhvuṃ**	*to learn*
સહેલું	**sahelum**	*easy*
અઘરું	**aghrum**	*difficult, hard*
ધીમે	**dhīme**	*slowly*

5 Take the following continuous present sentences and turn them into commands or requests. Use the following example to guide you:

મારો દીકરો બજારે જાય છે, દીકરા ...! māro dīkro bajāre jāy che, dīkrā...!

→ **દીકરા, બજારે જા!** dīkrā, bajāre jā!

a **દીપકભાઈ મારે ત્યાં આવે છે. દીપકભાઈ...!**
Dīpakbhāi māre tyāṃ āve che. Dīpakbhāī...!

b **શોભા કામ કરે છે. શોભા...!**
Śobha kām kare che. Śobhā...!

c **આનલ અને ઉદિતા મારી વાત સાંભળે છે. આનલ અને ઉદિતા...!**
Ānal ane Uditā mārī vāt sāṃbhaḷe che. Ānal ane Uditā...!

d **રચનાબેન મને સામાન આપે છે. રચનાબેન, જરા...!**
Racnāben mane sāmān āpe che. Racnāben, jarā...!

e **નીલા ઘેર નથી જતી. નીલા...!**
Nīlā gher nathī jatī. Nilā...!

6 Change the following sentences so that they include કોઈ koī, કંઈ kaṃī, કશું kaśuṃ or કેટલાંક keṭlāṃk instead of the underlined form. Use the following example to guide you:

તમને <u>આ</u> ચોપડી ગમે છે? tamne <u>ā</u> copḍī game che?

→ તમને <u>કોઈ</u> ચોપડી ગમે છે? tamne <u>koī</u> copḍī game che?

a દુકાનમાં <u>એ</u> મળતું નથી.
dukānmāṃ <u>e</u> maḷtuṃ nathī.

b <u>આ</u> કામ રહે છે?
<u>a</u> kām rahe che?

c <u>આ લોકોને</u> શહેર ગમે છે.
<u>ā lokone</u> śaher game che.

d <u>આ</u> દહાડે મારે ત્યાં આવજો!
<u>ā</u> dahāḍe māre tyāṃ āvjo!

e તે <u>ખૂબ</u> અભ્યાસ કરતો નથી.
te <u>khūb</u> abhyās karto nathī.

સમજયા/સમજયાં? SAMJYĀ/SAMJYĀṂ? *DO YOU UNDERSTAND?*

Read the following passage.

મહેર અને ફિરદોસ મિસ્ત્રી શિક્ષકો છે. એમને એક દીકરો અને એક દીકરી છે. દીકરાનું નામ રેશાદ છે અને દીકરીનું નામ અનાહિતા છે. તેઓ નાનાં છે અને નિશાળે જાય છે. તેઓ મુંબઈમાં રહે છે. એમનું મકાન ઘણું નાનું છે પણ શહેરમાં જ છે. મુંબઈમાં ઘણા લોકો શહેરથી દૂર રહે છે કારણ કે શહેરનાં મકાનો બહુ મોંઘાં છે. મકાન બહુ સારું છે. એમાં બે સૂવાના ઓરડા, એક રહેવાનો ઓરડો, નાનું રસોડું, અને નાહવાનો ઓરડો છે.

Maher ane Phirdos Mistrī śikṣako che. emne ek dīkro ane ek dīkrī che. dīkrānuṃ nām Reśād che ane dīkrī nuṃ nām Anāhitā che. teo nānāṃ che ane niśāḷe jāy che. teo Muṃbaīmām rahe che. emnuṃ makān ghaṇuṃ nānuṃ che paṇ śahermāṃ j che. Muṃbaimāṃ ghaṇā loko śaherthī dūr rahe che kāraṇ ke śahernāṃ makāno bahu moṃghāṃ che. makān bahu sāruṃ che. emāṃ be sūvānā orḍā, ek rahevāno orḍo, nānuṃ rasoḍuṃ, ane nāhvāno orḍo che.

Answer the following questions based on the paragraph you have just read.

1 આ મકાનમાં કેટલા માણસો રહે છે?
ā makānmāṃ keṭlā māṇaso rahe che?

2 મહેર અને ફિરદોસ શું કામ કરે છે?
Maher ane Phirdos śuṃ kām kare che?

3 એમના દીકરાનું નામ શું છે?
emnā dīkrānuṃ nām śuṃ che?

4 અનાહિતાને કેટલી બહેનો છે?
Anāhitāne keṭlī baheno che?

Test yourself

How would you do the following in Gujarati?

1. Ask someone where they live.
2. Say that you like London.
3. Ask Deepakbhai what is on the table.
4. Tell Deepakbhai that there is nothing in the market.
5. Ask Samir what work he does.
6. Tell your daughter to wash your new shirt.

SELF CHECK

	I CAN...
○	... talk about where I live and ask others questions about where they live.
○	... talk about my family.
○	... express opinions.
○	... give commands.

4 આપણે શું કરીશું?
āpṇe suṃ karīśuṃ?
What shall we do?

In this unit you will learn how to:

- ***talk about future events.***
- ***say you are hungry and thirsty and talk about what you like to eat.***
- ***talk about clothing and styles of dress.***
- ***talk about how you feel and what you know.***

ગુજરાત અને ગુજરાતીઓ gujarāt ane gujarātīo
Gujarat and Gujaratis

In Gujarat people wear many different kinds of clothing, from more traditional Gujarati styles to the latest international designer fashions. Occasion and location often dictate what is appropriate to wear. For example, at a Gujarati wedding women often wear quite costly and ornate saris and jewellery.

Ahmedabad, the seventh largest city in India and the largest city of Gujarat, used to be the capital of Gujarat until Gandhinagar, just outside of today's Ahmedabad, was built in the 1960s. Ahmedabad was founded in 1411 by Ahmad Shah, who established the independent Islamic kingdom of Gujarat. There are many beautiful buildings dating from this time, images of which can be found in George Michell and Snehal Shah's lavishly illustrated book *Ahmadabad*. For several centuries Ahmedabad has also been an important textile and industrial centre, sometimes called the Manchester of India. If you ever visit the city, be sure to take a walking tour of the old part of town to see the older buildings. This is called the Heritage Walk and details can be found online at www.egovamc.com/AhmCity/Heritage.aspx. If you are interested in textiles you can visit the Calico Museum of Textiles (www.calicomuseum.com).

Vocabulary builder

રજા (f.)	rajā	*holiday*
આવતી કાલ (f.)	āvtī kāl	*tomorrow*
આપણે જઈશું	āpṇne jaīśuṃ	*we will go*
કેવી રીતે	kevī rīte	*in what way, in what manner*
ટ્રેનમાં	ṭrenmāṃ	*by train*
આવશે	āvśe	*he/she/it will come*
સાથે	sāthe	*together*
આપણે શું કરીશું?	āpṇe śuṃ karīśuṃ?	*what will we do?*
આપણે રહીશું?	āpṇe rahīśuṃ?	*will we stay?*
માસી (f.)	māśī	*aunt* (mother's sister)
મામા	māmā	*uncle* (mother's brother)
હું બતાવીશ	huṃ batāvīś	*I will show you*
તને ખબર છે કે…	tane khabar che ke…	*you know that…*
જૂનાં જૂનાં	jūnaṃ jūnaṃ	*very old*
વગેરે	vagere	*etc.*
નદી (f.)	nadī	*river*
તું જાણે છે?	tuṃ jāṇe che?	*do you know?*
સાબરમતી	sābarmatī	*Sabarmati* (name of a river)
ગાંધીજી	gāṃdhījī	*Gandhi*
આશ્રમ (m.)	āśram	*ashram*
તમે મને ત્યાં લઈ જશો?	tame mane tyāṃ laī jaśo?	*will you take me there?*
ખુબ મઝા આવશે, મા	khūb majhā āvśe, mā	*it will be great fun, mother*
એને ઈસ્પિતાલમાં થોડું કામ રહે છે	ene ispitālmāṃ thoḍuṃ kām rahe che	*she has a little work left in the hospital*
થોડા દિવસો પછી	thoḍā divaso pachī	*after a few days*
ત્યારે	tyāre	*then*
સૌરાષ્ટ્ર (n.)	saurāṣṭra	*Saurashtra* (peninsular Gujarat)
આપણે ફરવા જઈશું	āpṇe pharvā jaīśuṃ	*we will tour around*
તૈયાર!	taiyār kar!	*get ready!*

04.01 Prabodh and his daughter Leena are talking about their forthcoming holiday.

1 Where are Prabodh and Leena going on holiday? What activities do they have planned and how will they travel to their destination?

Dialogue 1

પ્રબોધ	**કાલથી મને થોડા દિવસની રજા મળશે. આવતી કાલે આપણે અમદાવાદ જઈશું.**
Prabodh	kālthī mane thoḍa divasnī rajā maḷśe. āvtī kāle āpṇe amdāvād jaīśuṃ.
લીના	**કેવી રીતે જઈશું? આપણે ટ્રેનમાં જઈશું?**
Līnā	kevi rite jaīśuṃ? āpṇe ṭrenmāṃ jaīśuṃ?
પ્રબોધ	**તારો ભાઈ આજે મુંબઈથી આવશે. આવતી કાલે આપણે સાથે ટ્રેનમાં જઈશું.**
Prabodh	tāro bhāī aje mumbāīthī āvśe. āvtī kāle āpṇe sāthe ṭrenmāṃ jaīśuṃ.
લીના	**આપણે અમદાવાદમાં શું કરીશું? આપણે શાંતામાસી અને વિનોદમામાને ત્યાં રહીશું?**
Līnā	āpṇe amdāvādmāṃ śuṃ karīśuṃ? āpṇe śāmta-māsi ane Vinodmāmāne tyāṃ rahīśuṃ?
પ્રબોધ	**હા, જરૂર. હું તને અમદાવાદ બતાવીશ. તને ખબર છે કે હું ત્યાં વિદ્યાર્થી હતો? શહેરમાં ઘણાં જૂનાં જૂનાં મકાનો છે અને મોટી મોટી દુકાનો વગેરે છે. નદી પણ છે. તું એનું નામ જાણે છે?**
Prabodh	hā, jarur. huṃ tane amadāvād batāvīś. tane khabar che ke huṃ tyāṃ vidyārtī hato? śaher māṃ ghaṇāṃ jūnāṃ jūnāṃ makāno che ane moṭī moṭī dukāno vagere che. nadī paṇ che. tuṃ enuṃ nām jāṇo che?
લીના	**હા, સાબરમતી છે. ગાંધીજીનો આશ્રમ એના પર છે. તમે મને ત્યાં લઈ જશો?**
Līnā	hā, sābarmatī che. Gāṃdhījīno āśram enā par che. tame mane tyāṃ laī jaśo?
પ્રબોધ	**હા, હું લઈ જઈશ! ખૂબ મઝા આવશે.**
Prabodh	hā, huṃ lai jaiś! khūb majhā āvśe.
લીના	**મા નહિ આવે?**
Līnā	mā nahi āve?
પ્રબોધ	**એને ઈસ્પિતાલમાં થોડું કામ રહે છે. તે થોડા દિવસો પછી આવશે. ત્યારે આપણે સૌરાષ્ટ્રમાં ફરવા જઈશું. ચાલો, સામાન તૈયાર કર!**
Prabodh	ene ispitālmāṃ thoḍuṃ kām rahe che. te thoḍā divaso pachī āvśe. tyāre āpṇe saurāṣṭramāṃ pharvā jaīśuṃ. cālo, sāmān taiyār kar!

2 True or false? Read and correct the following sentences based on the information given in the dialogue.

a આ લોકો ગાડીમાં અમદાવાદ જશે.
ā loko gāḍīmāṃ amdāvād jaśe.

b અમદાવાદમાં તેઓ લીનાના કાકાને ત્યાં રહેશે.
amdāvādmāṃ teo Linānā kākāne tyāṃ raheśe.

c લીનાની મા અમદાવાદ નહિ આવશે.
Līnānī mā amdāvād nahi āvśe.

3 Answer the following questions based on what you learned in the dialogue.

a લીના, અમદાવામાં શું કરશે?
Līnā, amdāvādmāṃ śuṃ karśe?

b પ્રબોધને લાગે છે કે લીનાને અમદાવાદ ગમશે?
Prabodhne lāge che ke Lināne amdāvād gamśe?

Language discovery

Read and listen to the dialogue again.

In this unit you will be learning how to discuss events that occur in the future. All of the underlined words in the dialogue are verbs in the future tense. How do the endings of these verbs differ from other verb endings you have already learned? Do you notice any patterns?

1 THE FUTURE TENSE

The future tense, as its name implies, is used for talking about future actions (*I shall go*, *he will see*, etc.). In Gujarati, it is formed by adding a set of future endings to the verb stem. For example:

Infinitive: કરવું **karvuṃ** *to do, to make*

Stem: કર **kar-**

Future: કરીશ **kariś** *I will do*

Singular			
First person	હું કરીશ	**huṃ karīś**	*I will do, make*
Second person	તું કરશે	**tuṃ karśe**	*you will do*
Third person	તે કરશે (and આ, એ કરશે)	**te karśe** (and **ā**, **e karśe**)	*he, she, it will do* (*and it, this, that will do*)

Plural			
First person	અમે કરીશું	**ame karīśuṃ**	*we will do* (exclusive)
Second person	આપણે કરીશું	**āpṇe karīśuṃ**	*we will do* (inclusive)
Third person	તમે કરશો	**tame karśo** **teo, te karśe**	*you will do* *they will do*

In order to form negatives, the future uses નહિ **nahi** or ન **na** *not*. For example:

હું નહિ/ન કરીશ	**huṃ nahi/na karīś**	*I will not do*

a Verbs that have more than one stem (and which behave irregularly in the present tenses) use the following stems in the future:

જવું **javuṃ** *to go* uses જ **ja-**. For example:

હું જઈશ	**huṃ jaīś**	*I will go*
તે જશે	**te jaśe**	*he/she/it will go*

થવું **thavuṃ** *to be* uses થ **tha-**. For example:

હું થઈશ	**huṃ thaīś**	*I will be*
તે થશે	**te thaśe**	*he/she/it will be*

જોવું **jovuṃ** *to see* uses જો **jo-**. For example:

હું જોઈશ	**huṃ joīś**	*I will see*
તે જોશે	**te jośe**	*he/she/it will see*

b Verbs that use two different stems in the present tenses (e.g. રહેવું **rahevuṃ** *to live, to stay*, કહેવું **kahevuṃ**, લેવું **levuṃ**) behave similarly in the future tense:

લેવું **levuṃ** *to carry, to take*, for example, uses the stem લે **le-** before present tense endings that begin with a consonant, and the stem લ **la-** before present tense endings that begin with a vowel. For example:

હું લઈશ	**huṃ laīś**	*I will take* (that is લ **la-** + ઈશ = લઈશ
તે લેશે	**te leśe**	*he/she/it will take*

Similarly, કહેવું **kahevuṃ** *to say* and રહેવું rahevuṃ *to live, to stay* use the stems કહે **kahe-** and રહે **rahe-** respectively before consonants, and કહ **kah-** and રહ **rah-** before vowels. For example:

હું કહીશ	**huṃ kahīś**	*I shall say*
તે કહેશે	**te kaheśe**	*he/she/it will say*
હું રહીશ	**hum rahīś**	*I shall stay*
તે રહેશે	**te raheśe**	*he/she/it will stay*

c The future of the verb હોવું **hovuṃ** *to be* is formed from the infinitive form of the verb, હોવું **hovuṃ**, which is quite distinct from its present forms such as છે **che**, etc. Before future tense endings that begin with vowels હોવું **hovuṃ** *to be* uses the stem હો **ho-**, and before vowels it uses હ **ha-**. For example:

હું હોઈશ	**huṃ hoīś**	*I will be*
તે હશે	**te haśe**	*he/she/it will be*

The future tense is used to refer to future action, to express probability or supposition, and for the future imperative (see Unit 3). For example:

તે કાલે આવશે	**te kāle āvśe**	*he will come tomorrow*
તે ઘેર હશે	**te gher haśe**	*he must be at home* (lit. *he will be at home*)
મારે ત્યાં ચા પીવા આવશો	**māre tyāṃ cā pīvā āvśo**	*please come to my place to drink tea* (lit. *you will come to my place to drink tea*)

1 You have now learned how to express actions that take place in the future. Test your knowledge of the future tense by changing all of the following simple present tense sentences into the future tense.

a હું તમને વાર્તા કઉં છું huṃ tamne vārtā kauṃ chuṃ.
b તે ઘેર નથી જાતી te gher nathī jātī.
c દીપકભાઈ બજાર માં છે પણ લીલાબેન નથી Dīpakbhāī bajār māṃ che, paṇ Līlāben nathī.
d આપણે ગુજરાત જાઈએ છીએ āpṇe gujarāt jāīe chīe.

2 EXPRESSIONS OF PURPOSE

The invariable verb ending વા **-vā** (a form of the infinitive ending વું **-vuṃ**) is added to verb stems to express intention or purpose such as કરવા **karvā** *to do* (from કરવું **karvuṃ** *to do, to make*). For example:

તે ફરવા જાય છે	**te pharvā jāy che**	*she is going for a walk*
હું ભાઈને મળવા જાઉં છું	**hum bhāīne maḷvā jāuṃ chuṃ**	*I am going to meet my brother*

The adverbial (see Unit 3) (ને) માટે **(ne) māṭe** *for the sake of, in order to* is occasionally used after the વા **-vā** form. For example:

તેઓ ગાંધીજીનો આશ્રમ જોવા માટે અમદાવાદ જશે	**teo Gāṃdhījīno āśram jovā māṭe amdāvād jaśe**	*they will go to Ahmedabad in order to see Gandhi's ashram*

2 Test your knowledge and translate these sentences from English into Gujarati.

a They will go to hear a story.

b Deepakbhai and Leelaben went home to wash their shirts.

c I do not go home to meet my sisters every day.

3 કે KE AND એમ EM

Direct speech is the term used when something that was previously said is reproduced. In English, direct speech is usually given within quotation marks. For example:

'Tomorrow we will go to Ahmedabad,' said Prabodh.

Indirect speech, or reported speech, is the term used when somebody reports what someone else has said. For example:

Prabodh said that tomorrow they would go to Ahmedabad.

As you can see, in this example several changes have been made to the original sentence: *we* has become *they*, and *will* has become *would*. However, in Gujarati reported speech appears in the same way as direct speech and is introduced by કે **ke** *that* or followed by એમ **em** *thus*.

કે **ke** *that* can also be used just as *that* is used in English. For example:

તેને ખબર છે કે આપણે આવીશું	**tene khabar che ke āpṇe āvīsuṃ**	*he knows that we will come*
મને લાગે છે કે તે આવશે	**mane lāge che ke te āvśe**	*I think that he will come*

એમ **em** *thus* is used when reported speech is given first. For example:

તમે શું કરો છો, એમ આ માણસોને પૂછીએ	**tame śuṃ karo cho, em ā māṇasone puchīe**	*let us ask these people what they are doing*
નહિ જા, એમ નોકરને કહો	**nahi jā, em nokarne kaho**	*tell the servant not to go*

Notice the difference in how direct speech is rendered in English and Gujarati. More literal translations of these two sentences would be: *'what are you doing,' thus let us ask these people* and *'do not go!' thus tell the servant.*

એમ **em** *thus* can also be used colloquially to express something similar to *really?* or *it's like that, is it?* which we might say in English after someone has made a declarative statement. For example:

લીલા	આ સાડી સારી નથી
Līlā	ā sāḍī sārī nathī
Leela	*This sari is not good.*
નીલા	એમ?
Nīlā	em?
Neela	*Really?*

4 REPETITION

Repetition of a word can serve several functions in Gujarati. Two frequent uses are as follows.

a The repetition of an adjective, usually with plural forms, emphasizes its intensity and can be translated into English as *very* and/or *many*. For example:

મોટી મોટી દુકાનો	**moṭī moṭī dukāno**	*very big shops*

b The repetition of pronouns suggests variety in the example below:

શું શું લેશો?	**śuṃ śuṃ leśo?**	*what things will you take?*

3 You have now learned how to use repetition and કે ke and એમ em. Make sure that you have understood these concepts by translating the following sentences from Gujarati into English.

a દીપકભાઈ નથી ગમતું કે અમદાવાદમાં એની બહેન નહિ હશે. Dīpakbhāī nathī gamto ke amdāvādmāṃ enī bahen nahi haśe.

b લીલાબેનની નાની નાની ચોપડીઓ નવી છે. Līlābenni nānī nānī copḍio navī che.

c તમે કેવી વાર્તા કહેશો ? જૂની કે નવી? tame kevī vārtā kaheśo? jūnī ke navī?

d મને ખબર છે કે મારી દીકરી ઘરે હતી! mane khabar che ke marī dīkrī ghare hatī!

Vocabulary builder

મોડું થાય છે	moḍuṃ thāy che	*it's getting late*
મને ભૂખ લાગે છે	mane bhūkh lāge che	*I'm hungry*
જમવું	jamvuṃ	*to eat, to dine*
મને ભાવે છે	mane bhāve che	*I like* (food, drink)
ખોરાક (m.)	khorāk	*food* (cuisine, style of food)
ખાવાનું (n.)	khāvānuṃ	*food*

પોતે	pote	*oneself, self*
હમેશાં	hameśāṃ	*always*
પોતાનું	potānuṃ	*(one's) own*
શાકાહારી	śākāhārī	*vegetarian*
માંસાહારી	māṃsāhārī	*non-vegetarian, carnivore*
શાક (n.)	śāk	*vegetable*
રોટલી (f.)	roṭlī	*bread*
દાળભાત (f.)	dāḷbhāt	*rice and lentils*
જલદી	jaldī	*quickly, soon*
બનાવું	banāvuṃ	*to make, to do*
કઈ જાતની મીઠાઈ	kaī jātnī mīṭhāī?	*what kind of sweets?*
ખાવું	khāvuṃ	*to eat*
ખાંડ (f.)	khāṃḍ	*sugar*
ખાંડ વગરનું	khāṃd vagarnuṃ	*sugarless*
પીવું	pīvuṃ	*to drink*
તાજું દૂધ	tājuṃ dūdh	*fresh milk*
હાથ (m.)	hāth	*hand, arm*

તમને ગુજરાતી ખોરાક ભાવે છે? TAMNE GUJARĀTĪ KHORĀK BHĀVE CHE?
DO YOU LIKE GUJARATI FOOD?

04.02 *Ashish and his English friend Steve are having a discussion.*

1 What does Ashish invite Steve to do? What kinds of questions do Ashish and Steve ask one another?

Dialogue 2

આશિષ	**મોડું થાય છે. મને ભુખ લાગે છે. સ્ટીવ, તમે મારે ત્યાં જમવા આવશો?**
Āśiṣ	moḍuṃ thāy che. mane bhūkh lāge che. Sṭīv, tame māre tyāṃ jamvā āvśo?
સ્ટીવ	**હું જરૂર આવીશ. મને ગુજરાતી ખોરાક બહુ ભાવે છે, પણ ખાવાનું કોણ તૈયાર કરશે?**
Sṭīv	hum jarūr āvīś. mane gujarātī khorāk bahu bhāve che, paṇ khāvānuṃ koṇ taiyār karśe?
આશિષ	**હું પોતે ખાવાનું તૈયાર કરીશ. તમને ખબર ન હતી કે હું હમેશાં મારું પોતાનું ખાવાનું તૈયાર કરું છું? તમે શાકાહારી છો?**
Āśiṣ	huṃ pote khāvānum taiyār karīś. tamne khabar na hatī ke huṃ hameśaṃ māruṃ potānuṃ khāvānuṃ taiyār karuṃ chuṃ? tame śākāhārī cho?

સ્ટીવ	હું માંસાહારી છું. પણ મને શાકાહારી ખાવાનું બહુ જ ભાવે છે.
Sṭīv	huṃ māṃsāhārī chuṃ, paṇ mane śākāhārī khāvānuṃ bahu j bhāve che.
આશિષ	ભલે. કંઈ વાંધો નહિ. હું શાક, રોટલી અને દાળભાત વગેરે જલદી બનાવીશ. તમને કઈ જાતની મીઠાઈ ભાવે છે?
Āśiṣ	bhale. kaṃī vāṃdho nahi. huṃ śāk, roṭlī ane dāḷbhāt vagere jaldī banāvīś. tamne kaī jātnī mīṭhāī bhāve che?
સ્ટીવ	હું મીઠાઈ નથી ખાતો. મને ખાંડ નથી ભાવતી. હું ખાંડ વગરની ચા પણ પીઉં છું.
Sṭīv	huṃ mīṭhāī nathi khāto. mane khāṃḍ nathī bhāvtī. huṃ khāṃḍ vagarnī cā paṇ pīuṃ chuṃ.
આશિષ	હું દૂધ લઈ આવું? રસોડામાં તાજું દૂધ છે.
Āśiṣ	huṃ dūdh laī āvuṃ? rasoḍāmāṃ tājuṃ dūdh che.
સ્ટીવી	હા, દૂધ લઈ આવજો.
Sṭīv	hā, dūdh laī āvjo.
આશિષ	ચાલો, આપણે હાથ ધોઈએ અને જમીએ. તે પછી આપણે ફરવા જઈશું.
Āśiṣ	cālo, āpṇe hāth dhoīe ane jamīe. te pachī āpṇe pharvā jaīśuṃ.

2 True or false? Read and correct the following sentences based on the information in the above dialogue.

a આશિષને ભૂખ લાગતી નથી.
Äśiṣne bhūkh lāgtī nathī.

b સ્ટીવને શાકાહારી ખોરાક નથી ભાવતો.
Śṭīvne śākāhārī khorāk nathī bhāvto.

c સ્ટીવને ખાંડ ભાવે છે.
Śṭīvne khāṃḍ bhāve che.

3 Answer the following questions.

a આશિષ કઈ જાતનું ખાવાનું બનાવશે?
Äśiṣ kaī jātnuṃ khāvānuṃ banāvśe?

b સ્ટીવ શું પીએ છે?
Śṭīv śuṃ pīe che?

Language discovery

Listen to the dialogue again.

a Pay special attention to the underlined words and phrases. Use the Vocabulary builder to guess what all of the underlined words and phrases have in common.

b You will notice that all of the phrases used to say that you like or dislike food are unique. However, they are similar to other expressions of like and dislike that you have already learned. In which ways are they similar? If you are unsure, look at the endings of the nouns and pronouns that go with these expressions.

c Ashish says that he will do something himself. Use the Vocabulary builder to work out what that is.

5 THE REFLEXIVE PRONOUN

The form of the pronoun used to say *myself*, *oneself*, etc. is called the reflexive pronoun. Its Gujarati form, પોતે **pote** *self*, is used to express emphasis. For example:

હું પોતે	**huṃ pote**	*I myself*
તે પોતે	**te pote**	*he himself, she herself*, etc.
હું પોતે રોટલી બનાવીશ	**huṃ pote roṭlī banāvīs**	*I will make the breads myself*

There is also a variable adjective પોતાનું **potānuṃ** *one's own*, which is used mainly to avoid ambiguity in sentences. As with many adjectives, nouns and clitics, the નું **-nuṃ** suffix is variable and will change according to gender, number, etc. For example:

તે પોતાને ગામ જાય છે	**te potāne gām jāy che**	*she is going to her own village* (i.e. not someone else's village
એ એની પોતાની ગાડી છે	**ā enī potānī gāḍī che**	*this is his own car* (i.e. not one that he has borrowed)

There is another form, પોતપોતાનું **potpotānuṃ**, which is used to mean *each to his/her own*. For example:

બધા લોકો પોતપોતાને ઘેર જાય છે	**badhā loko potpotāne gher jāy che**	*everyone is going to their own home*

6 MORE IMPERSONAL VERBS

In Unit 3 some impersonal verbs were introduced, including ગમવું **gamvuṃ** *to like* and લાગવું **lāgvuṃ** *to seem*. In this unit you will meet more frequently used impersonal verbs. Like all impersonal verbs, the ones introduced here also use the clitic ને **-ne**, which modifies the corresponding nouns, proper nouns and pronouns.

ભાવવું **bhāvvuṃ** *to like* is a verb that is only used to express a liking for food and drink. For example:

તમને ગુજરાતી ખોરાક ભાવે છે?	**tamne gujarātī khorāk bhāve che?**	*do you like Gujarati food?*

આવડવું **āvaḍvuṃ** *to know (how to), to understand* is used in a similar way as the verb *to understand* in English. For example:

મને ગુજરાતી આવડે છ	**mane gujarātī āvaḍe che**	*I understand Gujarati*

However, it should be noted that if you want to say that you know how to do something, the suffix તાં **-tāṃ** will be added to the stem of the verb that describes the thing that you know how to do. For example:

Infinitive: વાંચવું **vāṃcvuṃ** *to read*

Stem: વાંચ **vaṃc-**

Suffix: તાં **tāṃ**

→ વાંચતાં **vāṃctāṃ** *I know how to read*

મને ગુજરાતી વાંચતાં આવડે છે પણ હિંદી વાંચતાં નથી આવડતું	**mane gujarātī vāṃctāṃ āvaḍe che paṇ hiṃdī vāṃctāṃ nathi āvaḍtuṃ**	*I know how to read Gujarati but I don't know how to read Hindi*

Some verbs have personal and impersonal forms with different meanings.

a Both forms of મળવું **maḷvuṃ** *to meet, to be found, to get* have already been introduced (see Unit 3). For example:

એને બહુ પૈસા નથી મળતા	**ene bahu paisā nathī maḷtā**	*he doesn't earn much money*
એ બહેનને મળવા જાય છે	**e bahenne maḷva jāy che**	*she is going to meet her sister*

b You were introduced to impersonal forms of લાગવું **lāgvuṃ** *to seem, to strike, to feel* in Unit 3. As you observed in the dialogue, however, લાગવું **lāgvuṃ** can also be used to express hunger and thirst. For example:

મને ભૂખ લાગે છે	**mane bhūkh lāge che**	*I feel hungry*
મને તરસ લાગે છે	**mane taras lāge che**	*I feel thirsty*

લાગવું **lāgvuṃ** is also used to express *feeling hot, tired*, etc. For example:

આજે ગરમી લાગે છે, ને?	**āje garmī lāge che, ne?**	*it's hot today, isn't it?*
છોકરીને થાક લાગે છે	**chokrīne thāk lāge che**	*the girl feels tired*

લાગવું **lāgvuṃ** also has a personal form meaning *to begin*. For example:

હું કામ કરવા લાગું?	**huṃ kām kārvā lāguṃ?**	*shall I begin to do some work?*

c The verb ચાલવું **cālvuṃ** *to walk, to move* can also be used idiomatically to mean *to be all right*. For example:

એમ નહિ ચાલે	**em nahi cāle**	*that won't do*
ચાલો તો એમ	**cāle to em**	*that's all right*

d The verb પડવું **paḍvuṃ** can mean *to fall*. For example:

ફળ ઝાડ પરથી પડે છે	**phaḷ jhāḍ parthī paḍe che**	*the fruit falls from the tree*

Indirectly, પડવું **paḍvuṃ** can also be used with ને **-ne** to mean *to happen* (lit. *to fall*). For example:

તમને ખબર પડે છે?	**tamne khabar paḍe che?**	*do you know about this?* (lit. *does this news fall to you?*)

પડવું **paḍvuṃ** can also be used indirectly as a verb of necessity. You will learn more about this in Unit 5.

e The only other common verb that is used indirectly is ફાવવું **phāvvuṃ** meaning *to be suitable* (the personal or direct meaning of the verb *to succeed* is rare). For example:

આ તમને ફાવે છે?	**ā tamne phāve che?**	*is this to your liking?* (lit. *is it suitable to you?*)

4 Now that you have learned more about how to talk about your feelings, likes and dislikes, and abilities, you will be able to answer the following questions in Gujarati! There are no answers in the Answer key for this exercise, because each answer will be uniquely yours. Here is an example to start you off:

તમને શું ભાવે છે? **tamne shuṃ bhāve che?** → મને ખાંડ ભાવે છે **mane khāṃḍ bhāve che** (*I like sugar*)

a તમને મીઠાઈ ભાવે છે? **tamne miṭhāī bhāve che?**

b તમને થાક લાગે છે કે ભૂખ લાગે છે? **tamne thāk lage che ke bhūk lage che?**

c આજે તમને કોને મળશે? **āje tamne kone maḷśe?**

7 TO KNOW

You have now seen several ways of saying *to know* in Gujarati. Let's review what you have learned thus far and meet some new ways to say that you know something.

a By using the word ખબર **khabar** *to know (something)*. For example:

મને ખબર છે કે નીલા ભારતમાં છે	**mane khabar che ke Nīlā bhāratmāṃ che**	*I know that Neela is in India*
તમને ખબર છે?	**tamne khabar che?**	*do you know (about this)?*

b By using the verb જાણવું **jāṇvuṃ** *to know, to have knowledge*. For example:

હું જાણું છું કે નીલા ભારતમાં છે	**huṃ jāṇuṃ chum ke Nīlā bhāratmāṃ che**	*I know that Neela is in India*

c By using the verb આવડવું **āvaḍvuṃ** *to know (how to do something)*. For example:

તમને આ વાર્તા આવડતી નથી	**tamne ā vārtā āvḍtī nathī**	*you do not know this story*
તમને ગુજરાતી આવડે છે?	**tamne gujarātī āvḍe che?**	*do you know Gujarati?*

d By using the verb ઓળખવું **oḷakhvuṃ** *to know, to be acquainted with, to be familiar with*. For example:

હું નીલાને ઓળખું છું	**hum Nīlāne oḷakhuṃ chuṃ**	*I know Neela*

Note that all these ways of expressing knowledge except for જાણવું **jāṇvuṃ** are used indirectly, that is, all pronouns in these constructions will take ને **-ne**.

5 Test how well you can express knowledge of people, things and activities by translating the following sentences in various tenses from Gujarati into English.

a તમને આ પાઠ આવડતો નથી tamne ā pāṭh āvḍto nathī

b છોકરીને આ કામ આવડતું નથી chokrīne ā kām āvḍtuṃ nathī

c દીપકભાઈ લીલાબેનને ઓળખે છે Dīpakbhāī Līlābenne oḷkhe che

d તેઓ જાણે છે કે તમને આ વાર્તા આવડતી હતી teo jaṇe che ke tamne ā vārtā āvḍtī hatī

e તેઓને ગુજરાતી આવડતી હશે teone gujarātī āvḍtī haśe!

NEW VOCABULARY

પાઠ (m.)	**pāṭh**	*lesson*

Practice

અભ્યાસ ABHYĀS

Here is a page from Javed's diary.

21 September

રજા! સવારે અને બપોરે હું ઘેર જ રહીશ. સાંજે હું વીરેનને મળવા બજારે જઈશ. તે પછી આપણે ખાવાનું અક્ષયને મળવા ત્યાં જઈશું. મને લાગે છે કે અક્ષયને શાકાહારી ખાવાનું બનાવતાં બરાબર આવડે છે. તે પછી આપણે સાથે ફરવા જઈશું. ખૂબ મઝા આવશે!

rajā! savāre ane bapore huṃ gher j rahīś. sāṃje huṃ Vīrenne maḷvā bajāre jaīś. te pachī āpṇe khāvānuṃ Akṣayne maḷvā tyāṃ jaīśuṃ. mane lage che ke Akṣayne śākāhārī khāvānuṃ banāvtāṃ barābar āvaḍe che. te pachī āpṇe sāthe pharvā jaīsuṃ. khūb majhā āvśe!

1 Answer the following questions in Gujarati about what Javed is going to do tomorrow.

a કાલે જાવેદ શું કરશે? kale Jāved śuṃ karśe?

b કાલે સાંજે તે ઘેર જ રહેશે? તે કોઈને ત્યાં જશે? kāle sāṃje te gher j raheśe? te koīne tyāṃ jaśe?

c તેને રજા મળશે? tene rajā maḷśe?

d તે શું તેઓ? કયાં, કયારે, અને કોની સાથે? te śuṃ tekho? kyāṃ, kyāre, ane konī sāthe?

e મઝા આવશે? majhā āvśe?

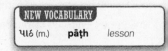

2 **Based on what you have learned in the unit, find the grammatical mistakes in these sentences.**

a હું ખાંડ નથી ભાવતો.
hum̤ khām̤ḍ nathī bhāvto.

b આપણે ફરવીએ જઈશું.
āpṇe pharvīe jaīśum̤.

c તમને ખબર છે એમ એ આવશે કે નહિ?
tamne khabar che em e āvśe ke nahi?

d આવતી કાલે તેઓ મારે ત્યાં હતાં.
āvtī kale teo māre tyām̤ hatām̤.

e એ પોતાનું ચા બનાવશે.
e potānum̤ cā banāvśe.

3 04.03 **You are at Ashish's house. Fill in your part of the dialogue.**

a	આશિષ	**આવો, આવો. કેમ છો?**
	Āśiṣ	āvo, āvo. kem cho?
	You	*Say that you're fine. Ask how he is.*
b	આશિષ	**મજામાં. બેસો, બેસો ને? તમને ભૂખ લાગે છે?**
	Āśiṣ	majāmām̤. beso, beso ne? tamne bhūkh lāge che?
	You	*Say you're not hungry.*
c	આશિષ	**તમે ચા લેશો?**
	Āśiṣ	tame cā leśo?
	You	*Say you aren't thirsty.*
d	આશિષ	**કંઈ વાંધો નહિ. શું ખબર છે?**
	Āśiṣ	kam̤ī vām̤dho nahi. śum̤ khabar che?
	You	*Say nothing special. Ask him where his son is today.*
e	આશિષ	**આજે એ એના મામાને ત્યાં છે. એ સાંજે આવશે.**
	Āśiṣ	āje e ena māmāne tyām̤ che. e sām̤je āvśe.
	You	*Suggest that you go to meet Steve. Tell him that Steve is American but he can speak Gujarati.*
	આશિષ	**ચાલો, આપણે જઈએ!**
	Āśiṣ	cālo, āpṇe jaīe!

NEW VOCABULARY
બેસવું **besvum̤** *to sit*

4 Steve is practising speaking Gujarati with Viren. His Gujarati is good, but he keeps making mistakes. Correct his parts of the dialogue.

સ્ટીવ	કેમ છે, વિરેન?
Sṭīv	kem che, Vīren?
વિરેન	**હું મજામાં છું. તમારું ગુજરાતી બહુ સારું છે. તમે શા માટે ગુજરાતી શીખો છો?**
Viren	huṃ majāmāṃ chuṃ. tamāruṃ gujarātī bahu sāruṃ che. tame śā māṭe gujarātī śīkho cho?
સ્ટીવ	**મારો પત્ની ગુજરાતી છે. એ હમેશાં ગુજરાતી જ બોલો.**
Sṭīv	māro patnī gujaratī che. e hameśāṃ gujarātī j bolo.
વિરેન	**મને બોલતાં આવડે છે પણ મને વાંચતાં લખતાં આવડતું નથી.**
Viren	mane boltāṃ āvaḍe che paṇ mane vāṃctāṃ lakhtāṃ āvaḍtuṃ nathī
સ્ટીવ	**તમે ખબર છો કે ગુજરાતી બહુ અઘરું નથી છે.**
Sṭīv	tame khabar cho ke gujarātī bahu aghruṃ nathī che.
વિરેન	**તમે કયાં શીખો છો? અહીંથી દૂર છે?**
Viren	tame kyāṃ śīkho cho? ahīṃthī dūr che?
સ્ટીવ	**અહીંથી બહુ દૂર નથી છે. તમે મારો સાથે શીખવો આવશો!**
Sṭīv	ahīṃthī bahu dūr nathī che. tame māro sāthe śikhvo āvśo!
વિરેન	**ખૂબ મઝા આવશે!**
Vīren	khūb majhā āvśe!

NEW VOCABULARY

શા માટે **śā māṭe?** *why? for what reason/purpose?*

5 Smita finds it difficult to wake up in the morning. Read the dialogue below to find out what her mother orders her to do, then complete Smita's replies. Use the indefinite present for the first two orders, the present continuous for the third order and the future for the last two orders.

લીલા	**બેટા, જલદી આવ! તારો નાસ્તો તૈયાર છે!**
Līlā	beṭā, jaldī āv! tāro nāsto taiyār che!
સ્મિતા	**હા, હું જલદી (આવવું).**
Smitā	hā, huṃ jaldī (āvvuṃ).

લીલા	**જલદી તૈયાર થા!**
Līlā	jaldī taiyār thā!
સ્મિતા	**હા, હું જલદી કપડાં (પહેરવું).**
Smitā	hā, huṃ jaldī kapḍāṃ (pahervuṃ).
લીલા	**નિશાળે જા! મોડું થાય છે!**
Līlā	niśaḷe jā! moḍuṃ thāy che!
સ્મિતા	**હા, હું (જવું).**
Smitā	ha, huṃ (javuṃ).
લીલા	**બપોરે તું શું કરશે?**
Līlā	bapore tuṃ śuṃ karśe?
સિમતા	**હું શહેર (જવું).**
Smitā	huṃ śaher (javuṃ).
લીલા	**અને પછી?**
Līlā	ane pachī?
સ્મિતા	**હું અહીં (આવવું).**
Smitā	huṃ ahīṃ (āvvuṃ).

NEW VOCABULARY

પહેરવું **pahervuṃ** *to wear, to dress*

સમજયા/સમજયાં? SAMJYĀ/SAMJYĀṂ? *DO YOU UNDERSTAND?*

Priya and Aanal meet at a shopping street in London. This dialogue uses all of the tenses that you have already learned including the future tense, which appears three times. Can you identify it?

પ્રિયા	**કેમ છે, આનલ? તું કયાં જાય છે?**
Priyā	kem che, Ānal? tuṃ kyāṃ jāy che?
આનલ	**હું થોડાં કપડાં ખરીદવા જાઉં છું. આવતે અઠવાડિયે હું ભારત જઈશ.**
Ānal	huṃ thoḍāṃ kapḍāṃ kharīdvā jāuṃ chuṃ, āvte aṭhvāḍiye huṃ bhārat jaīś.
પ્રિયા	**કેમ લંડનમાં કપડાં ખરીદે છે? અહીં બધું જ મોંઘું છે. ભારતમાં સારાં અને સસ્તાં કપડાં મળે છે.**
Priyā	kem laṃḍanmāṃ kapḍāṃ kharīde che? ahīṃ badhuṃ j moṃghuṃ che. bhāratmāṃ sārāṃ ane sastāṃ kapḍāṃ maḷe che.
આનલ	**પણ ત્યાં સ્ત્રીઓ ઘાઘરા અને ઓઢણી કે સાડીઓ પહેરે છે, ને?**
Ānal	paṇ tyāṃ strīo ghāgharā ane oḍhaṇī ke sāḍīo pahere che, ne?

પ્રિયા	હા, પણ શહેરોમાં સ્ત્રીઓ બધી જાતનાં કપડાં પહેરે છે. સારું કાપડ પણ મળે. માશીના દરજીને કાપડ આપજે અને તે જલદી તારાં કપડાં સીવશે.
Priyā	hā, paṇ śaheromāṃ strīo badhī jātnāṃ kapḍāṃ pahere che. sāruṃ kāpaḍ paṇ male. Māśīnā darjine kapad āpje ane te jaldī tārāṃ kapḍāṃ sīvśe.
આનલ	ભલે. પ્રિયા, મને કહેજે, તું કોઈ દિવસે અંગ્રેજી પહેરવેશ પહેરે છે?
Ānal	bhale. Priyā, mane kaheje, tuṃ koī divase aṃgrejī paherveś pahere che?
પ્રિયા	ના, કદી નહિ. અંગ્રેજી કપડાં મને નથી ગમતાં. હું હમેશાં સાડી પહેરું છું.
Priyā	nā, kadī nahi. aṃgrejī kapḍāṃ mane nathī gamtāṃ. huṃ hameśāṃ sāḍī paheruṃ chuṃ

NEW VOCABULARY

કપડાં (n.pl.)	**kapḍāṃ**	*clothes*
ખરીદવું	**kharidvuṃ**	*to buy*
સ્ત્રી (f.)	**stri**	*woman*
ઘાઘરો (m.)	**ghāgharo**	*skirt*
ઓઢણી (f.)	**oḍhaṇī**	*scarf, veil*
સાડી (f.)	**sāḍī**	*sari*
પહેરવું	**pahervuṃ**	*to wear, to dress*
બધી જાતનું	**badhi** jātnuṃ	*every kind of*
કાપડ (n.)	**kāpaḍ**	*cloth*
દરજી (m.)	**darjī**	*tailor*
સીવવું	**sīvvuṃ**	*to sew*
પહેરવેશ (m.)	**paherveś**	*dress, costume*
કદી નહિ	**kadī nahī**	*never*

Test yourself

How would you do the following in Gujarati?

1 Ask Deepakbhai if he likes Gujarati food.

2 Tell Leela that you can speak and write in Gujarati.

3 Say that Neela's daughters will like Ahmedabad.

4 Say that you are hungry but that you will not eat any sugar.

5 Say that you know that there are many small notebooks in the market.

6 Ask your friend Rekha if she likes to wear a veil.

SELF CHECK

	I CAN...
○	... talk about future events.
○	... say I am hungry and thirsty and talk about what I like to eat.
○	... talk about clothing and styles of dress.
○	... talk about how I feel and what I know.

5 તમારે શું જોઈએ છે?
tamāre śuṃ joīe che
What do you need?

In this unit you will learn how to:

- ***express need, necessity and desire.***
- ***name members of the extended family.***
- ***say what you want in a shop.***
- ***talk about your daily routine.***

If you are learning Gujarati script, you should now try to avoid reading the transliterated passages. From this unit onwards, transliterations for dialogues will be given separately from the script to help you do this.

ગુજરાત અને ગુજરાતીઓ gujarāt ane gujarātīo
Gujarat and Gujaratis

In many Hindu Gujarati homes there is a મંદિર **maṃdir**, *temple* or *area kept for worship*. Some families may decide to keep a whole room for this purpose, while others will designate a space within a common living area. Many families keep pictures or images of gods in their home and honour these deities by burning incense and offering food items. Images may include those of Ambaji (the mother goddess), Shiv, Vishnu (in his incarnation as Ram or Krishna), the saint Jalaram, or Sahajanand Swami, the founder of the Swaminarayan sect.

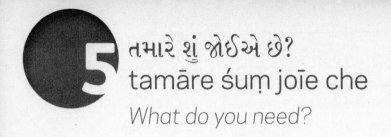

ʖhrinathji, a form of the Hindu deity Krishna who is central to the Vallabh
ʖampraday, the Vaishnav community that you learned about in the
Religion in Gujarat' section at the beginning of this book.

Vocabulary builder

મારે નવાં કપડાં જોઈએ છે	māre navāṃ kapḍāṃ joīe che	*I need some new clothes*
પંજાબી સૂટનું કાપડ	paṃjābī sūṭnuṃ kāpaḍ	*cloth for a Punjabi suit*
જોડો (m.)	joḍo	*shoe*
કદાચ	kadāc	*perhaps*
ચણિયા-ચોળી (f.)	caṇiyā-coṭī	*skirt and bodice*
મદદ (f.)	madad	*help, aid*
રોજનાં કપડાં (n.pl.)	rojnāṃ kapḍāṃ	*everyday clothes*
જરૂર પડે છે	jarur paḍe che	*it is necessary*
રોકડા પૈસા (m.pl.)	rokḍā paisā	*change*
બેન્કમાંથી પૈસા ઉપાડવા	benkmāṃthī paisā upāḍvā	*to take money out of the bank*
હોટેલ (f.)	hoṭel	*hotel, café*
મોંઘું પડશે	moṃghuṃ paḍśe	*it will be expensive*
બોલાવવું	bolāvvuṃ	*to call, to invite, to summon*
મારે જોઈતી ચીજો	māre joītī cījo	*the things which I need*
લઈ લેવું	lī levuṃ	*to get, to take*
તૈયાર થવું	taiyār thavuṃ	*to get (oneself) ready*

મારે નવાં કપડાં જોઈએ છે MĀRE NAVĀṂ KAPDĀṂ JOĪE CHE *I NEED SOME NEW CLOTHES*

05.01 *Veena and Meena live in Mumbai.*

1 What is the main topic of Veena and Meena's conversation?

Dialogue 1

વીણા	મારે નવાં કપડાં જોઈએ છે. ચાલો, આપણે બજારમાં જઈએ.
મીના	મારે પંજાબી સૂટનું કાપડ જોઈએ છે અને મારા ભાઈને જોડાની જરૂર છે. કદાચ હું મારી બહેનને માટે કાપડ લઈશ. કઈ દુકાનમાં મળશે?
વીણા	મુંબઈમાં ઘણી મોટી દુકાનો હોય છે. 'કલા નિકેતન' માં સારું પણ મોંઘું કાપ[ડ] મળશે. સાડીઓ, ચણિયા-ચોળી અને પંજાબી સુટો, બધી જાતનો માલ છે!
મીના	મારે તારી મદદ જોઈશે. મારે મોંઘું કાપડ નથી જોઈતું. મારે રોજનાં કપડાંની જરૂર પડે છે.
વીણા	મારી પાસે રોકડા પૈસા નથી. હું બેન્કમાંથી પૈસા ઉપાડીશ અને ત્યાંથી આપ[ણે] કાપડ લઈશું અને પછી આપણે હોટેલમાં ચા પીવા જઈશું.
મીના	હોટેલમાં મોંઘું પડશે.

વીણા	કંઈ વાંધો નહિ. હું પૈસા આપીશ. સાંજે હું દરજીને બોલાવીશ. મારો દરજી સારાં કપડાં સીવે છે.
મીના	સારું. હું મારી જાઈતી ચીજો લઈ લઈશ.
વીણા	ચાલો, જલદી તૈયાર થા!
Vīṇā	māre navāṃ kapḍāṃ joīe che. cālo, āpṇe bajārmāṃ jaīe.
Mīnā	māre paṃjābī sūṭnuṃ kāpaḍ joīe che ane mārā bhāīne joḍānī jarūr che. kadāc huṃ mārī bahenne māṭe kāpaḍ laīś. kaī dukānmāṃ malśe?
Vīṇā	muṃbaīmāṃ ghaṇī moṭī dukāno hoy che. 'Kalā Niketan' māṃ sāruṃ paṇ moṃghuṃ kāpaḍ maḷśe. sāḍīo, caṇiya-coli ane paṃjābī sūṭo, badhī jātno māl che!
Mīnā	māre tārī madad joīśe. māre moṃghuṃ kāpaḍ nathī joītuṃ. māre rojnāṃ kapḍāṃnī jarūr paḍe che.
Vīṇā	mārī pāse rokḍā paisā nathī. huṃ benkmāṃthī paisā upāḍīś ane tyāṃthī āpṇe bajārmāṃ jaīśuṃ. āpṇe kāpaḍ laīśuṃ ane pachī āpṇe hoṭālmāṃ cā pīvā jaiśuṃ.
Mīnā	hoṭelmāṃ moṃghuṃ paḍśe.
Vīṇā	kaṃī vāṃdho nahi. huṃ paisā āpīś, sāṃje huṃ darjīne bolavīś. māro darjī sārāṃ kapḍāṃ sīve che.
Mīnā	sāru huṃ mārī joītī cījo laī laīś.
Vīṇā	cālo, jaldī taiyār thā!

2 True or false? Read and correct the following sentences based on the information given in the above dialogue.

a મુંબઈમાં મોટી દુકાનો નથી.
muṃbaīmāṃ moṭī dukāno nathī.

b મીનાને મોંઘું કાપડ જોઈએ છે.
Mīnane moṃghuṃ kāpaḍ joīe che.

c વીણા પાસે રોકડા પૈસા છે.
Vīṇā pāse rokḍā paisā che.

3 Answer the following questions.

a તમને લાગે છે કે મીના પાસે બહુ પૈસા છે?
tamne lāge che ke Mīnā pāse bahu paisā che?

b કોને કાપડ જોઈએ છે?
kone kāpaḍ joīe che?

Language discovery

Read and listen to the dialogue again.

a Pay special attention to the underlined words and phrases. Can you see what all these words and phrases have in common? What do they allow the speakers in the dialogue to express to each other?

b You may have noticed by now that many English words are used regularly by Gujarati speakers. Can you find two words in the dialogue that you can identify as English words?

It is clear that some of the English words used by Gujarati speakers came into the language because they are words for Western ideas or objects such as ટ્રેન **ṭren** *train*. The reason for other English loan words is less clear. For example there is no obvious reason why a Gujarati speaker would use the English રૂમ **rūm** *room*, for which there are perfectly adequate Gujarati words. When you practise speaking in Gujarati with a Gujarati speaker, it is a good idea to use an English word if you don't know the Gujarati equivalent. You may find that the other person will suggest the Gujarati word, but at least it will allow you to keep the conversation going!

1 NEED, NECESSITY, DESIRE

You have already learned about the impersonal construction and use of જોઈએ **joīe** *(is) wanted, (is) needed* (see Unit 3), which expresses need or desire. જોઈએ **joīe** is actually the third person singular present tense form of the verb જોઈવું **joīvuṃ** *to need, to want.*

In addition to this form, the verb જોઈવું **joīvuṃ** also appears as a present variable participle જોઈતું (જોઈતીલ જોઈતો, etc.), and as a regular future tense verb (e.g. જોઈશે in the third person singular).

a As you have already encountered, when the જોઈએ **joīe** form is used, the meaning will be *to need* or *to want*. The noun or pronoun to which the need refers will be followed by the suffix ને **-ne** and changed accordingly (for pronouns followed by ને **-ne** see Point 2). In such constructions, the thing wanted or needed is treated as the subject of the sentence, following the same rules of agreement as other impersonal constructions. For example

મારે નવાં કપડાં જોઈએ છે	**māre navāṃ kapḍāṃ joīe che**	*I want/need new clothes*
મારે નવાં કપડાં નથી જાઈતાં	**mārenavāṃ kapḍāṃ nathī joītāṃ**	*I don't want/need new clothes*

| ામને પૈસા જોઈએ. | **temne paisā joīe** | *they want/need money* |
| ામને બીજું શું જોઈએ. | **tamne bījuṃ śuṃ joīe?** | *what else do you want/ need?* |

n these examples you can see that જોઈએ **joīe** can be used with or without he auxiliary verb: that is simply as જોઈએ **joīe** (without the auxiliary), or as ોઈએ છે **joīe che** (with the auxiliary). In the negative we may see either જોઈતું થી **joītuṃ nathī**, which is variable and agrees with the object needed (as n the second example), or ન/નહિ જોઈએ **na/nahi joīe**, which simply means *it s not needed* or *I don't want it.*

The future tense જોઈશે **joīśe** (negative નહિ જોઈશે **nahi joīśe**).

● The adjectival form જોઈતું **joītuṃ** is used to mean *necessary*. For example:

| ારે પાસે જોઈતા પૈસા નથી | **mārī pāse joītā paisā nathī** | *I do not have the necessary money with me* |

f you want to express a greater degree of necessity, the construction ી જરૂર (પડવી) **-nī jarūr (paḍvī)** *is necessary* can be used. For example:

| ને નવા જોડાની જરૂર છે | **mane navā joḍānī jarūr che** | *I need some new shoes* |
| ને માટે મોંઘા કાપડની જરૂર નથી | **ene māṭe momghā kāpaḍnī jarūr nathī** | *there is no need for expensive cloth for that* |

ou will have another opportunity to look at this point later in this unit.

2 PRONOUNS AND NOUNS AS AGENTS

Although most speakers of Gujarat use ને **ne** forms with the verbs of need, necessity, and desire, some Gujarati speakers insist that special forms are used in the written language. These special forms are called agential orms, because the subject becomes the agent of the verb. These forms are made by adding એ **-e** to the base or stem form of the noun (see Unit 2). n such cases, pronouns use the following special agential forms along vith the ને **ne** forms. For example:

| ીણા નવાં કપડાં જોઈએ છે | **Vīnāe navāṃ kapḍāṃ joīe che** | *Veena wants/needs some new clothes* |
| ારે નવાં કપડાં નથી જોઈતાં | **māre navāṃ kapḍāṃ nathī joītāṃ** | *I don't want/need new clothes* |

	Independent form of pronoun		Pronoun with ને ne		Pronoun with એ -e agential endings	
Singular						
First person	હું	**huṃ**	મને	**mane**	મારે	**māre**
Second person	તું	**tuṃ**	તને	**tane**	તારે	**tāre**
Third person	તે	**te**	તેને	**tene**	તેણે	**teṇe**
	એ	**e**	એને	**ene**	એણે	**eṇe**
	આ	**ā**	આને	**āne**	આણે	**āṇe**
	કોઈ	**koī**	કોઈને	**koīne**	કોઈએ	**koīe**
	કોણ	**koṇ**	કોને	**kone**	કોણે	**koṇe**
Plural						
First person	અમે	**ame**	અમને	**amne**	અમારે	**amāre**
Second person	આપણે	**āpṇe**	આપણને	**āpaṇne**	આપણે	**āpṇe**
Third person	તમે	**tame**	તમને	**tamne**	તમારે	**tamāre**
	તેઓ	**teo**	તેઓને	**teone**	તેઓએ	**teoe**
			તેમને	**temne**	તેમણે	**temne**

You will have another opportunity to look at this point in Unit 6.

1 Now that you have learned new ways to express need and desire translate the following sentences from Gujarati to English, or from English to Gujarati.

a Those little girls need many new notebooks.

b **તમને બીજું શું જોઈએ ? ઘરમાં બહુ સામાન છે.** tamne bījuṃ śuṃ joīe? gher māṃ bahu samān che!

c I need a new shirt from the market.

d **દીપકભાઈને નવાં કપડાં નથી જોઈતાં** Dīpakbhāīne navāṃ kapḍāṃ nathī joītāṃ.

3 THE HABITUAL PRESENT

In addition to the continuous present which you met in Unit 1 and Unit 2, Gujarati also has a habitual present. Whereas the continuous present is used for particular or specific statements, the habitual form is used to express universal truths and general statements.

The forms of the habitual present of the verb **હોવું hovuṃ** *to be* are as follows:

Singular			
First person	હું હોઉં છું	**huṃ houṃ chuṃ**	*I am*
Second person	તું હોય છે	**tuṃ hoy che**	*you are*
Third person	તે હોય છે (and આ, એ છે)	**te hoy che** (and **ā**, **e che**)	*he, she, it is* (and *it, this, that is*)

Plural			
First person	અમે હોઈએ છીએ આપણે હોઈએ છીએ	**ame hoīe chīe** **āpṇe hoīe chīe**	*we are* (exclusive) *we are* (inclusive)
Second person	તમે હો છો	**tame ho cho**	*you are*
Third person	તેઓ, તે હોય છે	**teo, te hoy che**	*they are*

For example:

અત્યારે તે ઘેર હોય છે	**atyāre te gher hoy che**	*he is (always/generally) at home now*
મારે સાત બહેન છે	**māre sāt bahen che**	*I have seven sisters*

The use of both the continous and habitual present tenses can also be compared in the following examples:

સાંજે લંડનના રસ્તા પર ઘણી ગાડીઓ હોય છે	**sāṃje laṃḍannā rastā par ghaṇī gāḍīo hoy che**	*in the evening, there are many cars on the road in London*

But:

આજે રસ્તા પર ઘણી ગાડીઓ છે	**āje rastā par ghaṇī gāḍīo che**	*there are many cars on the road today*

The negative form of the present habitual uses નથી **nathī**, and so is indistinguishable from the continuous present. For example:

અત્યારે તે ઘેર છે	**atyāre te gher che**	*he is at home now*
અત્યારે તે ઘેર હોય છે	**atyāre te gher hoy che**	*he is (always/generally) at home now*
અત્યારે તે ઘેર નથી	**atyāre te gher nathī**	*he is not at home now* (negative of both the above sentences)

હોય **hoy** can also be used as an auxiliary to the main verb of a sentence. For example:

અત્યારે તે ઘેર જાય છે	**atyāre te gher jāy che**	*she is going home now*

But:

અત્યારે તે ઘેર જતી હોય છે	**atyāre te gher jatī hoy che**	*she always goes home now* (habitually at this time of day)
અત્યારે તે ઘેર જતી નથી	**atyāre te gher jatī nathī**	*she is not going home now; she does not go home now* (habitually at this time of day)

Some speakers feel that this form of negation in the continuous and habitual present tenses is ambiguous and therefore prefer to use the invariable form હોતી નથી **hotī nathī** *is not* (with a continuous or habitual sense). For example:

અત્યારે તે ઘેર હોતી નથી	**atyāre te gher hotī nathī**	*he is not at home now*
અત્યારે તે ઘેર જતી હોતી નથી	**atyāre te gher jatī hotī nathī**	*she is not going home now; she does not go home now* (habitually at this time of day)

2 Now you can express things that happen habitually. Make the following sentences distinctly habitual by inserting the appropriate auxiliary forms such as હોતી hotī or હોય hoy in the following sentences. Here is an example to start you off:

હું ઘેર છું **huṃ gher chuṃ** *I am home* → હું ઘેર હોઉં છું **huṃ gher houṃ chuṃ** → *I am (regularly or habitually) home*

a એ લોકો અમદાવાદમાં છે e loko amdāvādmāṃ che

b મારી બહેન ના બગીચામાં ચાર કમળો છે! mārī bahen nā bagīcā māṃ cār kamaḷ che!

c હું રોજ દીપકભાઈ ની ત્યાં જતી નથી huṃ roj Dīpakbhāī nī tyāṃ jatī nathī

NEW VOCABULARY

કમળ (n.)	**kamaḷ**	*lotus*

4 FURTHER USES OF નું -NUṂ

You first met નું **-nuṃ** in Unit 3 as a possesive suffix. નું **-nuṃ** can also be added to nouns and clitics to create an adjectival form. You will find that this simple formation allows you to create a large number of phrases from your existing vocabulary. For example:

રોજનાં કપડાં	**rojnāṃ kapḍāṃ**	*everyday clothes* (lit. *clothes of the everyday*)
પાસેનું ગામ	**pāsenuṃ gām**	*the nearby village*
ગામના લોકો	**gāmnā loko**	*village people*
મારી પાસેના પૈસા	**mārī pasenā paisā**	*the money I have with me*
પંજાબી સૂટનું કાપડ	**paṃjābī sūṭnuṃ kāpaḍ**	*cloth for a Punjabi suit*
ઘરના ઓરડાઓ	**gharnā orḍāo**	*the rooms in the house*
એકનું એક છોકરું	**eknuṃ ek chokruṃ**	*an only child*
એકની/એક છોકરી/છોકરો	**eknī ek chokrī**	*an only daughter/son*

Complex adverbials (see Unit 3) may also add નું **-num̩** to form adjectival phrases in the same way. For example:

ખાંડ વગરની ચા	**khām̩d vagarnī cā**	*sugarless tea*
ભારત અંગેની વાત	**bhārat am̩genī vāt**	*talk about India*
મુંબઈ તરફની બસ	**mum̩baī taraphnī bas**	*the Mumbai bus, the bus for Mumbai*

3 Use some of the new words and phrases that you have just learned with નું -num̩ to translate the following sentences from English into Gujarati.

a I don't like sugar, please give me sugarless tea.
b Where is the bus for Mumbai?
c My daughter needs a new Punjabi suit.

Vocabulary builder

તારે ચા પીવી છે?	tāre cā pīvī che?	*would you like to drink tea?*
અત્યારે	atyāre	*now*
મારે ઘેર જવું જોઈએ	māre gher javum̩ joīe	*I should go home*
મારે ઘણું કામ કરવું પડશે	māre ghaṇum̩ kām karvum̩ paḍśe	*I have a lot of work I must do*
માબાપ (n.pl.)	mābāp	*parents*
તેઓ પાછાં આવશે	teo pāchām̩ āvśe	*they will come back/ return*
એ પહેલાં	e pahelām̩	*before that*
સાફ કરવું	sāph karvum̩	*to clean*
તો	to	*then*
વહેલી સવારે	vahelī savāre	*in the early morning*
ઊઠવું	ūṭhvum̩	*to rise, to get up*
મારે વહેલું ઊઠવું પડશે	māre vahelum̩ ūṭhvum̩ paḍṣe	*I shall have to get up early*
વિમાનમથક (n.)	vimānmathak	*airport*
મારી પાસે વખત નથી	marī pāse vakhat nathī	*I don't have time*
તો ઘેર તારે શું કામ કરવું પડે?	to gher tāre śum̩ kām karvum̩ paḍe?	*then what work is there for you to do at home?*
થાળી (f.)	thāḷī	*thali, plate*
મદદ કરવી	madad karvī	*to help*
માસી અને કાકા	māsī ane kākā	*uncle and aunt*
નોકરી (f.)	nokrī	*service, employment*

વિષે	viṣe	*about*
વાત કરવી	vāt karvī	*to chat*
જરૂર આવજે	jarūr āvje	*please do come* (agrees with **tuṃ**)
કોઈ પણ દિવસે	koī paṇ divase	*any day*
પાછું જવું	pāchuṃ jāvuṃ	*to go back*
ઇન્શાઅલ્લાહ!	inśāallāh!	*God willing!*

મારે ઘેર જવું જોઇએ MĀRE GHER JAVUṂ JOĪE I SHOULD GO HOME NOW

05.02 *Ali and Akshay are students in London.*

1 Ali wants to talk to Akshay, but Akshay is busy. What is he busy with?

Dialogue 2

અલી	કેમ છે, અક્ષય? તારે ચા પીવી છે?
અક્ષય	ના, અત્યારે મારે ઘેર જવું જોઈએ. ત્યાં મારે ઘણું કામ કરવું પડશે. કાલે મારાં માબાપ ભારતથી પાછાં આવશે અને એ પહેલાં મારે ઘરના બધા ઓરડા સાફ કરવા જોઈએ.
અલી	તો વહેલી સવારે ઊઠજે અને બધું કામ કરજે! હવે ચા પીવા જઈએ!
અક્ષય	ના, કાલે મારે વહેલું ઊઠવું પડશે કારણ કે મારે એમને લેવા વિમાનમથક જવું પડશે. મારી પાસે વખત નથી.
અલી	તો ઘેર તારે શું કામ કરવું પડે?
અક્ષય	મારે થાળી સાફ કરવી પડે.
અલી	આ મોટું કામ નથી. તો શું તારે મારી સાથે ચા પીવી નથી?
અક્ષય	મારે ઘણુંબધું કરવું પડે છે. તું શા માટે મને મદદ નથી કરતો?
અલી	ના, મારે ઘેર મારું પોતાનું કામ કરવું પડે છે. પણ મારે માસી અને કાકાને મળવા આવવું જોઈએ. મારે કાકાની સાથે મારી નોકરી વિષે થોડી વાત કરવી છે.
અક્ષય	જરૂર આવજે, કોઈ પણ દિવસે. તેઓ હમેશાં સવારે વહેલા ઊઠે છે.
અલી	પણ હું વહેલી સવારે નથી ઊઠતો! તો પણ હું જલદી આવીશ. ચાલો, હવે મારે પણ ઘેર પાછું જવું જોઈએ. કાલે મળીશું, ઇન્શાઅલ્લાહ!
Alī	kem che, Akṣay? tāre cā pīvī che?
Akṣay	nā, atyāre māre gher javuṃ joīe. tyāṃ māre ghaṇuṃ kām karvuṃ paḍśe. kāle mārāṃ mābāp bhāratthī pāchāṃ āvśe ane e pahelāṃ māre gharnā badhā orḍā sāph karvā joīe.

Alī to vahelī savāre ūṭhje ane badhuṃ kām karje! have cā pīvā jaīe!

Akṣay nā, kāle māre vaheluṃ uṭhvuṃ paḍśe kāraṇ ke māre emne levā vimānmathak javuṃ paḍśe. mārī pāse vakhat nathī.

Alī to gher tāre śuṃ kām karvuṃ paḍe?

Akṣay māre thāḷī sāph karvī paḍe.

Alī ā moṭuṃ kām nathī. to śuṃ tāre mārī sāthe cā pīvī nathī?

Akṣay māre ghaṇuṃbadhuṃ karvuṃ paḍe che. tuṃ śa māṭe mane madad nathī karto?

Alī nā, māre gher maruṃ potānuṃ kām karvuṃ paḍe che. paṇ māre māsī ane kākāne maḷvā āvvuṃ joīe. māre kākānī sāthe mārī nokrī viṣe thoḍī vāt karvī che.

Akṣay jarūr āvje, koī paṇ divase. teo hameśāṃ savāre vahelā ūṭhe che.

Alī paṇ huṃ vahelī savāre nathī ūṭhto! to paṇ huṃ jaldī āvīś, cālo, have māre paṇ gher pāchuṃ javuṃ joīe. kāle maḷīśuṃ, inśāallāh!

2 True or false? Read and correct the following sentences based on the information given in the dialogue.

a અક્ષયનાં માબાપ ઘેર જ છે.
Akṣavnāṃ mābāp gher j che.

b કાલે અક્ષય ઘેર જ રહેશે.
kāle Akṣay gher j raheśe.

c અલી અક્ષયનાં માબાપને ઓળખતો નથી.
Alī Akṣaynāṃ mābāpne oḷakhto nathī.

3 Answer the following questions based on what you learned in the dialogue.

a અક્ષયને શું કામ કરવું પડશે?
Akṣayne śuṃ kām karvuṃ paḍśe?

b અલીએ અક્ષયને મદદ કરવી છે?
Alīe Akṣayne madad karvī che?

Language discovery

Read and listen to the dialogue again.

a Pay special attention to all of the underlined words and phrases. What do these words and phrases have in common?

b Use the Vocabulary builder to figure out what these words and phrases mean. You will already be familiar with some of them. Which ones are new to you?

5 TRANSITIVE AND INTRANSITIVE VERBS

In English some verbs take a direct object (see Unit 3). These are called transitive verbs. For example:

to need: I need some new clothes

to give: I gave him some money

Other verbs do not require a direct object and are called intransitive verbs. For example:

to come: I came (to your house)

to go: I went (to your house)

Gujarati also has transitive and intransitive verbs, and the distinction between the two is of great importance. In future vocabulary lists, transitive verbs will be marked (tr.) and intransitive verbs (intr.). For example:

મારો ભાઈ મને પૈસા આપે છે	**māro bhāī mane paisā āpe che**	*my brother gives me money*
હું તમને જોઉં છું	**huṃ tamne jouṃ chuṃ**	*I see you*

But:

હું તને બજારમાં મળીશ	**huṃ tane bajārmāṃ maḷīś**	*I'll meet you in the market*
હું રોજ આવું છું	**huṃ roj āvuṃ chuṃ**	*I come every day*

The first two examples show the use of transitive verbs, whose objects are પૈસા **paisā** and તમને **tamne** respectively, and the second two examples show the use of intransitive verbs. While in the third example તને **tane** may appear to be the direct object, it is, in fact, the indirect object of the intransitive verb મળવું **maḷvu**ṃ *to meet*.

6 MORE ON NEED, NECESSITY AND DESIRE

જોઈએ **joīe** and other expressions of need, necessity and desire are used not only with nouns, but also in conjunction with other verbs (*I need to go, I want to sing a song*). When જોઈએ **joīe** is used with intransitive verbs the intransive verb will remain in its infinitve form. When used with transitive verbs, the verb's ending will vary according to the gender and number of the direct object, using the same pattern as variable adjectives.

When the form જોઈએ **joīe** is used in this way with other verbs it conveys the idea of duty, obligation or necessity. For example:

મારે ઘેર જવું જોઈએ (છે)	**māre gher javuṃ joīe (che)**	*I ought to go home*
મારે આ ચોપડી વાંચવી જોઈએ (છે)	**māre ā copḍī vāṃcvī joīe (che)**	*I ought to read this book*

જોઈએ **joīe** is unique in that there is no difference in meaning between its usage in the continuous present and the indefinite present tenses.

Desire can also be expressed in a similar fashion without using જોઈએ **joīe**. This is done by taking the infinite form of a verb (i.e. verb stem + વું **vuṃ**) and adding હોવું **hovuṃ**. For example:

મારે ઘેર જવું છે	**māre gher javuṃ che**	*I want to go home*
મારે આ ચોપડી વાંચવી છે	**māre ā copḍī vāṃcvī che**	*I want to read this book*

Similarly, the infinitive form of a verb plus વું પડવું **vuṃ paḍvuṃ** (lit. *to fall*) has the sense of *must* or *have to*. For example:

મારે ઘેર જવું પડે છે	**māre gher javuṃ paḍe che**	*I must go home*
મારે આ ચોપડી વાંચવી પડે છે	**māre ā copḍī vāṃcvī paḍe che**	*I have to read this book*

There is no distinct negative form of the infinite verb + જોઈએ **joīe** in Gujarati.

To make such sentences negative, use the same pattern of negation that you would for infinite verbs + છે **che**. For example:

મારે ઘેર જવું નથી	**māre gher javuṃ nathī**	*I don't want to/ have to go home*
મારે આ ચોપડી વાંચવી નથી	**māre ā copḍī vāṃcvī nathī**	*I don't want to read this book*

The constructions that use infinitive verbs + પડે છે **paḍe che** are negated as follows:

મારે ઘેર જવું નથી પડતું	**māre gher javuṃ nathī paḍtuṃ**	*I don't need to go home*
મારે આ ચોપડી વાંચવી નથી પડતી	**māre ā copḍī vāṃcvī nathī paḍtī**	*I don't need to read this book*

4 You have now learned more ways to express need, necessity and desire. Practise what you have learned by translating the following sentences from English to Gujarati, or Gujarati to English.

a I don't want/have to go to America, I want/have to go to India.
b વિદ્યાર્થીઓને રોજ ક્લાસ માં જવું પડતું હતું vidyārtīone roj klāsmāṃ javuṃ paḍtuṃ hatuṃ
c In Gujarat you have to speak Gujarati.
d મારે ઘેર જવું જોઈએ māre gher javuṃ joīe

NEW VOCABULARY

ક્લાસ (f.) **klās** *class* (an English loan word)

7 AGREEMENT OF ADJECTIVES FUNCTIONING AS ADVERBS

In the same way that adjectives describe nouns, adverbs (as the name implies) describe the way in which the action of a verb is performed. In English many adverbs end in *-ly*: *she ran quickly*, *we sing loudly*, etc. Sometimes adverbs seem to be more loosely connected with the action of the verb. For example, *I will be there soon, they arrived together.*

You have already learned that there are variable and invariable adjectives in Gujarati. Most Gujarati adverbs are invariable, but there are four common variable adverbs, i.e. adverbs that vary like adjectives. These are વહેલું **vahelum̩** *early*, મોડું **moḍum̩** *late*, પાછું **pāchum̩** *back* and પહેલું **pahelum̩** *first*. These words are variable in four different ways:

a If the verb is intransitive and the subject is in the independent form, the adverb agrees with the subject. For example:

તે કાલે પાછી આવશે	**te kāle pāchī āvśe**	*she will come back tomorrow*

b If the verb is intransitive but the subject is in any form other than the independent form, the adverb will be used in its stem form. For example:

એને કાલે પાછું આવવું છે	**eṇe kāḷe pāchum̩ āvvum̩ che**	*she should come back tomorrow*

c If the verb is transitive and an object is present, the adverb agrees with the object. For example:

એ નાસ્તો વહેલો ખાય છે	**e nāsto vahelo khāy che**	*she eats her breakfast early, she has an early breakfast*

d If the verb is transitive and an object is not present, the adverb shows neuter singular agreement. For example:

એ વહેલું ખાય છે	**e vahelum̩ khāy che**	*she eats early*

Note the contrast in the following expressions:

તે સવારે વહેલો ઊઠે છે	**te savāre vahelo ūṭhe che**	*he gets up early in the morning*
તે વહેલી સવારે ઊઠે છે	**te vahelī savāre ūṭhe che**	*he gets up early in the morning*

8 KINSHIP AND POLITENESS

Parents of one's friends and friends of one's parents, as well as much older acquaintances, may be referred to generically as Aunt and Uncle, sometimes preceded by the person's first name (e.g. રમેશકાકા **Rameśkākā** *Ramesh Uncle*). It is also common to simply refer to men as કાકા **kākā** (lit. *father's brother, uncle*) and to women as માસી/માશી **māsī/māśī** (lit. *mother's sister, aunt*).

Kinship terms are far more complicated than they are in English in that there are specific words for aunts and uncles according to their exact relationship to the speaker. For example, there is a different word for *mother's sister* (માશી **māśī**) and for *wife of father's brother* (કાકી **kākī**).

The number of kinship terms may be daunting at first, but if you try to work out what you would call your own relatives in Gujarati, you may find this a useful way of remembering the words. It will also help you to talk about your own family, even if you may still be a little vague about exact terms of kinship for other people's families!

This system, which seems rather complicated to people from small nuclear or one-parent families, is understandable in many Indian extended families where women traditionally leave their parents' home and village (પિયર **piyar**) after marriage to go to live in their in-laws' home (સાસરિયાં **sāsariyāṃ**) with their husband, his parents and other family members. Extended family relationships are especially important from the point of view of ritual, for example in certain communities the bride's મામા **māmā** *mother's brother* will give her away at her wedding, and relationships are traditionally strictly hierarchical. In some more traditional families a woman may not address or even show her face in front of her જેઠ **jeṭh** *husband's older brother*, while she has a close relationship with her દિયર **diyar** *husband's younger brother*.

Older family members may be addressed by their title or by specific terms of address, while younger family members may be called by their first name or a nickname.

Gujarati Muslims often use the same kinship terms as Gujarati Hindus, except for the use of the terms શૌહર **śauhar** *husband*, બીબી **bībī** *wife* and વાલિદ **vālīd** *father*.

Practice

1 Answer these questions in Gujarati about the things you have to do every day. Use the following example to guide you.

તમે નોકરી કરો છો? હા ... **tame nokrī karo cho? hā...**

હા, મારે નોકરી કરવી પડે છે. **hā, māre nokrī karvī paḍe che.**

a તમે વહેલા/વહેલાં ઊઠો છો? હા, ...
tame vahelā/vahelāṃ ūṭho cho? hā,...

b તમે ખાવાનું તૈયાર કરો છો? હા, ...
tame khāvānuṃ taiyār karo cho? hā,...

c તમે આવ-જા કરો છો? ના, ...
tame āv-jā karo cho? nā,...

d તમે ઘર સાફ કરો છો? ના, ...
tame ghar sāph karo cho? nā,...

e તમે વહેલા/વહેલાં સુઈ જાઓ છો? હા, ...
tame vahelā/vahelāṃ sūī jāo cho? hā,...

2 Correct and rewrite these sentences.

a સુથાર વહેલા કામ શરૂ કરે છે.
suthār vahelā kām śarū kare che.

b મારે ઘણો અભ્યાસ કરવું પડે છે.
māre ghaṇo abhyās karvuṃ paḍe che.

c પ્રબોધ અને એની દીકરીને વહેલાં નીકળવાં પડે છે.
Prabodh ane enī dīkrīne vahelāṃ nīkaḷvāṃ paḍe che.

d ચાલો, હું જવું જોઈએ.
cālo, huṃ javuṃ joīe.

e તમારે હાથ ધોવી જોઈએ, એમ છોકરીઓને કહો!
tamāre hāth dhovī joīe, em chokrīone kaho!

NEW VOCABULARY

સુથાર (m.)	**suthār**	*carpenter*
શરૂ કરવું	**śarū karvuṃ**	*to begin*

3 The following dialogue has been mixed up. Find what has been put out of place and rearrange the sentences into a coherent order.

અલી	તારી સાથે લાવજે ને! મઝા આવશે!
હેલન	મારે જવું છે. આવતા વરસે હું જવા ધારું છું. તું ઉનાળામાં જાય છે ને?
અલી	તારું ગુજરાતી હવે ઘણું સારું છે. તારે હવે થોડા વખતમાં ગુજરાત જવું જોઈએ.
હેલન	મારી મા નાતાલમાં મારે ત્યાં છે તેથી મારે અહીં રહેવું પડશે.
અલી	હા, કારણ કે ઉનાળામાં મને રજા મળે છે. પણ ત્યારે ત્યાં ભારે ગરમી હોય છે. તારે શિયાળામાં જવું જોઈએ.
Alī	tārī sāthe lāvje ne! majhā āvśe!
Helen	māre javuṃ che. āvtā varse huṃ javā dhāruṃ chuṃ, tuṃ unāḷāmāṃ jāy che ne?
Alī	tāruṃ gujarātī have ghaṇuṃ sāruṃ che. tāre have thoḍā vakhtmāṃ gujarāt javuṃ joīe.

Helen	mārī mā nātālmāṃ māre tyāṃ āve che tethī māre ahīṃ rahevuṃ paḍśe.
Alī	hā, kāraṇ ke unāḷāmāṃ mane rajā maḷe che. paṇ tyāre tyāṃ bhāre garmī hoy che. tāre śiyāḷāmāṃ javuṃ joie.

NEW VOCABULARY

ઉનાળો (m.)	**unāḷo**	*summer*
નાતાલ (f.)	**nātāl**	*Christmas*
ભારે	**bhāre**	*very, heavy*
શિયાળો (m.)	**śiyāḷo**	*winter*

4 Leela is offering Meena some advice. Complete the dialogues using the correct form of the word in brackets.

મીના	માશી, મારે નવાં કપડાં (ખરીદવું).
Meena	*Auntie, I want some new clothes.*
લીલા	તારે ભારતીય કપડાં (પહેરવું).
Leela	*You should wear Indian clothes.*
મીના	કાલે મારે બજારે (જવું).
Meena	*I want to go to the market tomorrow.*
લીલા	તારે (વહેલું) (નીકળવું).
Leela	*You should set out early in the morning.*
મીના	મારે નીલાને (મળવું).
Meena	*I want to see Neela.*
લીલા	અત્યારે તે ઓફિસે (જવું).
Leela	*She always goes to the office now (at this time).*
મીના	મારે અહીં થોડી વાર (રહેવું).
Meena	*I want to stay here for a while.*
લીલા	તારે ઘેર (પાછું) (જવું).
Leela	*You must go back home.*
Mīnā	māśi, māre navāṃ kapḍāṃ (kharīdvuṃ).
Līlā	tāre bhāratīy kapḍāṃ (pahervuṃ).
Mīnā	kāle māre bajāre (javuṃ).
Līlā	tāre (vaheluṃ) (nīkaḷvuṃ).
Mīnā	māre Nīlāne (maḷvuṃ).
Līlā	atyāre te ophise (javuṃ).
Mīnā	māre ahīṃ thoḍī vār (rahevuṃ).
Līlā	tāre gher (pāchuṃ) (javuṃ).

Read the following passage.

ગામડામાં અમારે થોડી જમીન છે, પણ તેઓ ખેડૂત નથી. તેઓ સુથાર છે. તેઓ પોતે ખેતરનું જોઈતું કામ કરે છે. અમારા ખેતરમાં અમે મગફળીનો પાક લઈએ છીએ. ચાર વરસથી હું બેન્કમાં નોકરી કરું છું.

હું વહેલી સવારે ઊઠું છું અને હું દાતણ કરું છું અને સ્નાન કરું છું. ઘરમાં અંબાજીનું મંદિર છે અને હું એની પૂજા કરું છું. પછી હું એમને માટે નાસ્તો તૈયાર કરું છું અને પછી હું ઓફિસ જવા નીકળું છું. હું બસમાં આવ-જા કરું છું અને રોજ બસો ચિકાર હોય છે અને લોકો બહુ ગડબડ કરે છે. રાતે હું કોઈ ચોપડી વાંચું છું અને પછી હું સુઇ જાઉં છું.

મારો નોકરી છોડવી છે પણ ગામડામાં લોકોને બહુ ઓછા પૈસા મળે છે અને મારે બેચાર વરસ સુધી નોકરી કરવી પડે એમ છે.

gāmḍāmāṃ amāre thoḍī jamīn che, paṇ teo kheḍūt nathī. teo suthār che. teo pote khetarnuṃ joītuṃ kām kare che. amārā khetarmāṃ ame magphaḷīno pāk lāīe chīe. cār varasthī huṃ beṃkmāṃ nokrī karuṃ chuṃ.

huṃ vahelī savāre ūṭhuṃ chuṃ ane huṃ dātaṇ karuṃ chuṃ ane snān karuṃ chuṃ. gharmām Aṃbājīnuṃ maṃdir che ane huṃ enī pūjā karuṃ chuṃ. pachī huṃ emne māṭe nāsto taiyār karuṃ chuṃ ane pachī huṃ ophis javā nīkaḷuṃ chuṃ. huṃ basmāṃ āv-jā karuṃ chuṃ ane roj baso cikār hoy che ane loko bahu garbaḍ kare che. rāte huṃ koī copḍī vāṃcuṃ chuṃ ane pachī huṃ sūī jāuṃ chuṃ.

māre nokrī choḍvī che paṇ gāmḍāmāṃ lokone bahu ochā paisā maḷe che ane māre becār varas sudhī nokrī karvī paḍe em che.

NEW VOCABULARY

ગામડું (n.)	gāmḍuṃ	*village*
જમીન (f.)	jamīn	*land, ground, floor*
તેઓ	teo	*he* (i.e., my husband)
ખેડૂત (m.)	kheḍūt	*farmer, peasant*
ખેતર (n.)	khetar	*field*
જોઈતું	joītuṃ	*necessary*
મગફળી (f.)	magphaḷī	*peanut*
પાક (m.)	pak	*crop*
વરસ (n.)	varas	*year*
દાતણ કરવું	dātaṇ karvuṃ	*to clean one's teeth*
સ્નાન કરવું	snān karvuṃ	*to have a bath*
અંબાજી	Aṃbājī	*Ambaji, Mother Goddess*
મંદિર (n.)	maṃdir	*temple, area of worship in the house*
પૂજા (f.)	pūjā	*worship*
ઓફિસ (f.)	ophis	*office*
નીકળવું	nīkaḷvuṃ	*to set out, depart*

બસ (f.)	bas	*bus*
આવ-જા કરવું	āv-jā karvuṃ	*to commute*
ચિકાર	cikār	*crowded*
ગરબડ કરવું (f.)	garbaḍ karvuṃ	*to make a lot of noise*
સુઈ જવું	sūī javuṃ	*to go to sleep*
છોડવું	choḍvuṃ	*to leave*
એમ છે	em che	*that's the way it is* (lit. *it is*)
વાણિયો (m.)	vāṇiyo	*merchant, Bania*

Answer the following questions:

1 **આ સ્ત્રી ક્યાં રહે છે?**
ā strī kyāṃ rahe che?

2 **એનો પતિ શું કામ કરે છે? વાણિયો છે?**
eno pati śuṃ kām kare che? vāṇiyo che?

3 **તે મંદિરમાં શું કરે છે?**
te maṃdirmāṃ śuṃ kare che?

4 **બપોરે તે ઘેર જમવા આવે છે?**
bapore te gher jamvā āve che?

5 **બસમાં તે મજામાં હોય છે?**
basmāṃ te majāmāṃ hoy che?

6 **તેને નોકરી ગમે છે?**
tene nokrī game che?

Test yourself

How would you do the following in Gujarati?

1 Say that Deepakbhai needs new shoes.

2 Say that the girls will have to go to class early every day.

3 Tell somebody that you need/want fresh milk from the market today.

4 Say that we (exclusive) are forced to go to sleep early.

5 Tell Deepakbhai that you do not take sugar in your tea.

6 Ask for new cloth for a shirt.

SELF CHECK

	I CAN...
○	. . . express need, necessity and desire.
○	. . . name members of the extended family.
○	. . . say what I want in a shop.
○	. . . talk about my daily routine.

6 હું ભારત ગયો
huṃ bhārat gayo
I went to India

In this unit you will learn how to:

- ***talk about a visit to India.***
- ***talk about what you did during your visit.***
- ***talk about what you did today.***
- ***talk about a visit to a friend.***
- ***give directions.***

ગુજરાત અને ગુજરાતીઓ gujarāt ane gujarātīo
Gujarat and Gujaratis

The Mumbai suburb of Juhu was a resort until the 1960s and 1970s when it became a fashionable place to live for those involved in Mumbai's huge film industry. India produces more films than any other country in the world, and the two main centres of industry are Madras, where films in south Indian languages (such as Tamil, Telugu and Malayalam) are produced, and Mumbai, where films in Hindi and other regional languages are produced. Gujarati films are made both in Mumbai and in various places in Gujarat, but in rather small numbers. Ask any taxi driver in Juhu to show you where the well-known film star Amitabh Bachan lives and they'll be able to show you, as his residence is a local landmark! The Hare Krishna Hare Rama temple is also something of a landmark in Juhu, where it attracts a large number of overseas followers of the Hare Krishna movement. It is also known for its excellent vegetarian restaurant, which is always crowded.

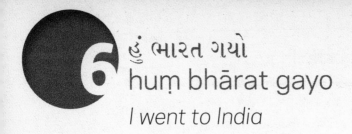

Vocabulary builder

ઘણા દિવસથી આપણે નથી મળ્યાં	ghaṇā divasthī āpṇe nathī maḷyāṃ	*we haven't met for many days*
હું દેશ ગયો હતો	huṃ deś gayo hato	*I went to India*
હું પરમ દિવસે જ પાછો આવ્યો	huṃ param divase j pācho āvyo	*I came back just the day before yesterday*
હું પહોંચ્યો	huṃ pahoṃcyo	*I arrived*
હું પહેલી રાતે હોટેલમાં રહ્યો	huṃ pahelī rāte hoṭelmāṃ rahyo	*I stayed in a hotel on the first night*
બીજે દિવસે	bīje divase	*the next day*
ત્યાંથી	tyāṃthī	*from there*
આગગાડીમાં	āggāḍīmāṃ	*in the train, by train*
વડોદરા	vaḍodrā	*Vadodara, Baroda*
ઊંચું	uṃcuṃ	*high*
છાપરા પરથી	chāprā parthī	*from the roof*
આખું	ākhum	*whole*
શહેર દેખાય છે	śaher dekhāy che	*the city can be seen; you can see the city*
મોદી	modī	*grocer*
આધુનિક	ādhunik	*modern*
એકદમ	ekdam	*completely, absolutely*
વાપરવું	vāparvuṃ	*to use*
લાકડાની પેટી	lākdānī peṭī	*wooden box*
તેઓ ચોપડામાં હિસાબ લખે છે	teo copḍāmāṃ hisāb lakhe che	*they keep their accounts in ledgers*
આ બધું તને કેવું લાગ્યું ?	ā badhuṃ tane kevuṃ lāgyuṃ?	*what did you think about all this?*
વ્યવસ્થા (f.)	vyavasthā	*arrangements*
રાજકોટ	rajkoṭ	*Rajkot*
બન્ને	banne	*both*
તેઓ મને શહેર જોવા લઈ ગયાં	teo mane śaher jovā laī gayāṃ	*they took me to see the city*
ટોપી	ṭopī	*hat*
લઈ આવવું	laī āvvuṃ	*to bring*
સૌ	sau	*all*
પરંતુ	paraṃtu	*but*
બહુ ઓછી વાર	bahu ochī vār	*seldom*
કોઈ પણ દિવસે	koi paṇ divase	*on any day at all*
હું માંદો પડયો	huṃ māṃdo paḍyo	*I fell ill*
ઓ બાપ રે બાપ!	o bāp re bāp!	*oh no!* (lit. *Oh father!*)

હવે તો તારી તબિયત સારી છે?	have to tārī tabiyat sārī che?	*but now your health is OK, isn't it?*
ભગવાનની કૃપા	Bhagvānnī kṛpā	*thank God!* (lit. *the mercy of God*)
હું પાતળો થયો	huṃ pātḷo thayo	*I became thin*
ઓહો	oho	*oh my*
મને તારી વાતની સમજ પડી	mane tārī vātnī samaj paḍī	*I understand what you're saying*
તું મજાક કરે છે	tuṃ majāk kare che	*you're joking*
નાસ્તો કરવો	nāsto karvo	*to have a breakfast, to have a snack*

હું ભારત ગયો HUṂ BHĀRAT GAYO *I WENT TO INDIA*

06.01 *Sameer Shah meets his mother's friend, Leela Patel, in the market.*

1 What does Sameer tell Leela? Where has Sameer visited and what did he do there?

Dialogue 1

લીલા	કેમ છે, સમીર? ઘણા દિવસથી આપણે નથી મળ્યાં.
સમીર	હું દેશ ગયો હતો. હું પરમ દિવસે જ પાછો આવ્યો.
લીલા	સારું. તું દેશમાં કયાં ગયો હતો?
સમીર	હું લંડનથી મુંબઈ ગયો હતો. હું વહેલી સવારે પહોંચ્યો તેથી હું પહેલી રાતે હોટેલમાં રહ્યો. બીજે દિવસે હું ત્યાંથી આગગાડીમાં વડોદરા ગયો અને હું કાકાને ત્યાં રહ્યો.
લીલા	એમનું ઘર કેવું લાગે છે? સરસ છે?
સમીર	બહુ જ સરસ છે.જૂનું અને ઊંચું છે. છાપરા પરથી આખું જૂનું શહેર દેખાય છે તેઓ મોટી છે અને એમની નાની દુકાન આધુનિક નથી. અમારી લંડનની દુકાન એકદમ જુદી છે.
લીલા	હા, અહીં આપણે કોમ્પ્યુટર વગેરે વાપરીએ છીએ. તે લોકો લાકડાની પેટીમાં રૂપિયા રાખે છે અને ચોપડામાં હિસાબ લખે છે. આ બધું તને કેવું લાગ્યું?
સમીર	એવી જુદી વ્યવસ્થા મને સરસ લાગી. ત્યાં મને આંનદ આવ્યો. થોડા દિવસ પછી હું રાજકોટ ગયો.
લીલા	રાજકોટમાં તું તારી માશીને મળ્યો?
સમીર	હા, હું સુરેશમામાને ત્યાં રહ્યો. તેઓ બન્ને મને શહેર જોવા લઈ ગયાં. હું મોટા ભાઈને માટે ટોપી અને બહેન ને માટે થોડી સાડીઓ લઈ આવ્યો.
લીલા	સાડીઓ તારી બહેનને ગમી?
સમીર	હા, સૌ ગમી, પરંતુ અહીં બહુ ઓછી વાર સાડીઓ પહેરે છે.
લીલા	તો દેશમાં મઝા આવી?

મીર	હા, ખૂબ, પણ ગરમીને કારણે કોઈ પણ દિવસે મને ભુખ નહિ લાગી. પાણી ખરાબ હતું અને હું માંદો પડયો અને ઇસ્પિતાલમાં જવું પડયું
ીલા	ઓ બાપ રે બાપ! હવે તો તારી તબિયત સારી છે?
મીર	હા, ભગવાનની કૃપા, પણ હું પાતળો થયો ને?
ીલા	ના, મને એમ નથી લાગતું. તું એકદમ સારો લાગે છે. ઓહો, હવે મને તારી વાતની સમજ પડી! તું મજાક કરે છે. ચાલ, મારે ત્યાં નાસ્તો કરવા આવજે!
.īlā	kem che, Samīr? ghaṇā divasthī āpṇe nathī maḷyāṃ.
Samīr	huṃ deś gayo hato. huṃ param divase j pācho āvyo.
.īlā	sāruṃ. tuṃ deśmāṃ kyāṃ gayo hato?
Samīr	huṃ laṃḍanthī muṃbaī gayo hato. huṃ vehelī savāre pahoṃcyo tethī huṃ pahelī rāte hoṭelmāṃ rahyo. bīje divase huṃ tyāṃthī āggāḍīmāṃ vaḍodrā gayo ane huṃ kākāne tyāṃ rahyo.
īlā	emnuṃ ghar kevuṃ lāge che? saras che?
Samīr	bahu j saras che. jūnuṃ ane uṃcuṃ che. chāprā parthī ākhuṃ jūnuṃ śaher dekhāy che. teo modī che ane emnī nānī dukān ādhunik nathī. amārī laṃḍannī dukān ekdam judī che.
īlā	hā, ahīṃ āpṇe kampyuṭar vagere vāparīe chīe. te loko lākḍānī peṭīmāṃ rūpiyā rākhe che ane copḍāmāṃ hisāb lakhe che. ā badhuṃ tane kevuṃ lāgyuṃ?
amīr	evī judī vyavasthā mane saras lāgī. tyāṃ mane ānaṃd āvyo. thoḍā divas pachī huṃ rājkoṭ gayo.
īlā	rājkoṭmāṃ tuṃ tārī māśīne maḷyo?
amīr	hā, huṃ sureśmāmāne tyāṃ rahyo. teo banne mane śaher jovā laī gayāṃ. huṃ moṭā bhāīne māṭe ṭopī ane bahenne māṭe thoḍī sāḍīo laī āvyo.
īlā	sāḍīo tārī bahenne gamī?
amīr	hā, sau gamī, paraṃtu ahīṃ bahu ochī vār sāḍīo pahere che.
īlā	to deśmāṃ majhā āvī?
amīr	hā, khūb, paṇ garmīne kāraṇe koī paṇ divase mane bhūkh nahi lāgī. pāṇī kharāb hatuṃ ane huṃ māṃḍo paḍyo ane ispitālmāṃ javuṃ paḍyuṃ.
īlā	o bāp re bāp! have to tārī tabiyat sārī che?
amīr	hā, Bhagvānnī krpā, paṇ huṃ pātḷo thayo ne?
īlā	nā, mane em nathī lāgtuṃ. tuṃ ekdam sāro lāge che. oho, have mane tārī vātnī samaj paḍī! tuṃ majāk kare che. cāl, māre tyāṃ nāsto karvā āvje!

2 **True or false? Read and correct the following sentences based on the information given in the dialogue.**

a સમીર પહેલી વાર પાકિસ્તાન ગયો.
Samīr pahelī vār Pākistān gayo.

b સમીર મુંબઈથી ભાવનગર ગયો.
Samīr Muṃbaīthī Bhāvnagar gayo.

c ભારતમાં સમીરની તબિયત સારી હતી.
Bhāratmāṃ Samīrnī tabiyat sārī hatī.

3 **Answer the following questions based on what you learned in th dialogue.**

a સમીરને ભારત દેશ ગમ્યો?
Samīrne Bhārat desh gamyo?

b સમીર કેમ મજાક કરે છે?
Samīr kem majāk kare che?

Language discovery

Read and listen to the dialogue again.

You have already learned how to talk about events and situations in the past, present and future. In this unit you will be learning how to use a different kind of past tense. All the underlined words and phrases highligh this new past tense. Can you see from the context of the dialogue how th past tense is different from the simple past that you learned in Unit 2?

1 PERFECTIVE VERBS: THE SIMPLE PAST

Intransitive and semi-transitive verbs

You were introduced to the past tense of the verb **હોવું hovuṃ** *to be* in Unit 2 (**હતું hatuṃ**), which is used for incompleted or habitual verbal actions. It is called the imperfective because it is not concerned with the perfection or completion of an action. It is clear that in the case of forms like *I was* there is no question of the action being completed. However, when the action of a verb actually is completed, a different past tense called the perfective is used. *I went* is a perfective form in English, while *was going, I used to go* are imperfective forms.

In order to conjugate a verb in the perfective tense the ending **યું -yuṃ** is added to the stem of the verb (that is, the verb without its infinitive ending **વું -vuṃ**). The ending **યું -yuṃ** is added to the last consonant of the stem to form a conjunct consonant. This ending follows the same patter ıs a variable adjective, although you should note that the feminine is 'ormed by adding . to the stem without ય **-ya**. For example:

આવવું **āvvuṃ** *to come* → આવ્યું **āvyuṃ** *came* (n.), આવ્યો **āvyo** *came* (m.), આવી **āvī** *came* (f.), etc.

નહિ **nahi** or ન **na** are used when putting the perfective in the negative. For example:

ન આવ્યો	**na āvyo**	*he did not come*

A few verbs, such as લેવું **levuṃ** *to take* and બેસવું **besvuṃ** *to sit*, take the irregular perfective endings ધું **-dhuṃ** or ઠું **-ṭhuṃ** rather than યું **-yuṃ**. For example:

લેવું **levuṃ** *to take* → લીધું **līdhuṃ** *took* (n.)

બેસવું **besvuṃ** *to sit* → બેઠું **beṭhuṃ** *sat* (n.)

Most intransitive verbs behave regularly, although જવું **javuṃ** *to go* forms its perfective past from the stem ગ **ga**, to give the forms ગયું **gayuṃ**, ગયો **gayo** and ગઈ **gaī**. For example:

લક્ષ્મીબેન ઘેર ગયાં	**Lakṣmīben gher gayāṃ**	*Lakshmiben went home*

The perfective endings of intransitive verbs agree with the grammatical subject of the verb, which appears in its independent form. For example:

મારો ભાઈ આવ્યો	**māro bhāī āvyo**	*my brother came*
તે આવી	**te āvī**	*she came*
છોકરું આવ્યું	**chokruṃ āvyuṃ**	*the child came*
સમીર માશીને મળ્યો	**Samīr māśīne maḷyo**	*Sameer met his aunt*

Semi-transitive verbs are verbs which, although transitive in meaning, behave in the perfective past like intransitive verbs. These verbs include:

અડવું	**aḍvuṃ**	*to touch*
ચૂકવું	**cūkvuṃ**	*to lose* (a game), *to miss* (a train, etc.)
જમવું	**jamvuṃ**	*to eat*
પામવું	**pāmvuṃ**	*to receive, to get, to experience*
બોલવું	**bolvuṃ**	*to tell* (intr. *to speak*)
ભણવું	**bhaṇvum**	*to study, to learn*

ભૂલવું	**bhūlvuṃ**	*to forget*
લાવવું	**lāvvuṃ**	*to bring*
વળગવું	**vaḷgvuṃ**	*to clasp, to embrace*
શીખવું	**śīkhvuṃ**	*to learn*
સમજવું	**samajvuṃ**	*to understand*
મળવું	**maḷvuṃ**	*to meet, to find*

For example:

વિરેન ચોપડી લાવ્યો	**Vīren copḍī lāvyo**	*Viren brought the book*
આનલ ગુજરાતી ભણી	**Ānal gujarātī bhaṇī**	*Aanal studied Gujarati*

When this form appears without an auxiliary verb in Gujarati, it represents the simple past tense. This tense is used to describe an action which has been completed (hence the name perfective for the ending in યું **-yuṃ**). It is used for the general narrative tense, that is, the tense used to tell a sequence of events or a story. For example:

તે ગયો	**te gayo**	*he went*
શું થયું?	**śuṃ thayuṃ?**	*what happened?*

1 Now that you have learned how to describe actions that occurred in the past with intransitive and semi-transitive verbs, test your knowledge by translating the following sentences from Gujarati to English or from English to Gujarati. Then try to generate as many sentences from the verbs listed above as you can. Try to use a variety of pronouns, not just *I*, and also a variety of genders, not just your own!

a He came home.
b What happened afterwards?
c તે જમવા માટે ક્યાં ગઈ? te jamvā maṭe kyāṃ gaī?

2 MORE PERFECTIVE VERBS: THE PERFECT AND THE REMOTE PAST

The perfective form with યું **-yuṃ**, etc. is also used with the auxiliaries છે **che**/નથી **nathī** and હતું **hatuṃ**/ ન હતું **na hatuṃ**, નહોતું **nahotuṃ**. The former is used for a present perfective tense, while the latter is used for the remote past. Here are several examples:

a Simple past (see Point 1 above)

મારી બહેન ગઈ	**mārī bahen gaī**	*my sister went*

lere went has no reference to present time and is used mostly as a arrative tense.

Perfect

ારી બહેન ગઈ છે	**mārī bahen gaī che**	*my sister has gone*

his sentence refers to a present state resulting from a previous action. hus its full meaning is she has gone and is still not here.

Remote past

ારી બહેન ગઈ હતી	**mārī bahen gaī hatī**	*my sister had gone*

his sentence means that there has been subsequent activity after the ıain verb, which represents remote action, and so its full meaning is *my ister had gone but she has now come back.*

/hen these tenses are used with certain verbs, the contrast between ıe three meanings described above is very clear. The most important of ıese verbs for you to note are બેસવું **besvuṃ** *to sit*, સૂવું **sūvuṃ** *to sleep* ıd પડવું **paḍvuṃ** *to lie, to fall*. For example:

બેસે છે	**te bese che**	*he is sitting down* (i.e. he is in the process of sitting down)
બેઠો છે	**te beṭho che**	*he is sitting* (i.e. he has sat down and is still sitting)
બેઠો હતો	**te beṭho hato**	*he was sitting down* (i.e. he had sat down and was still sitting)

You have now learned to make even more complex sentnces about events in the past. Translate the following sentences from Gujarati into English to test your comprehension.

a **હું ગામ ગઈ હતી પણ મારો ભાઈ શહેર માં ગયો છે.** huṃ gām gaī hātī, paṇ maro bhaī śaher māṃ gayo che.

b **શું લાવ્યો છો?** shuṃ lāvyo cho?

c **શું થયું હતું?** śuṃ thāyuṃ hatuṃ?

d **એ છોકરી આવી છે.** e chokrī āvī che.

e **લીલાબેન ઘેર બેઠી હતી.** Līlāben gher beṭhī hātī.

วu will have another opportunity to look at perfective verbs later in this unit.

ADVERBIAL FORMATIONS

lany complex adverbials (see Unit 3 and Appendix 2) are also used ithout the નું **-nuṃ** ending in a purely adverbial manner. For example:

અંદર આવો	**aṃdar āvo**	*come in*
બહાર જાઓ	**bahār jāo**	*go out*
આગળ જાઓ	**āgaḷ jāo**	*go ahead*
એ નીચે રહે છે	**e nīce rahe che**	*he/she lives downstairs*
એ ઉપર રહે છે	**e upar rahe che**	*he/she lives upstairs*
આ તરફ જાઓ	**ā taraph juo**	*look this way*
આ બાજુ આવો	**ā bāju āvo**	*come to this side, come over here*
જમણી તરફ જાઓ	**jamṇī taraph jāo**	*go to the right*
ડાબી બાજુ જાઓ	**ḍābī bāju jāo**	*go to the left*

Some adjectives take the **એ -e** ending and are then used adverbially:

ધીમે	**dhīme**	*quietly, slowly*
ધીરે, ધીરે ધીરે	**dhīre, dhīre dhīre**	*slowly*
સીધા	**sīdhā**	*straight ahead*
ભલે	**bhale**	*good, well done!, it's good that...*
ભલે પધાર્યા	**bhale padhāryā**	*it's good that you have come, welcome!*

3 Translate the following sentences into Gujarati.

a Deepakbhai, go slowly on the road!

b Leela lives upstairs, where do you live?

c No, don't go there, turn left!

Vocabulary builder

પીધું	pīdhuṃ perfective of **પીવું** pīvuṃ	*to drink*
ખાધું	khādhuṃ perfective of **ખાવું** khāvuṃ	*to eat*
બાઈ (f.)	bāī	*woman, servant*
ચૂકવું (intr.)	cūkvuṃ	*to miss* (train)
જગ્યા (f.)	jagyā	*place*
પરીક્ષા આપવી	parīkśā āpvī	*to sit an exam*
તેઓ બહાર ગઈ	teo bahār gaī	*they've gone away*
સમાચાર (m.pl.)	samācār	*news*
ચોરી (f.)	corī	*theft*

મેં છાપામાં વાંચ્યા	meṃ chāpāmāṃ vāṃcyā	*I read it (i.e. the news) in the newspaper*
જણાવવું (tr.)	jaṇāvvuṃ	*to inform*
હકીકત (f.)	hakīkat	*fact, news, detailed account*
ચોર (m.)	cor	*thief*
તેણે કારકુન પાસે પૈસા માગ્યા	teṇe kārkun pāse paisā māgyā	*he asked the clerk for money*
ના પાડવી	nā pāḍvī	*to refuse*
તોફાન (n.)	tophān	*fight (lit. storm)*
પછાડવું (tr.)	pachāḍvuṃ	*to knock down*
પોલીસ (m.)	polīs	*police*
પકડવું (tr.)	pakaḍvuṃ	*to catch*
ખરેખર?	kharekhar?	*really?*
ફિલ્મ (f.)	philm	*film, movie*
ઠીક!	ṭhīk!	*OK!*
આરામ કરવો	ārām karvo	*to have a rest*

તમે આજે શું કર્યું? TAME ĀJE ŚUṂ KARYUṂ? *WHAT DID YOU DO TODAY?*

06.02 Leela and Prabodh Parikh both live in the suburbs of Mumbai, but Leela teaches in a women's university in the town.

1 What kind of questions does Prabodh ask Leela? What information do Prabodh and Leela learn about one another?

Dialogue 2

બોધ	લીલા, તું કયાં ગઈ? શું કરે છે?
ીલા	સવારથી હું કામ કરું છું. સવારે મેં નાસ્તો તૈયાર કર્યો. <u>નિશાએ</u> દૂધ નહિ પીધું અને <u>નિમિષે</u> કશું ખાધું નહિ. બાઈ આવી અને તે પછી હું નીકળી. હું ટ્રેન ચૂકી અને બસમાં ઘણા લોકો હતા તેથી મને જગ્યા નહિ મળી.
બોધ	યુનિવર્સિટીમાં શું થયું?
ીલા	પરમ દિવસે <u>વિદ્યાર્થિનીઓએ</u> પરીક્ષા આપી. તો તેઓ બહાર ગઈ. ગઈ કાલે <u>મેં</u> બેંકમાંથી ઓછા પૈસા લીધા તો મારે આજે ફરીથી જવું પડયું. <u>કોઈએ</u> તમને આજના સમાચાર કહ્યા?
બોધ	કયા સમાચાર? ચોરી અંગેના? મેં છાપામાં વાંચ્યા.
લા	તો કેમ તમે મને આ વાત જણાવી નહિ?
બોધ	કારણ કે મેં અત્યારે જ આ વાત વાંચી. <u>કોઈએ</u> તને બધી હકીકત કહી?
લા	ના. શું થયું?

પ્રબોધ એક ચોર બેન્ક ઓફ ઇન્ડિયામાં ગયો; તેણે કારકુન પાસે પૈસા માગ્યા. કારકુને ના પાડી અને તોફાન થયું. કારકુને ચોરને જમીન પર પછાડયો. પછી પોલીસે ચોરને પકડયો.

લીલા ખરેખર? તમે આજે શું કર્યું? તમે ચોપડી વાંચી?

પ્રબોધ ના, મેં એક બહુ સરસ ફિલ્મ જોઈ.

લીલા ઠીક! આરામ કરો. તમે કેટલું બધું કામ કર્યું!

Prabodh Līlā, tuṃ kyāṃ gaī? śuṃ kare che?

Līlā savārthī huṃ kaṃ karuṃ chuṃ, savāre meṃ nāsto taiyār karyo. Niśāe dūdh nahi pīdhuṃ ane Nimiśe kaśuṃ khādhuṃ nahi. bāī āvī ane te pachī huṃ nīkaḷī. huṃ ṭren cūkī ane basmāṃ ghaṇā loko hatā tethī mane jagyā nahi maḷī.

Prabodh yunivarsiṭīmaṃ suṃ thayuṃ?

Līlā param divase vidyārthinīoe parīkśā āpī. to teo bahār gaī. gaī kāle meṃ beṃkmāṃthī ochā paisā līdhā to māre āje pharīthī javuṃ paḍyuṃ. koīe tamne ājnā samācār kahyā?

Prabodh kayā samācār? corī aṃgenā? meṃ chāpāmām vāṃcyā.

Līlā to kem tame mane ā vāt jaṇāvī nahi?

Prabodh kāraṇ ke meṃ atyāre j ā vāt vāṃcī. koīe tane badhī hakīkat kahī?

Līlā nā. śuṃ thayuṃ?

Prabodh ek cor beṃk oph Inḍiyāmāṃ gayo; teṇe kārkun pāse paisā māgyā. kārkune nā pāḍī ane tophān thayuṃ. kārkune corne jamīn par pachāḍyo. pachī polīse corne pakḍyo.

Līlā kharekhar? tame āje śuṃ karyuṃ? tame copḍī vāṃcī?

Prabodh nā, meṃ ek bahu saras philm joī.

Līlā thīk! ārām karo. tame keṭluṃ badhuṃ kām karyuṃ!

2 True or false? Read and correct the following sentences based on the information given in the dialogue.

a આજે લીલાએ કશું કામ ન કર્યું.
āje Līlāe kaśum kām na karyuṃ.

b લીલા બસમાં આવ–જા કરે છે.
Līlā basmām āv-jā kare che.

c કારકુને ચોરને પૈસા આપ્યા.
kārkune corne paisā āpyā.

3 Answer the following questions based on what you learned in the dialogue.

a લીલાને કેમ બેન્કમાં જવું પડ્યું?
Līlāne kem beṃkmāṃ javuṃ paḍyuṃ?

b આજે પ્રબોધે શું કર્યું?
āje Prabodhe śuṃ karyuṃ?

Language discovery

Read and listen to the dialogue again.

a Pay special attention to the underlined words. All of these words are verbs – can you guess which tense these verbs are conjugated in here?

b How do the pronominal forms that agree with the underlined verbs appear different to you? Do you notice any patterns?

4 MORE PERFECTIVE VERBS: TRANSITIVE VERBS

Transitive verbs are conjugated in the simple past tense in the same way as intransitive verbs. However, transitive verbs in the simple past yield a slightly different sentence structure because the subject does not appear n the independent form, but rather with an agential suffix **એ -e** added (see Point 5 below), and the verb agrees with its direct object. For example:

બાપે દીકરીને ફૂલ આપ્યું	**bāpe dīkrīne phūl āpyuṃ**	*the father* (agent) *gave his daughter* (indirect object) *a flower* (direct object)

n this sentence, the verb agrees with the direct object of the verb (the ieuter singular word ફૂ, **phūl** *flower*). Note the agential ending **એ -e**, added ɔ બાપ **bāp** *father*.

ં ફિલ્મ જોઈ	**meṃ philm joī**	*I saw a film*

he verb in this sentence also agrees with the direct object of the verb eminine singular **ફિલ્મ philm** *film*). As displayed in the table on the next age **મેં meṃ** is the agential form of the first person singular pronoun.

MORE PRONOUNS AND NOUNS AS AGENTS

addition to the forms given in Unit 5, there are further agential forms pronouns that are used as agents with the simple past of transitive ːrbs. Most of these are formed by adding **એ -e** to the independent rm of the pronoun (e.g **કોઈએ koīe**, **કોણે koṇe**, **આપે āpe**, **તેઓએ teoe**, etc.).

Some pronouns whose independent forms end in એ **-e**, are the same in the agential form (e.g. અમે **ame**, આપણે **āpṇe**, તમે **tame** etc.). The singular pronouns have the special forms મેં **meṃ** and તેં **teṃ**.

	Agential forms of the pronoun with verbs of need, necessity and desire		Agential forms of pronoun with past tenses in યું yuṃ	
Singular				
First person	મારે	**māre**	મેં	**meṃ**
Second person	તારે	**tāre**	તેં	**teṃ**
Third person	તેણે	**teṇe**	તેણે	**teṇe**
	એણે	**eṇe**	એણે	**eṇe**
	આણે	**āṇe**	આણે	**āṇe**
	કોઈએ	**koīe**	કોઈએ	**koīe**
	કોણે	**koṇe**	કોણે	**koṇe**
Plural				
First person	અમારે	**amāre**	અમે	**ame**
Second person	આપણે	**āpṇe**	આપણે	**āpṇe**
Third person	તમારે	**tamāre**	તમે	**tame**
	આપે	**ape**	આપે	**āpe**
	તેઓએ	**teoe**	તેઓએ	**teoe**
	તેમણે	**temṇe**	તેમણે	**temṇe**
	એમણે	**emṇe**	એમણે	**emṇe**

There are also agential forms of nouns. These add the agential ending એ **-e** to the base form or to the stem form. For example:

છોકરે મને ચોપડી આપી	**chokre mane copḍī āpī**	*the boy gave me the book*

Or:

છોકરાએ મને ચોપડી આપી	**chokrāe mane copḍī āpī**	*the boy gave me the book*
પુરુષોએ કશું કામ ન કર્યું	**puruśoe kaśuṃ kām na karyuṃ**	*the men did not do any work*

Possessive adjectives agreeing with nouns that carry an agential ending may appear with the base form + એ -e or in the independent form. For example:

તમારે છોકરે મને ચોપડી આપી	**tamāre chokre mane copḍī āpī**	*your boy gave me the book*
તમારા છોકરે મને ચોપડી આપી	**tamārā chokre mane copḍī āpī**	*your boy gave me the book*

મારા છોકરાએ મને ચોપડી આપી	**tamārā chokrāe māne copḍī āpī**	*your boy gave me the book*

4 You have already learned several ways in which pronouns change their forms according to various grammatical structures. Now you have also learned how pronouns change in the past tense with intransitive verbs. Test your knowledge by translating the following sentences from English to Gujarati.

a Deepakbhai's wife gave a new notebook to the student (male).
b We (inclusive female) saw that old film at home.
c She ate Gujarati food.

NOTES ON GENDER

s you have already seen, some nouns have forms in both masculine/ euter and feminine in order to show a contrast between objects that are rge or coarse and objects that are small or fine. For example:

ેપડો	**copḍo**	*ledger*	ચોપડી	**copḍī**	*book*
ટલો	**roṭlo**	*thick bread*	રોટલી	**roṭlī**	*thin bread*
ટલું	**māṭlum̩**	*big earthenware pot*	માટલી	**māṭlī**	*small earthenware pot*
ડું	**gāḍum̩**	*cart*	ગાડી	**gāḍī**	*carriage, motor car*

EXPRESSIONS FOR NOW

ujarati has three words for now, અત્યારે **atyāre**, હવે **have** હમણાં and **amṇām̩**. These all have slightly different meanings and cannot be used terchangeably.

અત્યારે **atyāre** means *now* in the sense of right now, immediately. or example:

ત્યારે મારે જવું જોઈએ	**atyāre māre javum̩ joīe**	*I must go right now.*

હવે **have** means *now*, *right now* after something else has happened. or example:

મે હવે ક્યાં જાઓ છો?	**tame have kyām̩ jāo cho?**	*where are you going now?*
ઓ માંદા હતા પણ હવે તેઓ સાજા થયા છે	**teo mām̩dā hatā paṇ have teo sājā thayā che**	*he was ill but now he is well*
ઓ ગયા છે. હવે હું મજામાં છું	**teo gayā che. have hum̩ majāmām̩ chum̩**	*he has gone. now I am happy*

c હમણાં **hamṇāṃ** means *now* in the sense of nowadays, these days withou reference to any specific time. For example:

નાણપણમાં તેઓ માંદા હતા. હમણાં તેઓ સાજા છે	**nāṇpaṇmāṃ teo māṃdā hata. hamṇāṃ teo sājā che**	*in his childhood he was ill. nowadays he is well*

Practice

અભ્યાસ ABHYĀS

Read this postcard that Farook has written to a friend in London.

અત્યારે હું વડોદરામાં છું. ગયે અઠવાડિયે હું ગુજરાત પહોંચયો હતો. હું રાજકોટ ગયો હતો અને ત્યાંથી હું ભાવનગર ગયો હતો. આવતે અઠવાડિયે હું મુંબઈ જઈશ અને ત્યાંથી હું પાછો આવીશ. મારે પાછા આવવું નથી! અહીં ખૂબ મઝા આવે છે. મારે ફરીથી આવવું છે. તું મારી સાથે આવશે, ને?

atyāre huṃ vaḍodrāmāṃ chuṃ. gaye aṭhvāḍiye huṃ gujarāt pahoṃcyo hato. huṃ rājkoṭ gayo hato ane tyāmthī huṃ bhāvnagar gayo hato. āvte aṭhvāḍiye huṃ muṃbaī jaīś ane tyāṃthī huṃ pācho āvīś. māre pāchā āvvuṃ nathī! ahīṃ khūb majhā āve che. māre pharīthī āvvuṃ che. tuṃ marī sāthe āvśe, ne?

1 Answer the following questions in Gujarati.

a ફારૂક ગુજરાતમાં કેટલાં અઠવાડિયાં રહ્યો?
Phārūk gujarātmāṃ keṭlāṃ aṭhvāḍiyāṃ rahyo?

b ફારૂક કયા શહેરોમાં રહ્યો?
Phārūk kayā śaheromāṃ rahyo?

c એને ભારત દેશ ગમ્યો?
ene bhārat desh gamyo?

d એણે ગુજરાત ફરીથી જવું છે?
eṇe gujarāt pharīthī javuṃ che?

e તમે કયારેય ગુજરાત ગયા છો?
tame kyārey gujarāt gayā cho?

NEW VOCABULARY

કયારેય **kyārey** *ev*

2 Read and correct the following sentences. Pay special attentio to transitive and agential (એ -e) forms.

a લીલા પરમ દિવસે એના ભાઈ જોઈ.
Līlā param divase enā bhāī joī.

b કોણ તમને આ ખબર કહ્યું?
koṇ tamne ā khabar kahyuṃ?

c તમે આ ચોરીની બાબતમાં કંઈ વાંચ્યા?
tame ā corīnī bābatmāṃ kaṃī vāṃcya?

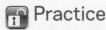

d તું એની વાત સાંભળ્યો?
tuṃ enī vāt sāṃbhaḷyo?

e નીલાએ મારા ભાઈને નથી મળી.
Nīlāe mārā bhāīne nathī maḷī.

> **NEW VOCABULARY**
>
> ની બાબતમાં **nī bābatmāṃ** *in the matter of, concerning*

3 06.03 **Fill in your part of the following dialogue.**

અલી	**કેમ છે? ઘણા દિવસથી આપણે નથી મળ્યા.**
Alī	kem che? ghaṇā divasthī āpṇe nathī maḷyā.
You	*Say you're pleased to see him. Say you haven't seen (met) him since last year.*
અલી	**મને ખબર છે. તું ક્યાં ગયો હતો?**
Alī	mane khabar che. tuṃ kyāṃ gayo hato?
You	*Tell him you went to India and you came back the day before yesterday.*
અલી	**મને તારો કાગળ હજી પણ મળ્યો નથી.**
Alī	mane tāro kāgaḷ hajī paṇ maḷyo nathī.
You	*Tell him that you're sorry and that you know that you're very lazy.*
અલી	**હું મજાક કરું છું, આજે તમારે કંઈ કામ કરવું પડશે?**
Alī	huṃ majāk karuṃ chuṃ, āje tamāre kaṃī kām karvuṃ paḍśe?
You	*Tell him 'nothing special.' Ask him why.*
અલી	**મારા કાકા અમદાવાદથી આવ્યા છે. તું મારી સાથે ઘેર આવજે!**
Alī	mārā kākā amdāvādthī āvyā c̣he. tuṃ mārī sāthe gher āvje!
You	*Say yes, you'd like to.*

> **NEW VOCABULARY**
>
> મને માફ કરો **mane māph karo** *I'm sorry*
> હજી પણ **hajī paṇ** *until now*

4 Complete the text below using the correct form of the verb in brackets.

The infinitive form of the verb (with the વું **-vuṃ** ending) is given in brackets. Before you do this exercise, you may wish to revisit the sections on the use of the past tenses, paying particular attention to the imperfect (હતું **hatuṃ**; see Unit 2), the simple past (ગયો **gayo**, etc.; see Point 1 above), and the remote past (ગયો હતો **gayo hato**, etc.; see Point 2 above).

શ્રીમતી પટેલ મોડાં (જાગવું) અને ખુશ ન (હોવું). બસ ભરચક (હોવું) અને એક છોકરો એમની સાડી પર ઊભો (રહેવું) અને એણે માફી ન (માગવું). એ શાકમારકેટ (જવું), શાકભાજી વાસી (હોવું). એમન સેક્રેટરી ગુસ્સે (હોવું). કારણ કે કોમ્પ્યુટર બગડી (જવું). જોકે સાંજે એમના મિત્રે એક નવી ફિલ્મ જોવા એમને (બોલાવવું) તેથી શ્રીમતી પટેલ આનંદમાં (આવવું).

Śrīmatī Paṭel moḍāṃ (jāgvuṃ) ane khuś na (hovuṃ). bas bharcak (hovuṃ) ane ek chokro emnī sāḍī par ūbho (rahevuṃ) ane eṇe māphī na (māgvuṃ). e śākmārkeṭ (javuṃ), śākbhājī vāsī (huvuṃ). emnāṃ sekreṭarī gusse (hovuṃ). kāraṇ ke kampyuṭar bagḍī (javuṃ). joke sāṃje emnā mitre ek navī philm jovā emne (bolāvvuṃ) tethī Srīmatī Paṭel ānaṃdmāṃ (āvvuṃ).

NEW VOCABULARY

જાગવું	**jāgvuṃ**	*to wake up*
ભરચક	**bharcak**	*full*
ઊભું	**ūbhuṃ**	*standing*
માફી માગવી	**maphī māgvī**	*to apologize*
શાકમારકેટ (f.n.)	**śākmārkeṭ**	*vegetable market*
શાકભાજી (n.pl.)	**śākbhājī**	*vegetables*
વાસી	**vāsī**	*stale, old*
સેક્રેટરી (f.)	**sekreṭarī**	*secretary*
બગડી જવું (intr.)	**bagḍī javuṃ**	*to get broken*
જોકે	**joke**	*although*

5 Complete the following dialogue by translating the English phrases in brackets into Gujarati.

માઈક	સાંભળો ભાઈ, હું હરે કૃષ્ણ હરે રામનું મંદિર શોધું છું, એ (*in which direction*) છે?
નટુભાઈ	જુઓ (on the right side) પોસ્ટ ઓફિસ છે. (*Opposite you*) જુહુ બજાર છે. (*Straight ahead*) જાઓ અને બજારમાં પહેલાં (*left side*) જાઓ. તમે હિંદુ ધર્મમાં વિશ્વાસ ધરાવો છો?
માઈક	ના, ભાઈ, હું ખ્રિસ્તી છું પણ લોકો કહે છે કે ત્યાંનું ખાવાનું બહુ સરસ છે અને એ લોકો બહુ માયાળુ છે.
Māīk	sāṃbhaḷo bhāī, huṃ Hare Kṛśṇa Hare Rāmnuṃ maṃdi śodhuṃ chuṃ, e (in which direction) che?
Naṭubhāī	juo, (*on the right side*) posṭ ophis che. (*Opposite you*) Juh bajār che. (*Straight ahead*) jāo ane bajār pehelāṃ (*left side*) jāo. tame Hiṃdu dharmmāṃ viśvās dharāvo cho?
Maik	nā, bhāī, huṃ Khristī chuṃ paṇ loko kahe che ke tyāṃnuṃ khāvānuṃ bahu saras che ane e loko bahu māyāḷu che.

NEW VOCABULARY

તરફ (f.)	**taraph**	*direction*
બાજુ (f.)	**bāju**	*side, direction*
જમણું	**jamṇuṃ**	*right*
સામું	**sāmuṃ**	*opposite*
સીધું	**sīdhuṃ**	*straight ahead*
ડાબું	**ḍābuṃ**	*left*
ડાબી બાજુમાં	**ḍābī bājumāṃ**	*on the left side*

...મજયા/સમજયાં? SAMJYĀ/SAMJYĀṂ? *DO YOU UNDERSTAND?*

...ead the following passage.

...ઈ કાલે મારા ખાસ મિત્ર તારીકે અમને જમવા બોલાવ્યા હતા. તેઓ અમારી સોસાયટીમાં રહે છે અને ...મારા ફ્લેટો સામસામે છેઃ અમે ૮ નંબરના ફ્લેટમાં રહીએ છીએ અને તારીક ૭ નંબરના ફ્લેટમાં રહે ... મેં બારણા પર ટકોરા માર્યા.

...રીક	સલામ અલેકુમ, કાસીમમિયાં! આવો આવો, કેમ છો? આવો નસરીન.
	વાલેકુમ સલામ! અમે મજામાં છીએ. કેમ છો?
...રીક	આવો, બેસો, ને? મારી બેગમ અંદર છે, તે જલદી આવે છે.
...સરીન	હું અંદર જાઉં. મારે ખુરશીદા સાથે બહુ વાતો કરવી છે.
...રીક	એ લોકો અંદર બહુ જ લાંબી વાત કરશે. ચાલો, આપણે ફરવા જઈએ.
...રશીદા	હેં, મેં સાંભળ્યું! આપણે જલદી જમીશું અને પછી આપણે ચારેય જણાં પાન ખાવા જઈશું

...મે આ બધું જ કર્યું અને પછી અમે ખુદા હાફિઝ કહી અને પોતપોતાને ઘેર પાછા ગયાં.

...aī kāle mārā khās mitra Tārīke amne jamvā bolāvyā hatā. teo amārī ...osāyaṭīmāṃ rahe che ane amārā phleṭo sāmsāme che: ame 8 ...aṃbarnā phleṭmāṃ rahīe chīe ane Tarīk 7 naṃbarnā phleṭmāṃ rahe ...he. meṃ bārṇā par ṭakorā māryā.

...ārīk	**salām alekum, Kāsīmmiyāṃ! āvo āvo, kem cho? āvo Nasrīn.**
...uṃ	**vālekum salāṃ! āme majāmāṃ chīe. kem cho?**
...ārīk	**āvo, beso ne? marī begum aṃdar che, te jaldī āve che.**
...asrin	**huṃ aṃdar jāuṃ. māre Khurśīdā sāthe bahu vāto karvī che.**

Tārīk e loko aṃdar bahu j lāṃbī vāt karśe. cālo, āpṇe pharvā jaīe.

Khurśīdā heṃ, meṃ sāṃbhaḷyuṃ! āpṇe jaldī jamīsuṃ ane pachī āpne cārey jaṇaṃ pān khāvā jaiśuṃ.

ame ā badhuṃ j karyuṃ ane pachī ame Khudā haphij kahī ane potpotāne gher pāchaṃ gayāṃ.

NEW VOCABULARY

પાન pān *paan* is the leaf of the betel tree. The leaf is often filled with different spices and sometimes also with tobacco, and is eaten or chewed (and then spat out) as a digestive aid after a meal.

1 True or false? Read and correct the following sentences based on the dialogue.

a તારીક અને કાસીમ ભાઈઓ છે.
Tārīk ane Kāsīm bhāīo che.

b આ લોકો સાથે રહે છે.
ā loko sāthe rahe che.

c તારીકની પત્ની બહાર ગઈ હતી.
Tarīknī patnī bahār gaī hatī.

2 Answer the following questions.

a નસરીન કેમ અંદર જાય છે?
Nasrīn kem aṃdar jāy che?

b આ લોકોનો ધર્મ શું છે? તેઓ કૃષ્ણ ભગવાનમાં વિશ્વાસ ધરાવે છે?
ā lokono dharm śuṃ che? teo Kṛṣṇa Bhagvānmāṃ viśvās dharāve che?

Test yourself

How would you do the following in Gujarati?

1. Tell your friend that you went to India and met your sister.
2. Ask Deepakbhai what he did today.
3. Say that you have arrived and that you want to eat now.
4. Tell your taxi driver to please go left, then right, then straight – but go slowly!
5. Tell Neela that the boy gave you the money, but that it was insufficient.
6. Say that you drank the cold water.

SELF CHECK

	I CAN...
○	. . . talk about a visit to India.
○	. . . talk about what I did during my visit.
○	. . . talk about what I did today.
○	. . . talk about a visit to a friend.
○	. . . give directions.

7 કેટલા વાગ્યા છે? kelā vāgyā che? *What's the time?*

In this unit you will learn how to:

- ***count in Gujarati.***
- ***tell the time.***
- ***talk about the seasons.***
- ***talk about possibilities and probabilities.***
- ***connect phrases and sentences in more idiomatic ways.***

ગુજરાત અને ગુજરાતીઓ gujarāt ane gujarātīo *Gujarat and Gujaratis*

Although the Hindu calendar uses solar years, it has lunar months in which the month is the interval between one new moon and the next. The lunar month is divided into two fortnights (પખવાડિયું **pakhvāḍiyuṃ**), the firs being the period from the new moon to the full moon, called શુદ્ધ **śuddh**, સુદ **sud** or શુક્લપક્ષ **śuklapakṣ** (*the light half of the month*), and the second being the time between the full moon and the new moon, વદ **vad**, વદી **vadī** or કૃષ્ણપક્ષ **kṛṣṇapakṣ** (*the dark half of the month*). A *leap month* (અધિકમાસ **adhikmās**) is added after every thirtieth month in order to compensate for the discrepancy between the lunar and solar calendars. The new year begins the day after Diwali, the festival of lights, which falls in autumn, i.e the first day of the light half of કારતક **kārtak**. In other parts of India, the Hindu year starts at different times; for example, in northern India it start on the first day of the dark half of ચૈત્ર **caitra**.

The fourteen days are called તિથિ **tithi** and each has its own name: પડવો **paḍvo**, બીજ **bījo**, ત્રીજ **trījo**, ચોથ **coth**, પાંચમ **pāṃcam**, છઠ **chaṭh**, સાતમ **sātam**, આઠમ **āṭham**, નોમ **nom**, દસમ **dasam**, અગિયારસ **agiyāras**, બારસ **bāras**, તેરસ **terus**, ચૌદસ **coudas**. Before any of these days, સુદ **sud** or વદ **vad**, is prefixed. The fifteenth day of સુદ **sud**, the full moon day, is પૂનમ **pūnam** or પૂર્ણિમા **pūṇimā**. The fifteenth day of સુદ **sud**, the new moon day, is called અમાસ **amās** or અમાવાસ્યા **amāvāsyā**.

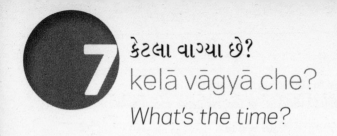

The lunar months do not correspond exactly with the Gregorian solar months (Western calendar months) but are approximately as follows:

Month	Season	
કારતક **kārtak**	શિયાળો **śyāḷo**	*October–November*
માગસર **māgsar**		*November–December*
પોષ **poṣ**		*December–January*
મહા **mahā**		*January–February*
ફાગણ **phāgaṇ**	ઉનાળો **unāḷo**	*February–March*
ચૈત્ર **chai**		*March–April*
વૈશાખ **vaiśākh**		*April–May*
જેઠ **jeṭh**		*May–June*
અષાઢ **āṣāḍh**	ચોમાસું **comāsuṃ**	*June–July*
શ્રાવણ **śrāvaṇ**		*July–August*
ભાદરવો **bhādravo**		*August–September*
આસો **aso**		*September–October*

In Gujarat, there are normally three seasons (ઋતુ) -શિયાળો (m.) **śiyāḷo** *winter*, ઉનાળો (m.) **unāḷo** *summer* and ચોમાસું (n.) **comāsuṃ** *rainy season*. However, the Sanskrit system of six seasons is also used. These begin in ચૈત્ર **caitra**, and each lasts for two months: વસંત (m.) **vasaṃt** *spring*, ગ્રીષ્મ (m.) **grīṣmā** *summer*; વર્ષા (f.pl.) **varṣā** *rains*, શરદ (f.) **śarad** *autumn*, હેમંત (m.) **hemaṃt** *winter* and શિશિર (m.) **śiśir** *cool season*. The last is also known as પાનખર (f.) **pānkhar** *autumn*.

Rather than using the Christian era, the Gujarati calendar usually uses the Vikrarma era વિક્રમ સંવત **vikram saṃvat**, abbreviated to VS. This corresponds to 56/7 B.C. (during the reign of King Vikram) so you have to subtract 56/7 to find the A.D. date.

Vocabulary builder

ટ્યૂબ (f.)	ṭyūb	*tube, underground railway*
કેટલા વાગ્યે?	keṭlā vāgye?	*at what time?*
સવા નવની ટ્યુબ	savā navnī yūb	*the 9.15 tube*
પોણા દસ	poṇā das	*a quarter to ten*
પોણા વાગ્યે પૂરા થાય છે	poa vāgye pūrā thāy che	*they finish at a quarter to one*
કેટલા વાગ્યા સુધી?	keṭlā vāgyā sudhī?	*until what time?*
સાડા ચાર	sāḍā cār	*half past four*

રોકાવું	rokāvuṃ	*to stay*
દોઢ	doḍh	*one and a half*
મુદત (f.)	mudat	*fixed time*
સંશોધન (n.)	saṃśodhan	*research*
પૂરું કરવું (tr.)	pūruṃ karvuṃ	*to finish*
નાટક (n.)	nāṭak	*play, drama*
ક્યારેય નહિ	kyārey nahi	*never*
લગભગ	lagbhag	*approximately*
સવા વાગ્યે	savā vāgye	*at a quarter past one*
અઢી વાગ્યે	aḍhī vagye	*half past two*
તારી ઘડિયાળમાં કેટલા વાગ્યા છે?	tarī ghaḍiyāḷmāṃ keṭlā vāgyā che?	*what's the time by your watch?*
દસમાં થોડીક મિનિટ બાકી છે	dasmāṃ thoḍīk miniṭ bākī che	*it's nearly ten o'clock*
તારી ઘડિયાળ આગળ જાય છે.	tārī ghaḍiyāḷ āgaḷ jāy che	*your watch is fast*
દસમાં દસ છે	dasmāṃ das che	*it's ten to ten*
બરાબર સવા વાગ્યે	barābar savā vāgye	*at a quarter past one sharp*

તું અહીંથી દૂર રહે છે? TUṂ AHĪṂTHĪ DŪR RAHE CHE? *DO YOU LIVE FAR FROM HERE?*

07.01 *In the students' coffee bar, Nisha Lakhani is talking to Ashish Jhaveri.*

1 Where does Ashish live? What does he tell Nisha about how he travels to and from university?

Dialogue 1

નિશા	તું અહીંથી દૂર રહે છે?
આશિષ	ના, પણ મારે ટ્યૂબમાં આવવું પડે છે.
નિશા	તારે કેટલા વાગ્યે યુનિવર્સિટી આવવા નીકળવું પડે છે?
આશિષ	હું સવા નવની ટ્યુબમાં આવું છું અને હું અહીં પોણા દસ વાગ્યે પહોંચું છું. સવારના વર્ગો દસ વાગ્યે શરૂ થાય છે અને પોણા વાગ્યે પૂરા થાય છે.
નિશા	તું કેટલા વાગ્યા સુધી અહીં રહે છે?
આશિષ	હું રોજ સાડા ચાર સુધી અહીં હોઉં છું.
નિશા	શાને માટે તું આખો દિવસ અહીં રોકાય છે?
આશિષ	હું દોઢ વરસ જ અહીં છું તેથી આ મુદતમાં મારે બધું સંશોધન પૂરું કરવું પડશે. મેં યુ.એસ. માં અભ્યાસ કર્યો હતો અને હું થોડા અઠવાડિયાં પહેલાં અહીં આવ્યો છું.

નિશા તું લંડન જોવા ગયો નથી?

આશિષ ના, મારી પાસે વખત નથી.

નિશા પણ તું લંડનમાં કયારેય નાટક જોવા ગયો છે ?

આશિષ ના, કયારેય નહિ.

નિશા એક દિવસ તું અમારા લોકોની સાથે આવજે. આજે તું મારી સાથે જમશે?

આશિષ હા, જરૂર. મારો વર્ગ લગભગ એક વાગ્યા સુધી ચાલશે. તો હું તને સવા વાગ્યે મળીશ.

નિશા ઠીક, પણ બપોરના વર્ગો અઢી વાગ્યે શરૂ થશે.

આશિષ તારી ઘડિયાળમાં કેટલા વાગ્યા છે?

નિશા દસમાં થોડીક મિનિટ બાકી છે.

આશિષ તારી ઘડિયાળ આગળ જાય છે. દસમાં દસ છે.

નિશા ચાલો, મારે જવું જોઈએ. આપણે બરાબર સવા વાગ્યે મળીશું.

Niśā tuṃ ahīṃthī dūr rahe che?

Āśis nā, paṇ māre ṭyūbmāṃ āvvuṃ paḍe che.

Niśā tāre keṭlā vāgye yunivarsiṭī āvvā nīkaḷvuṃ paḍe che?

Āśis huṃ savā navnī ṭyūbmaṃ āvuṃ chuṃ ane huṃ ahīṃ poṇā das vāgye pahoṃcuṃ chuṃ. savārnā vargo das vāgye śarū thāy che ane poṇā vāgye pūrā thāy che.

Niśā tuṃ keṭlā vāgyā sudhī ahīṃ rahe che?

Āśis huṃ roj sāḍā cār sudhī ahīṃ houṃ chuṃ.

Niśā śāne māṭe tuṃ ākho divas ahīṃ rokāy che?

Āśis huṃ doḍh varas j ahīṃ chuṃ tethī ā mudatmāṃ māre badhuṃ saṃśodhan pūruṃ karvuṃ paḍśe. meṃ yu.es.māṃ abhyās karyo hato ane huṃ thoḍāṃ aṭhvāḍiyāṃ pahelāṃ ahīṃ āvyo chuṃ.

Niśā tuṃ laṃḍan jovā gayo nathī?

Āśis nā, mārī pāse vakhat nathī.

Niśā paṇ tuṃ laṃḍanmāṃ kyārey nāṭak jovā gayo che?

Āśis nā, kyārey nahi.

Niśā ek divas tuṃ amārā lokonī sāthe āvje. āje tuṃ mārī sāthe jamśe?

Āśis ha, jarūr. māro varg lagbhag ek vāgyā sudhī cālśe. to huṃ tane savā vāgye maḷīś.

Niśā ṭhīk, paṇ bapornā vargo aḍhī vāgye śarū thaśe.

Āśis tārī ghaḍiyāḷmāṃ keṭlā vāgyā che?

Niśā dasmāṃ thoḍīk miniṭ bākī che.

Āśis tārī ghaḍiyā āga jāy che. dasmāṃ das che.

Niśā cālo, māre javuṃ joīe. āpṇe barābar savā vāgye maḷīśuṃ.

2 True or false? Read and correct the following sentences based on the information given in the dialogue.

a આશિષ પોણા નવની ટ્યુબમાં આવે છે.
Āśiṣ poṇā navnī ṭyūbmāṃ āve che.

b સવારના વર્ગો દસ વાગ્યે શરૂ થાય છે
savārnā vargo savā das vāgye śarū thāy che.

c બપોરના વર્ગો સાડા બે વાગ્યે શરૂ થાય છે.
bapornā vargo sāḍā be vāgye śarū thāy che.

3 Answer the following questions based on what you learned in the above dialogue.

a આશિષ શું કામ કરે છે?
Āśiṣ śuṃ kām kare che?

b આશિષને લંડન ગમે છે?
Āśiṣne Laṃḍan game che?

Language discovery

Read the dialogue again. What do all the underlined words or phrases have in common? Look at the Vocabulary builder to help you figure this out.

1 NUMERALS

Cardinal numbers (1, 2, 3, etc.)

Gujarati numbers are not as straightforward as numbers in English. Instead of the consistent English forms such as *twenty-two*, *thirty-three*, etc., Gujarati has more variable forms such as બાવીસ **bāvīs** (22), બત્રીસ **batrīs** (32), બેતાળીસ **betāḷīs** (34), બાવન **bāvan** (52). They must be learnt by heart up to one hundred (see Appendix 5). However, in most circumstances, you can get by using English numbers, so if you have limited time, you can learn up to 20 and come back to this section later.

After 100, numbers are regular, but you should note that unlike in English, in Gujarati *and* is not used to join them (for example, *one hundred and one*

English numbers with more than four figures are grouped in thousands. This is usually indicated by a comma in the numeric form, for example, 1,000 and 10,000, 100,000 and 1,000,000. This grouping is seen also in the vocabulary, for in these examples, only 1,000 and 1,000,000 (a thousand and a million) have their own terms; the other words use compound forms (ten thousand, a hundred thousand, etc.) In Gujarati, owever, after *one thousand*, which has its own special word (હજાર **hajār**), ıe higher numbers group into hundreds (e.g. 1,00,000), so there are ɔecial words for *a hundred thousand* (લાખ **lākh**), *ten million* (કરોડ **karoḍ**), tc., but not for one million (૧૦,૦૦,૦૦૦ દલ લાખ **daslākh** *ten lakhs*).

૦૦	એકસો, સો	**ekso so**
૦૧	એકસોએક	**ekso ek**
૦૦	બસો, બસેં	**baso, basem̩**
૦૦	ત્રણસો, ત્રણસેાં	**traṇso, traṇsom̩**
,૦૦૦	હજાર, સહસ્ત્ર	**hajār, sahasra**
૧૦૧	એક હજાર એકસો એક	**ek hajār ekso ek**
૦,૦૦૦	દસ હજાર	**dashajār**
,૦૦,૦૦૦	લાખ	**lākh lac, lakh,** *one hundred thousand*
૦,૦૦,૦૦૦	દસ લાખ	**daslākh** *one million*
,૦૦,૦૦,૦૦૦	કરોડ	**karoḍ crore**, *ten million*
,૦૦,૦૦,૦૦,૦૦૦	અબજ	**abaj** *a thousand million*

ardinal numbers up to 19 are masculine, whereas numbers above 19 ·e feminine. This is relevant to the agreement of પોણું **poṇum̩** and ધું **ardhum̩** (see below).

so, હજાર hajār, લાખ lākh and કરોડ karo are all masculine.

rdinal numbers (1st, 2nd, 3rd, etc.)

હેલું	**pahelum̩**	*first*
જું	**bījum**	*second* (also means *other*)
જું	**trījum̩**	*third*
થું	**cothum̩**	*fourth*
ંચમું	**pām̩cmum̩**	*fifth*
ઠું	**chaṭhṭhum̩**	*sixth*
ાતમું	**sātmum̩**	*seventh*

'ith numbers higher than સાતમું **sātmum̩**, મું **mum̩** is added to the cardinal ımber. For example:

કસો એકમું	**ekso ekmum̩**	*101st*
કસો પચાસમું	**ekso pacāsmum̩**	*150th*

Fractions

A system based on Sanskrit numerals is used for mathematical fractions. For example:

એક દ્વિતીયાંશ	**ek dvitīyāṃś**	*half*
એક તૃતીયાંશ	**ek tr̥tīyāṃś**	*a third*
એક ચતુર્થાંશ	**ek caturthāṃś**	*a quarter*

However, the more common forms are as follows:

પા	**pā**	*a quarter*
અર્ધું	**ardhuṃ**	*(a) half*
સાડા	**sāḍā**	*a half times*
પોણું	**poṇuṃ**	*three-quarters, a quarter less than*
સવા	**savā**	*one and a quarter, a quarter more than*
દોઢ	**doḍh**	*one and a half, one and a half times*
અઢી	**aḍhī**	*two and a half, two and a half times*

a પા **pā** may be used as a noun to mean *a quarter*, or as an invariable adjective to mean *a quarter* of the noun that it describes. It is not used with numbers apart from સો **so**, હજાર **hajār** and લાખ **lākh**, but even with these it is rarely used. For example:

પા કિલો	**pā kilo**	*a quarter of a kilo*
પા કલાક	**pā kalāk**	*a quarter of an hour*

b અર્ધું **ardhuṃ** is used as a noun to mean *a half*, or as a variable adjective to mean *half* of the noun that it describes. It is not used with cardinal numbers (e.g. *eight and a half*, where સાડા આઠ **sāḍā āṭh** is used), although it is used with સો **so**, હજાર **hajār** and લાખ **lākh** (which are all masculine). For example:

અર્ધો કિલો	**ardho kilo**	*half a kilo*
અર્ધો કલાક	**ardho kalak**	*half an hour*
અર્ધો લાખ	**ardho lakh**	*half a lakh, 50,000*

c સાડા **sāḍā** is an invariable adjective and is used with numbers over two to mean *a half more of the total*. With cardinal numbers it means *and a half*, but when it is used with ત્રણસો, ચાર હજાર **traṇso cār hajār** etc. it means *with a half more of the second number of the compound* (i.e., 50 or 500). સાડા **sāḍā** is never used with the singular forms સો **so**, હજાર **hajār** or લાખ **lākh**, etc. (અર્ધું **ardhuṃ** is used instead). For example:

સાડા ત્રણ	**sāā tra**	*3.5*

But:

સાડા ત્રણસો	**sāḍā traṇso**	*350*
સાડા ચાર હજાર	**sāḍā cār hajār**	*4,500*

d પોણું **poṇuṃ** is a variable adjective meaning *a quarter less than*, that is *three-quarters* of the noun that it describes. With cardinal numbers it means *and minus a quarter*, but with સો **so**, હજાર **hajār** and લાખ **lākh**, etc., it means *three-quarters of the total*.

Since numbers between 19 and 99 are feminine the feminine word પોણી **poṇī** is used, whereas સો **so**, હજાર **hajār** and લાખ **lākh** are all masculine and thus take પોણો **poṇo**/ પોણા **poṇā**. For example:

પોણો રૂપિયો	**poṇo rūpiyo**	*three-quarters of a rupee, 75 paisa*
પોણા ત્રણ	**poṇā traṇ**	*2.75*
પોણી વીસ	**poṇī vīs**	*19.75*
પોણો સો	**poṇo so**	*75* (but પોણી સો **poṇī** so *99.75*)
પોણા બસો	**poṇā baso**	*175* (but પોણી બસો **poṇī baso** *199.75*)
પોણા છ હજાર	**poṇā cha hajār**	*5,750*

e સવા **savā** is an invariable adjective meaning *a quarter more than*. With cardinal numbers it means *and a quarter*, but with સો **so**, હજાર **hajār** and લાખ **lākh**, etc., it means *with a quarter more of the total*. For example:

સવા બે	**savā be**	*2.25*
સવા વીસ	**savā vīs**	*20.25*

But:

સવા સો	**savā so**	*125*
સવા બસો	**savā baso**	*225*

f દોઢ **doḍh** *one and a half* can be used as a noun or an adjective, but only on its own or with સો **so**, હજાર **hajār** and લાખ **lākh**, etc., where it means *with half as much again of the total*. It takes singular forms, unlike in English, where *one and a half* is plural. For example:

દોઢ રૂપિયો	**doḍh rūpiyo**	*one and a half rupees*
દોઢસો	**doḍhso**	*150*

g અઢી **aḍhī** *two and a half* behaves as દોઢ **doḍh** and is the only one of the fractions to use plural forms. For example:

અઢી રૂપિયા	**aḍhī rūpiyā**	*two and a half rupees*
અઢી સો	**aḍhī so**	*250*
અઢી કરોડ	**aḍhī karod**	*25 million*

2 TELLING THE TIME

In order to tell the time in Gujarati, it is important that you learn, or at least start to learn, the cardinal numbers given in Point 1 above and in Appendix 5. The fractions are used, and there is a section below showing the special use of the fractions between 12 o'clock and 2.30. The times with fractions (including દોઢ **doḍh** *one and a half, half past one*) all take વાગ્યો **vāgyo** in the singular, except for અઢી **aḍhī** (*two and a half, half past two*), which takes વાગ્યા **vāgyā** in the plural.

The verb વાગવું **vāgvuṃ** *to strike* is used for times on the hour and at a quarter past, a quarter to and half past the hour. *What's the time?* is **કેટલા વાગ્યા છે? keṭlā vāgyā che?** and *at what time?* is કેટલા વાગ્યે છે? **keṭlā vāgye che?**

Practise by looking at your watch every now and then and trying to work out how you would say the time in Gujarati.

		it's...
o'clock		
નવ વાગ્યા (સવારે, રાતે) છે	**nav vāgyā (savāre, rāte) che**	*9.00 (a.m/p.m.)*
બરાબર નવ વાગ્યા છે	**barābar nav vāgyā che**	*exactly 9.00*
quarter past		
સવા નવ વાગ્યા છે	**savā nav vāgyā che**	*9.15*
half past		
સાડા નવ વાગ્યા છે	**sāḍā nav vāgyā che**	*9.30*
quarter to		
પોણા નવ વાગ્યા છે	**poṇā nav vāgyā che**	*8.45*
minutes past the hour		
નવને પાંચ (મિનિટ) થઈ છે	**navne pāṃc (miniṭ) thaī che**	*9.05*
નવ ઉપર પાંચ થઈ છે	**nav upar pāṃc thaī che**	*9.05*
નવ વાગ્યા પછી થોડીક મિનિટો થઈ છે	**nav vāgyā pachī thoḍīk miniṭo thaī che**	*a few minutes after 9 o'clock*
minutes to the hour		
નવમાં પાંચ કમ છે	**navmāṃ pāmc kam che**	*8.55*
નવમાં થોડીક મિનિટો બાકી છે	**navmāṃ thodīk miniṭo bākī che**	*a few minutes before 9 o'clock*

The following times use the fractions introduced in Point 1 above:

પોણો વાગ્યો છે	**poṇo vāgyo che**	*12.45*
એક વાગ્યો છે	**ek vāgyo che**	*1.00*
સવા વાગ્યો છે	**savā vāgyo che**	*1.15*
દોઢ વાગ્યો છે	**doḍh vāgyo che**	*1.30*
પોણા બે વાગ્યા છે	**poṇā be vāgyā che**	*1.45*
અઢી વાગ્યા છે	**aḍhī vāgyā che**	*2.30*
બપોર ના બાર વાગ્યા છે	**bapornā bār vāgyā che**	*12.00 noon*
રાત ના બાર વાગ્યા છે	**rātnā bār vāgyā che**	*12.00 midnight*
કેટલા વાગ્યે (or વાગે)	**keṭlā vāgye (or vāge)?**	*At what time?*
હું આઠ વાગ્યે અહીં આવું છું	**huṃ āṭh vāgye ahīṃ āvuṃ chuṃ**	*I come here at 8 o'clock*
તે સવા વાગ્યે આવ્યો	**te savā vāgye āvyo**	*he came at a quarter past one*
તે નવ વાગ્યાના સમયે અહીં આવે છે	**te nav vāgyā nā samaye ahīṃ āve che**	*she comes here at 9 o'clock*
તેઓ સવારે દસમાં પાંચ કમે પહોંચશે	**teo savāre dasmāṃ pāṃc kame pahoṃcśe**	*they will arrive at five to ten in the morning*
દુકાન સાતને વીસે બંધ થશે	**dukān sātne vīse baṃdh thaśe**	*the shop will close at twenty past seven*
હું રોજ સાડા સાત સુધી અહીં રહું છું	**huṃ roj sāḍā sāt sudhī ahīṃ j rahuṃ chuṃ**	*I stay here until half-past seven every day*
બપોરે બાર વાગ્યે થાય	**bapore bār vāgye thāy che**	*midday is at 12 o'clock*
મધરાત રાત્રિના બાર વાગ્યે થાય છે	**madhrāt rātrinā bār vāgye thāy che**	*midnight is at 12 o'clock at night*
મ.પૂ. (મધ્યાહ્ન પૂર્વ)	**ma. pū. (madhyāhn pūrva)**	*a.m.*
મ.પ. (મધ્યાહ્ન પછી)	**ma. pa. (madhyāhn pachī)**	*p.m.*

1 Now that you have learned how to tell time and about numbers in Gujarati ask Deepakbhai the following questions in Gujarati.

- **a** Do you come here at 9 o'clock every day?
- **b** What time will you go tomorrow?
- **c** What will we do at 2 o'clock?
- **d** This shirt is 100 rupees!

Vocabulary builder

મેં ચાર દિવસ પહેલાં મારો સામાન તૈયાર કરવા માંડયો	meṃ cār divas pahelāṃ māro sāmān taiyār karvā māṃḍyo	*I began to pack my belongings four days ago*
મારા ભાઈનો ફોન નથી આવ્યો	mra bhino phon nathi avyo	*my brother didn't phone me*
મેં એમને ફોન કર્યો	meṃ emne phon karyo	*I called him*
તેઓ બહારગામ ગયા હશે	teo bahārgām gayā haśe	*he must have gone away (lit. out of town/the village)*
તું પહોંચીને એમને ફોન કરજે	tuṃ pahoṃcīne emne phone karje	*please call him when you arrive*
અમારા સમાચાર સાંભળીને તેઓ રાજી થશે	amārā samācār sāṃbhaḷīne teo rājī thaśe	*he'll be pleased to hear our news*
હું કાગળ લખવા લાગી પણ હજીય પૂરો થયો નથી	huṃ kāgaḷ lakhvā lāgī paṇ hajīy pūro thayo nathī	*I started to write a letter but I haven't finished it yet*
કશી ચિંતા ન કરશો	kaśī ciṃtā na karśo	*don't worry at all*
તેઓ જલદી આવતા હશે	teo jaldī āvtā haśe	*he should be coming soon*
એમનું કામ પૂરું થયું હશે	emnuṃ kām pūruṃ thayuṃ haśe	*he must have finished his work*
આપણે અહીં થોડી વાર બેસીને એમની રાહ જોઈએ	āpṇe ahīṃ thoḍī vār besīne emnī rāh joīe	*let's sit here for a while and wait for him*
અમે ઘેર પહોંચ્યાં તે પહેલાં વરસાદ પડવા લાગ્યો	ame gher pahomcyāṃ te pahelāṃ varsād paḍvā lāgyo	*it began to rain before we reached home*

સાંભળ્યું છે કે તું દેશ જશે MEṂ SĀṂBHALYUṂ CHE KE TUṂ DEŚ JAŚE

'VE HEARD YOU'RE GOING TO INDIA

07.02 *Leela Patel has heard that her friend's daughter, Nisha Lakhani, is going to India, and wants her to take a message.*

1. **What does Leela tell Nisha?**

Dialogue 2

લીલા	ગઈ કાલે હું અહીં આવી હતી પણ તને ન મળી. તારા બાપુજીએ મને કહ્યું કે તું દેશ જશે.
નીશા	હા, હું પરમ દિવસે જાઉં છું, મેં ચાર દિવસ પહેલાં મારો સામાન તૈયાર કરવા માંડયો. તમે મુંબઈમાં કયારે આવશો?
લીલા	મને ખબર નથી. મારા ભાઈનો ફોન નથી આવ્યો. મેં એમને ફોન કર્યો પણ તેઓ બહારગામ <u>ગયા હશે</u>. તું <u>પહોંચીને</u> એમને ફોન કરજે. અમારા સમાચાર <u>સાંભળીને</u> તેઓ <u>રાજી થશે</u>. હું કાગળ લખવા લાગી પણ હજીય પૂરો થયો નથી.
નીશા	ભલે. પહોંચીને જ હું કાકાને ફોન કરીશ. કશી ચિંતા ન કરશો. પ્રબોધકાકા કયાં છે?
લીલા	તેઓ બજારમાંથી મારા ભાઈને માટેની કેટલીક ચીજો લઈને આવશે. કેટલા વાગ્યા છે? ચાર? તેઓ જલદી આવતા હશે. એમનું કામ પૂરું થયું હશે. આપણે અહીં થોડી વાર બેસીને એમની રાહ જોઈએ.
નીશા	મને લાગે છે કે વરસાદ પડશે. આપણે તમારે ત્યાં જઈએ.
લીલા	મને નથી લાગતું કે પડે, પણ ગઈ કાલે હું અને તારા કાકા ફરવા ગયાં હતાં અને અમે ઘરે પહોંચ્યાં તે પહેલાં વરસાદ પડવા લાગ્યો. ચાલો, જલદી જઈએ.
Līla	gaī kāle huṃ ahīṃ āvī hatī paṇ tane na maḷī, tārā bāpujīe mane kahyuṃ ke tuṃ deś jaśe.
Niśā	hā, huṃ param divase jāuṃ chuṃ, meṃ cār divas pahelāṃ māro sāmān taiyār karvā māṃḍyo. tame muṃbaīmāṃ kyāre āvśo?
Līlā	mane khabar nathī. mārā bhāīno phon nathī āvyo. meṃ emne phon karyo paṇ teo bahārgām <u>gayā haśe</u>. tuṃ pahoṃcīne emne phon karje. amārā samācār <u>sāṃbhaḷīne</u> teo <u>rājī thaśe</u>. huṃ kāgaḷ lakhvā lāgī paṇ hajīy pūro thayo nathī.
Niśā	bhale. <u>pahoṃcīne</u> j huṃ kākāne phon karīś. kaśī ciṃtā na karśo. Prabodhkākā kyāṃ che?

Līla teo bajarmāṃthī mārā bhāīne māṭenī keṭlīk cījo laīne āvśe. keṭlā vāgyā che? cār? teo jaldī āvtā haśe. emnuṃ kām pūruṃ <u>thayuṃ hāse</u>. āpṇe ahīṃ thoḍī vār besīne emnī rāh joīe.

Niśā mane lāge che ke varsād paḍśe. āpṇe tamāre tyāṃ jaīe.

Līla mane nathī lāgtuṃ ke paḍe, paṇ gaī kāle huṃ ane tārā kākā pharvā gayāṃ hatāṃ ane ame gher pahoṃcyāṃ te pahelāṃ varśād paḍvā lāgyo. cālo, jaldī jaīe.

2 True or false? Read and correct the following sentences based on the information in the above dialogue.

a નીશા ગઈ કાલે એનો સામાન તૈયાર કરવા માંડયો.
Niśā gaī kāle eno sāmān taiyār karvā māṃḍyo.

b લીલાના ભાઈ મુંબઈમાં હશે.
Līlānā bhāī muṃbaīmāṃ haśe.

c લીલાએ કહ્યું કે પ્રબોધ ઘેર જ હશે.
Līlāe kahyuṃ ke Prabodh gher j haśe.

3 Answer the following questions.

a પ્રબોધ નું કામ પૂરું થયું છે?
Prabodhnuṃ kām pūruṃ thayuṃ che?

b લીલાને લાગે છે કે વરસાદ પડશે?
Līlāne lāge che ke varsād paḍśe?

Language discovery

Read and listen to the dialogue again.

a Pay special attention to the underlined words or phrases and use the Vocabulary builder to figure out what they have in common.

b In this unit you will be learning about gerunds, or terms that express *having done* something or *once X has been done do Y*. There are three such terms in the dialogue. Can you find them? Here is a hint: the three terms all end in -ઈને **īne.**

3 THE GERUND (E.G. *HAVING DONE*)

If two or more sentences include sequential actions being performed by the same subject they are usually combined to form one sentence. When such sentences are formed in Gujarati, all but the main verb (the last verb will take the invariable ending ઈ **-ī** or ને **-īne** added to the root. This form is called the gerund. If there is more than one gerund in a sentence, the first gerund will usually end in ઈ **-ī**, while the subsequent ones will end in ઈને **-īne**. This form is roughly equivalent to saying in English *having done X, he did Y*, etc. If the main verb is transitive then the subject appears in the agential form. For example:

કરવું **karvuṃ** *to do, to make* → કરી **karī**, કરીને **karīne**

કામ કરો અને પછી ઘેર જાઓ	**kām karo ane pachī ghẹr jāo**	*do your work and then go home*

Or:

કામ કરીને (કરી) અને પછી ઘેર જાઓ	**kām karīne (karī) gher jāo**	*do your work and then go home*
કામ કરીને એ ઘેર ગયો	**kām karīne e gher gayo**	*he did his work and went home*
હું બજારમાં ગઈ અને પછી હું અહીં આવી	**huṃ bajārmāṃ gaī ane pachī huṃ ahīṃ āvī**	*I went to the market and then came here*

Or:

હું બજારમાં જઈને અહીં આવી	**huṃ bajārmāṃ jaīne ahīṃ āvī**	*I went to the market and then came here*
તે અમારી પાસે આવ્યો અને તેણે કહ્યું કે...	**te amārī pāse āvyon ane teṇe kahyuṃ ke...**	*he came to us and laughed and then said that...*
અમારી પાસે આવી તેણે હસીને કહ્યું કે	**amārī pāse āvi teṇe hasīne kahyuṃ ke...**	*he came to us and laughed and then said that...*

The construction હસીને **hasine** may also be translated as *smiling* or *laughing*.

Gerund constructions can be used in several idiomatic phrases:

a થઈને **thaīne** (lit. *having been*) is used to mean *via* or *by way of*. For example:

વારડેન રોડ થઈને આવો	**vārḍen roḍ thaīne āvo**	*come via Warden Road*

b કરીને **karīne** (lit. *having done*) is used idiomatically as follows:

મહેરબાની કરીને	**maherbānī karīne**	*please (do me a favour)*
ખાસ કરીને	**khās karīne**	*especially*

c જાણી જોઈને **jāṇi joīne** (lit. *having known, having seen*) means *deliberately*. For example:

મેં જાણી જોઈને આ કાગળ લખ્યો	**meṃ jāṇī joīne ā kāgaḷ lakhyo**	*I wrote this letter deliberately*

2 Gerunds are fairly straightforward. Make sure you have understood how they work by replacing અને પછી ane pachī *and then* **or અને ane** *and* **in the following sentences with a gerund.**

a હું ઘેર ગઈ અને પછી મેં એને ફોન કર્યો huṃ gher gaī ane pachī meṃ ene phon karyo.

b અમારા સમાચાર સાંભળો અને પછી તેઓ રાજી થયા amārā samācār sāṃbaḷyo ane pachī teo rājī thayā.

c અયાં બેસો અને એમની રાહ જોઈએ ayāṃ beso ane emnī rāh joīe.

> **NEW VOCABULARY**
>
> ફોન કરવું **phone karvuṃ** *to call on the phone*

4 EXPRESSIONS FOR *TO BEGIN*

The verbs લાગવું **lāgvuṃ** and માંડવું **māṃḍvuṃ** are used with the invariable ending વા **-vā** to mean *to begin*. For example:

a લાગવું **lāgvuṃ** is used intransitively. For example:

એ કામ કરવા લાગ્યો	**e kām karvā lāgyo**	*he began to work*
એ કાગળ લખવા લાગ્યો	**e kāgaḷ lakhvā lāgyo**	*he began to write a letter*

b This construction with the verb માંડવું **māṃḍvuṃ** is irregular. While its meaning is the same as that of લાગવું **lāgvuṃ**, the sentence is constructed according to whether or not the verb is being used as a transitive or intransitive (you should note that માંડવું **māṃḍvuṃ** *to place* is generally considered a transitive verb). For example:

વરસાદ પડવા માંડયો	**varsād paḍvā māṃḍyo**	*it began to rain*

Or:

વરસાદે પડવા માંડયું	**varsāde paḍvā māṃḍyuṃ**	*it began to rain*
એણે કામ કરવા માંડયું	**eṇe kām karvā māṃḍyuṃ**	*he began to work*
હું કામ કરવા લાગું?	**huṃ kāṃ karvā lāguṃ?**	*may I help you?* (lit. *shall I start some work?*)

એ કામ કરવા માંડયો **e kāṃ karvā māṃḍyo** is not a proper construction

c If what is begun is a noun rather than a verb, the expression શરૂ કરવું **saru karvuṃ** is used. For example:

મેં કામ શરૂ કર્યું	**meṃ kām śarū karyuṃ**	*I began the work*

3 Test your understanding of how to talk about beginning something by translating the following sentences into English:

a કામ શરૂ કરો kām śurū karvo

b એ પાણી પીવા લાગ્યું ee pāṇī pīvā lāgyuṃ

c વરસાદ પડવા માંડ્યો varsād paḍvā māṃḍyo

5 POSSIBILITY AND PROBABILITY

The future tense of હોવું **hovuṃ** (હશે **haśe**, etc.) can be used on its own to express an action in the future. For example:

તમે કયારે મુંબઈ હશો?	**tame kyāre muṃbaī haśo?**	*when will you be in Mumbai?*

This tense is also used to express supposition, probability or uncertainty, rather like the English *he'll be at home now*. The tense is used either on its own or as an auxiliary verb, replacing છે **che**, etc. with તું **-tuṃ** ending imperfectives or યું **-yuṃ** ending perfectives. The negative form is the invariable નહિ/ન હોય **nahi/na hoy**. For example:

તે ઘેર હશે/તે ઘેર નહિ હોય	**te gher haśe/te gher nahi hoy**	*he must/mustn't be at home*
તે આવતો હશે/તે આવતો નહિ હોય	**te āvto haśe/te āvto nahi hoy**	*he must/mustn't be coming*
તે આવી હશે/તે આવી નહિ હોય	**te āvī haśe/ te āvī nahi hoy**	*she must/mustn't have come*

4 Now that you have learned how to express possibility and probability, translate the following sentences from Gujarati to English or English to Gujarati.

a તે માણસ ગાંડો હશે/હોય te māṇas gāṃḍo haśe/hoy

b Today I ought to receive a letter.

c આ છોકરો હોશિયાર હશે/હોય ā chokro bahu hośiyār haśe/hoy

d She must be coming home now.

NEW VOCABULARY

ગાંડો હોવું **gāṃḍo hovuṃ** *to be angry*

Practice

1 Write out the following passage to practise using the Gujarati script. Use gerunds (see Point 3) to link sentences together where possible:

ગામડામાં અમારે થોડી જમીન છે, પણ તેઓ ખેડુત નથી. તેઓ સુથાર છે. તેઓ પોતે ખેતરનું જોઈતું કામ કરે છે. અમારા ખેતરમાં અમે મગફળીનો પાક લઈએ છીએ. ચાર વરસથી હું બેંકમાં નોકરી કરું છું.

હું વહેલી સવારે ઊઠું છું અને હું દાતણ કરું છું અને સ્નાન કરું છું. ઘરમાં અંબાજીનું મંદિર છે અને હું એની પૂજા કરું છું અને પછી હું ઓફિસ જવા નીકળું છું, હું બસમાં આવ-જા કરું છું અને રોજ બસો ચિકાર હોય છે અને લોકો બહુ ગડબડ કરે છે. રાતે હું કોઈ ચોપડી વાંચું છું અને પછી હું સૂઈ જાઉં છું.

મારે નોકરી છોડવી છે પણ ગામડામાં લોકોને બહુ ઓછા પૈસા મળે છે અને મારે બેચાર વરસ સુધી નોકરી કરવી પડે એમ છે.

gāmdāmāṃ amāre thoḍī jamīn che, paṇ teo kheḍut nathī. teo suthār che. teo pote khetarnuṃ joītuṃ kām kare che. amārā khetarmaṃ ame magphaḷīno pāk laīe chīe. cār varasthī huṃ beṃkmāṃ nokrī karuṃ chuṃ

huṃ vahelī savāre ūṭhuṃ chuṃ ane huṃ dātaṇ karuṃ chuṃ ane snān karuṃ chuṃ. gharmaṃ Aṃbājīnuṃ maṃdir che ane huṃ enī pūjā karuṃ chum, pachī huṃ emne māṭe nāsto taiyār karuṃ chuṃ ane pachī huṃ ophis java nīkalum chuṃ, huṃ basmāṃ āv-jā karuṃ chuṃ ane roj baso cikār hoy che ane loko bahu gaḍbaḍ kare che. rāte huṃ koī copḍi vāṃcuṃ chuṃ ane pachī huṃ suī jāuṃ chuṃ.

māre nokrī choḍvī che paṇ gāmḍāmāṃ lokone bahu ochā paisā maḷe che ane māre becār varas sudhī nokrī karvī paḍe em che.

2 Read the Introduction to Gujarat section at the beginning of this book and then answer the following questions:

a ગુજરાતની વસ્તી કેટલી છે?
gujarātnī vasti keṭlī che?

b ગુજરાતનો કિનારો કેટલો લાંબો છે?
gujarātno kināro keṭlo lāṃbo che?

c ગુજરાતમાં એક વરસમાં કેટલો વરસાદ પડે છે?
gujarātmāṃ ek varasmāṃ keṭlo varsād paḍe che?

d ગુજરાતમાં કેટલા લોકોને લખતાં વાંચતાં આવડે છે?
gujarātmāṃ keṭlā lokone lakhtāṃ vāṃctām āvaḍe che?

e તમને ખબર છે કે ભારતની વસ્તી કેટલી છે?
tamne khabar che ke bhāratnī vastī ketḷī che?

NEW VOCABULARY

વસતી (f.)	**vasti**	*population*
કિનારો (m.)	**kināro**	*shore, coast, bank*

3 Say what the time is in Gujarati as indicated on the following clock faces:

1

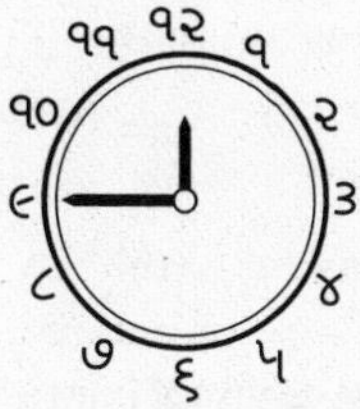

2

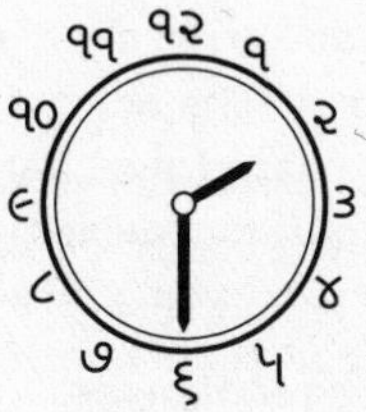

3

4

5

6

4 Fill in your part of the following dialogue.

સુરેશ	**તમે સવારે કેટલા વાગ્યે ઓફિસ જાઓ છો?**
Sureś	tame savāre keṭlā vāgye ophise jāo cho?
You	*Tell him that you go out at 9 o'clock.*
સુરેશ	**તમે બસમાં આવ–જા કરો છો?**
Sureś	tame basmāṃ āv-jā karo cho?
You	*Tell him that you commute by train.*
સુરેશ	**તમે ઓફિસ મોડા પહોંચતા હશો.**
Sureś	tame ophis moḍā pahoṃctā haśo.
You	*Tell him that you arrive at about 10.30.*
સુરેશ	**તમે કેટલા વાગ્યા સુધી ત્યાં કામ કરો છો?**
Sureś	tame keṭlā vāgyā sudhī tyāṃ kām karo cho?
You	*Tell him you work until 6 o'clock in the evening.*

સમજયા/સમજયાં? SAMJYA/SAMJYAṂ? DO YOU UNDERSTAND?

As this is the final unit in *Get started in Gujarati*, we are testing your comprehension skills and omitting the transliteration of the following passage. The passage contains many English words in Gujarati script. By doing this exercise, you will be able to see how much revision of the script will be needed if you decide to continue learning to read and write in Gujarati beyond the introductory level covered in this book.

અઠવાડિયાના સાત દિવસ હોય છે (રવિવાર, સોમવાર, મંગળવાર, બુધવાર, ગુરુવાર, શુક્રવાર અને શનિવાર).

વરસના બાર મહિના હોય છે (જાન્યુઆરી, ફેબ્રુઆરી, માચ, એપ્રિલ, મે, જૂન, જૂલાઈ, ઓગસ્ટ, સપ્ટેમ્બર, ઓકટોબર,નવેમ્બર, ડિસેમ્બર).

શિયાળો, ઉનાળો, અને ચોમાસું, એ વરસની ત્રણ ઋતુ છે.

ઉનાળો લગભગ માર્ચમાં બેસે છે. ગુજરાતમાં ઉનાળામાં ખૂબ ગરમી પડે છે. ધરતી સુકાઈ જાય છે અને બહુ જ ધૂળ હોય છે. ચોમાસાના પહેલા બે મહિનામાં વરસાદ પડે છે. ગરમી ઓછી થાય છે અને ઝાડપાન ચોળ્ખાં લાગે છે. શિયાળો નવેમ્બરમાં બેસે છે. દિવસે ગરમી તથા ઠંડી લાગતી નથી પણ રાતે કોઈ કોઈ વાર ઠંડી લાગે છે. રોજ આકાશ સાફ હોય છે. આ ઋતુ ઘણી સુંદર હોય છે.

1 True or false? Read and correct the following sentences.

- **a** અઠવાડિયાના આઠ દિવસ હોય છે.
- **b** ગુજરાતમાં પાંચ ઋતુ હોય છે.
- **c** ચોમાસાના છેલ્લા બે મહિનામાં વરસાદ પડે છે.

2 Answer the following questions.

- **a** ચોમાસું ક્યારે બેસે?
- **b** ચોમાસું ક્યાં સુધી ચાલે છે?

Test yourself

How would you do the following in Gujarati?

1. Ask how many rupees the tea was and what time it is.
2. Tell Deepakbhai that you leave the house to go to work every day at 6 a.m.
3. Ask how many times a week Leela goes to meet her family in the village.
4. Say that you began your work after you drank tea.
5. Say that you did your work until 5 o'clock and then went home and ate dinner.
6. Ask what season it is and what month of the year.

SELF CHECK

I CAN...
. . . count in Gujarati.
. . . tell the time.
. . . talk about the seasons.
. . . talk about possibilities and probabilities.
. . . connect phrases and sentences in more idiomatic ways.

Appendix 1

Conjunct consonants

ક્ + ક = ક્ક	જ્ + ર = જ્ર	દ્ + ર = દ્ર	મ્ + ય = મ્ય
ક્ + ખ = ક્ખ	જ્ + વ = જ્વ	દ્ + વ = દ્વ	મ્ + ર = મ્ર
ક્ + ટ = ક્ટ	ટ્ + ટ = ટ્ટ	ધ્ + ય = ધ્ય	મ્ + લ = મ્લ
ક્ + ત = ક્ત	ટ્ + ઠ = ટ્ઠ	ધ્ + વ = ધ્વ	મ્ + હ = મ્હ
ક્ + મ = ક્મ	ટ્ + ય = ટ્ય	ન્ + ત = ન્ત	ય્ + ય = ય્ય
ક્ + ય = ક્ય	ટ્ + ર = ટ્ર	ન્ + દ્ + ર = ન્દ્ર	ર્ + થ = ર્થ
ક્ + ર = ક્ર	ઠ્ + ઠ = ઠ્ઠ	ન્ + ધ = ન્ધ	લ્ + ક = લ્ક
ક્ + લ = ક્લ	ઠ્ + ય = ઠ્ય	ન્ + ન = ન્ન	લ્ + દ = લ્દ
ક્ + વ = ક્વ	ડ્ + ડ = ડ્ડ	ન્ + મ = ન્મ	લ્ + પ = લ્પ
ક્ + શ = ક્શ	ડ્ + ર = ડ્ર	ન્ + ય = ન્ય	લ્ + મ = લ્મ
ક્ + ષ = ક્ષ	ઢ્ + ય = ઢ્ય	ન્ + વ = ન્વ	લ્ + ય = લ્ય
ક્ષ્ + મ = ક્ષ્મ	ણ્ + ટ = ણ્ટ	ન્ + હ = ન્હ	વ્ + ય = વ્ય
ક્ + સ = ક્સ	ણ્ + ઠ = ણ્ઠ	પ્ + ત = પ્ત	વ્ + ર = વ્ર
ખ્ + ય = ખ્ય	ણ્ + ડ = ણ્ડ	પ્ + ન = પ્ન	વ્ + વ = વ્વ
ગ્ + દ = ગ્દ	ણ્ + ય = ણ્ય	પ્ + પ = પ્પ	શ્ + ક = શ્ક
ગ્ + ધ = ગ્ધ	ત્ + ક = ત્ક	પ્ + ય = પ્ય	શ્ + ચ = શ્ચ
ગ્ + ન = ગ્ન	ત્ + ત = ત્ત	પ્ + ર = પ્ર	શ્ + ન = શ્ન
ગ્ + મ = ગ્મ	ત્ + ત્ + વ = ત્ત્વ	પ્ + લ = પ્લ	શ્ + ય = શ્ય
ગ્ + ય = ગ્ય	ત્ + થ = ત્થ	પ્ + સ = પ્સ	શ્ + ર = શ્ર
ગ્ + ર = ગ્ર	ત્ + ન = ત્ન	બ્ + જ = બ્જ	શ્ + લ = શ્લ
ગ્ + લ = ગ્લ	ત્ + પ = ત્પ	બ્ + દ = બ્દ	શ્ + વ = શ્વ
ગ્ + વ = ગ્વ	ત્ + મ = ત્મ	બ્ + ધ = બ્ધ	ષ્ + ક = ષ્ક
ઘ્ + ન = ઘ્ન	ત્ + ય = ત્ય	બ્ + બ = બ્બ	ષ્ + ટ = ષ્ટ
ઘ્ + ય = ઘ્ય	ત્ + ર = ત્ર	બ્ + ચ = બ્ચ	ષ્ + ટ્ + ર = ષ્ટ્ર
ઘ્ + ર = ઘ્ર	ત્ + વ = ત્વ	બ્ + ર = બ્ર	ષ્ + ઠ = ષ્ઠ
ઙ્ + ક = ઙ્ક	ત્ + સ = ત્સ	ભ્ + ય = ભ્ય	ષ્ + ણ = ષ્ણ
ચ્ + ચ = ચ્ચ	ત્ + સ્ + ય = ત્સ્ય	ભ્ + ર = ભ્ર	ષ્ + પ = ષ્પ
ચ્ + છ = ચ્છ	થ્ + ય = થ્ય	મ્ + ન = મ્ન	ષ્ + મ = ષ્મ
ચ્ + ય = ચ્ય	દ્ + દ = દ્દ	મ્ + પ = મ્પ	ષ્ + ય = ષ્ય
જ્ + જ = જ્જ	દ્ + ધ = દ્ધ	મ્ + બ = મ્બ	ષ્ + વ = ષ્વ
જ્ + ગ = જ્ઞ	દ્ + મ = દ્મ	મ્ + ભ = મ્ભ	સ્ + ત્ + ર = સ્ત્ર
જ્ + ય = જ્ય	દ્ + ય = દ્ય	મ્ + મ = મ્મ	સ્ + થ = સ્થ
સ્ + થ્ + ય = સ્થ્ય	સ્ + મ = સ્મ	સ્ + સ = સ્સ	હ્ + ર = હ્ર
સ્ + ન = સ્ન	સ્ + ય = સ્ય	હ્ + ન = હ્ન	હ્ + લ = હ્લ
સ્ + ક = સ્પ	સ્ + ર = સ્ર	હ્ + મ = હ્મ	હ્ + વ = હ્વ
સ્ + ફ = સ્ફ	સ્ + વ = સ્વ	હ્ + ય = હ્ય	

Appendix 2

Adverbials

Adverbials, when preceded by a form of નું **nuṃ** (e.g. છોકરાની પાસે **chokrānī pāse** *with the child*), are called complex adverbials as opposed to simple adverbials, which are used after stem forms of nouns and pronouns (e.g. મેજ પર **mej par** *on the table*). Some of these forms are preceded by ની **nī**, others by ને **ne** and others by ના **na**. There is no rule, but each form must be learned. The most common adverbials are given here in alphabetical order. You may find it easier to learn them by writing them out in groups according to the form of નું **nuṃ** that they use. Remember that these forms are not mandatory when preceded by a noun (e.g. છોકરાની પાસે **chokrānī pase** *with the child* or છોકરા પાસે **chokrā pase** *with the child*), but must be used when preceded by a pronoun (e.g. એની પાસે **enī pāse** *with him/her*).

ના અંગે	**nā aṃge**	*with regard to, about*
ની અંદર	**nī aṃdar**	*inside*
ની આગળ	**nī āgaḷ**	*in front of, further on*
ની/ના ઉપર	**nī/nā upar**	*above*
ને કારણે	**ne kāraṇe**	*because of*
ની તરફ	**nī taraph**	*towards, in the direction of*
ની તરીકે	**nī tarīke**	*in the character of, as*
ને દરમિયાન	**ne darmiyān**	*in the course of, during*
ની નજીક	**nī najīk**	*near, close to* (in space or time)
ની નીચે	**nī nīce**	*below*
ની પછી	**nī pachī**	*after, subsequent to*
ની/ના પહેલાં	**nī/nā pahelāṃ**	*before, sooner than*
ની પાછળ	**nī pāchaḷ**	*after, behind*
ની પાસે	**nī pāse**	*at the side of, near, by*
ની પૂઠે	**nī pūṭhe**	*behind*
ના પ્રમાણે	**nā pramāṇe**	*by the standard of, according to*
ની બદલે	**nī badle**	*in exchange for, instead of*
ની બહાર	**nī bahār**	*outside of*
ને માટે	**ne māṭe**	*for the sake of, in order to*

ને લીધે	**ne līdhe**	*because of, owing to, for the sake of*
ના વગર	**nā vagar**	*without, except*
ની વચ્ચે	**nī vacce**	*in the middle*
ની વડે	**nī vaḍe**	*by, with, by means of*
ના વિના	**nā vinā**	*without, except*
ના વિષે	**nā viṣe**	*in the matter of, about*
ની સાથે	**nī sāthe**	*with*
ની સામે	**nī sāme**	*opposite*
ના સિવાય	**nā sivāy**	*except, besides*
ના સુધી	**nā sudhī**	*until, as far as*

Appendix 3

Verbs with perfective forms other than યું yuṃ

Besides યું **yuṃ**, there are two other suffixes used for forming perfective endings, namely ધું **dhuṃ**, and ઠું **thuṃ**. The first is used more with vowels, while verbs stems ending in ; always take ઠું **ṭhuṃ**.

The most common verbs that take ધું **dhuṃ** in their perfective forms are:

કરવું	**karvuṃ**	*to do, to make*	→ કર્યું, કીધું	**karyuṃ, kīdhuṃ**
કહેવું	**kahevuṃ**	*to say*	→ કહ્યું, કીધું	**kahyuṃ, kīdhuṃ**
ખાવું	**khāvuṃ**	*to eat*	→ ખાધું	**khādhuṃ**
દેવું	**devuṃ**	*to give*	→ દીધું	**dīdhuṃ**
બીવું	**bīvuṃ**	*to fear*	→ બીધું	**bīdhuṃ**
પીવું	**pīvuṃ**	*to drink*	→ પીધું	**pīdhuṃ**
લેવું	**levuṃ**	*to take*	→ લીધું	**līdhuṃ**

The most common verbs that take ઠું **thuṃ** in their perfective forms are:

દેખવું **dekhvuṃ** *to see* → દીઠું **dīṭhuṃ** (this verb is rarely used; જોવું **jovuṃ** *to see* is more common).

નાસવું	**nāsvuṃ**	*to flee*	→ નાઠું	**nāṭhuṃ**
પેસવું	**pesvuṃ**	*to enter*	→ પેઠું	**peṭhuṃ**
બેસવું	**besvuṃ**	*to sit*	→ બેઠું	**beṭhuṃ**

Other endings in the perfective:

મરવું	**marvuṃ**	*to die*	→ મુઉ (મુઈ)	**muuṃ** (**muī**)
સૂવું	**suvuṃ**	*to sleep*	→ સૂતું	**sutuṃ**
હોવું	**hovuṃ**	*to be*	→ હતું	**hatuṃ**

Appendix 4

Dictionary order

The dictionary order for Gujarati is as follows, working vertically down the columns. Syllables with **anusvāra** follow those without: e.g. ઠરવું **tharvuṃ** precedes ઠંડી **ṭhaṃḍī**. Syllables with **visarga** follow these: e.g. દુંદુભિ **duṃdubhi** precedes દુઃખ **duḥkh**. Conjunct forms of a consonant come after all non-conjunct forms: thus ત્રણ **traṇ** comes after તરફ **taraph**.

It is important to learn this order, otherwise you will not be able to use the Glossary in this book, nor use a dictionary for more advanced work. However, you will find that you will begin to learn it as you go through the course and start to use the Glossary.

અ	**a**	ક	**ka**	ઠ	**ṭha**	બ	**ba**
આ	**ā**	ખ	**kha**	ડ	**ḍa**	ભ	**bha**
ઇ	**i**	ગ	**ga**	ઢ	**ḍha**	મ	**ma**
ઈ	**ī**	ઘ	**gha**	ણ	**ṅa**	ય	**ya**
ઉ	**u**	ઙ	**ṅ**	ત	**ta**	ર	**ra**
ઊ	**ū**	ચ	**ca**	થ	**tha**	લ	**la**
ઋ	**ṛ**	છ	**cha**	દ	**da**	વ	**va**
એ	**e**	જ	**ja**	ધ	**dha**	શ	**śa**
ઐ	**ai**	ઝ	**jha**	ન	**na**	ષ	**ṣa**
ઓ	**o**	ઞ	**ña**	પ	**pa**	સ	**sa**
ઔ	**au**	ટ	**ṭa**	ફ	**pha**	હ	**ha**
						ળ	**ḷa**

Appendix 5

Numerals

1	૧	એક
2	૨	બે
3	૩	ત્રણ
4	૪	ચાર
5	૫	પાંચ
6	૬	છ
7	૭	સાત
8	૮	આઠ
9	૯	નવ
10	૧૦	દસ
11	૧૧	અગિયાર
12	૧૨	બાર
13	૧૩	તેર
14	૧૪	ચૌદ
15	૧૫	પંદર
16	૧૬	સોળ
17	૧૭	સત્તર
18	૧૮	અઢાર
19	૧૯	ઓગણીસ
20	૨૦	વીસ
21	૨૧	એકવીસ
22	૨૨	બાવીસ
23	૨૩	ત્રેવીસ
24	૨૪	ચોવીસ
25	૨૫	પચ્ચીસ
26	૨૬	છવીસ
27	૨૭	સત્તાવીસ
28	૨૮	અટ્ઠાવીસ
29	૨૯	ઓગણત્રીસ
30	૩૦	ત્રીસ
31	૩૧	એકત્રીસ
32	૩૨	બત્રીસ
33	૩૩	તેત્રીસ
34	૩૪	ચોત્રીસ
35	૩૫	પાંત્રીસ
36	૩૬	છત્રીસ
37	૩૭	સાડત્રીસ
38	૩૮	આડત્રીસ
39	૩૯	ઓગણચળીસ
40	૪૦	ચાળીસ
41	૪૧	એકતાળીસ
42	૪૨	બેતાળીસ
43	૪૩	તેતાળીસ
44	૪૪	ચુંમાળીસ
45	૪૫	પિસ્તાલીસ
46	૪૬	છેંતાળીસ
47	૪૭	સુડતાળીસ
48	૪૮	અડતાળીસ
49	૪૯	ઓગણપચાસ
50	૫૦	પચાસ
51	૫૧	એકાવન
52	૫૨	બાવન
53	૫૩	ત્રેપન
54	૫૪	ચોપન
55	૫૫	પંચાવન
56	૫૬	છપ્પન
57	૫૭	સત્તાવન
58	૫૮	અટ્ઠાવન
59	૫૯	ઓગણસાઠ
60	૬૦	સાઠ
61	૬૧	એકસઠ
62	૬૨	બાસઠ
63	૬૩	ત્રેસઠ
64	૬૪	ચોસઠ
65	૬૫	પાંસઠ
66	૬૬	છાસઠ
67	૬૭	સડસઠ
68	૬૮	અડસઠ
69	૬૯	ઓગણોતેર
70	૭૦	સિત્તેર
71	૭૧	એકોતેર
72	૭૨	બોંતેર
73	૭૩	તોંતેર
74	૭૪	ચુંમોતેર
75	૭૫	પંચોતેર
76	૭૬	છોંતેર
77	૭૭	સીતોતેર
78	૭૮	ઈકોતેર
79	૭૯	ઓગણએંસી
80	૮૦	એંસી
81	૮૧	એકયાસી
82	૮૨	બ્યાસી
83	૮૩	ત્યાસી
84	૮૪	ચોરાસી
85	૮૫	પંચ્યાસી
86	૮૬	છયાસી
87	૮૭	સત્યાસી
88	૮૮	અઠયાસી
89	૮૯	નેવ્વાસી
90	૯૦	નેવું
91	૯૧	એકાણુ
92	૯૨	બાણું
93	૯૩	ત્રાણું
94	૯૪	ચોરાણું
95	૯૫	પંચાણું
96	૯૬	છણ્ણું
97	૯૭	સતાણું
98	૯૮	અટ્ઠાણું
99	૯૯	નવાણું
100	૧૦૦	એકસો

KEY TO THE EXERCISES

UNIT 1

How are you?

1 Namste!, describe themselves as Gujarati. No they haven't met before
2 **a** **હા, લીલાબેન ગુજરાતી છે.** hā, Līlāben gujarātī che. **b** **ના, તેઓ ગુજરાતી છે.** nā, teo gujarātī che. **3 a** **હા, દીપકભાઈ ગુજરાતી છે.** hā, Dīpakbhāī gujarātī che. **b** **ના, નીલા અમેરિકન નથી.** nā, Nīlā amerikan nathī.

Language discovery

a હું ગુજરાતી	huṃ gujarātī
b તમે લોકો પંજાબી	tame loko paṃjābī
c તું ભારતીય	tuṃ bhāratīy
d તે પાકિસ્તાની	te pākistānī
e અમે અંગ્રેજ	ame aṃgrej
f તેઓ બંગાળી	teo baṃgāḷī

a I am Gujarati. **b** You are Punjabi. **c** You are Indian. **d** He/she is Pakistani. **e** We are English. **f** They are Bengali.

1 **a** છું chuṃ **b** છો cho **c** છે che **d** છે che **e** છીએ chīe **f** છે che

2 **a** **ના, હું ભારતીય નથી.** nā, huṃ bhārtīy nathī /**હા, હું ભારતીય છું.** hā, huṃ bhārtīy chuṃ **b** **ના, હું અંગ્રેજ છું.** nā, huṃ aṇgrej chuṃ /**ના, હું અંગ્રેજ નથી.** nā, huṃ angrej nathī **c** **ના, હું અમેરિકન નથી.** nā huṃ amerikan nathī /**હા, હું અમેરિકન છું.** hā, huṃ amerikan chuṃ

3 **a** This is Deepakbhai **b** Is this Deepakbhai? **c** This is not Deepakbhai **d** Greetings! How are you, Leelaben? Are you Indian? **e** Yes, I am Gujarati. Are you Indian? **f** No, I am not Indian – goodbye!

This is my older brother

1 **a** Two brothers. **b** Elder brother Setu, Younger brother Samir

2 **a** **હા, સેતુ હોશિયાર છે.** hā, Setu hośiyār che. Setu is clever.
b **ના, મોટી બહેન શ્રુતિ છે.** nā, moṭī bahen Śruti che. No, elder sister is Shruti.

3 **a** **ના, મોટી બહેન શ્રુતિ છે.** nā, moṭī bahen Śruti che. **b** **હા, શ્રુતિ લાંબી છે.** hā, Śruti lāṃbī che.

Language discovery

a Describe the nouns. e.g. elder brother
b moto –to agree with the noun. e.g. moto bhai, moti bahen

4 **a** **વાંદરો** vāṇḍro (m.) → **વાંદરી** vāṇḍrī (f.) **કૂતરો** kūtro (m.) → **કૂતરી** kūtrī (f.)
b **લાકડાં** lākḍāṃ **જીવડાં** jīvḍāṃ **બારીઓ** bārīo **બગીચાઓ/બગીચો** bagīchāo/bagīcho

5 a આ ખુરશી નવો/નવી છે. ā khurśī navo/navī che. **b ના, આ ખુરશી જૂનું/જૂની છે.** nā, ā khurśī jūnuṃ/jūnī che. **c એ છોકરા ચોકખી/ચોકખા છે.** e cokrā cokkhī/cokkhā che. **d આ બગીચો મેલું/મેલો છે.** ā bagīcho meluṃ/melo che.
6 a ના, આ જૂની ખુરશી છે. nā, ā jūnī khūrśī che **b એ ચોકખા છોકરા છે.** e cokkhā chokrā che. **c આ મેલો બગીચો છે.** ā melo bagīco che.
7 c આ ખુરશી નવી છે, પણ એ ખુરશી જૂની છે. ā khurśī navī che, paṇ e khurśī jūnī che. **f આ ખુરશી નવી છે અને ચોકખી પણ છે.** ā khurśī navī che ane cokkhī paṇ che.

Practice

1 a હું મજામાં છું. huṃ majāmāṃ chuṃ. **b આવજો!** āvjo! **c હા, હું ગુજરાતી છું.** hā, huṃ gujarātī chuṃ. **d ના, એ ગુજરાતી છે.** nā, e gujarātī che. **e હા, હું અંગ્રેજ છં.** ha, hum amgrej chum.
2 a છે. che **b છે, છે.** che, che **c છો** cho **d છુ** chum **e છો, છું** cho, chum
3 સોનલ મજામાં છે. તે ગુજરાતી છે. તે ભારતીય છે. Sonal majamam che. te gujarati che. te bharatiy che.
5 a તેઓ teo **b એ** e **c તેઓ** teo **d યે** e **e તેઓ** teo
6 મોટું, સારા, મોટા, સફેદ, લાલ, સાફ. motum, sārā, moṭā, saphed, lāl, sāph
7a ના, ચાર ખુરશી નથી, ત્રણ ખુરશી છે. nā, cār khursī nathī, tran khursī che.
b ના, ખુરશીઓ સફેદ નથી, તે લાલ છે. na, khursīo saphed nathī, te lāl che.
c ના, મેજ ગંદુ નથી, તે સાફ છે. nā, mej gaṃduṃ nathī, te sāph che.
d હા, ખુરશીઓ સાફ છે. hā, khursīo sāph che.

Do you understand?

1 ના, તે લોકો ગુજરાતી છે. nā, te loko gujarati che. **2 ના, બે છોકરા છે.** nā, be chokrā che. **3 હા, ફિરોઝ ડોકટર છે.** hā, Phiroj ḍokṭar che. **4 ના, મોટો છોકરો અદનાન છે.** nā, moṭo chokro Adnān che.

Test yourself

1 નમસ્તે! કેમ છો?
2 આવજો.
3 દીપકભાઈ ભારતીય છે?
4 હું અમેરિકન છું, પણ નીલાબેન પાકિસ્તાની છે.
5 આ નાના છોકરાઓ અમેરિકન છે?
6 આ નાની ખુરશી છે, પણ પેસી મોટી ખુરશી છે.

UNIT 2

In the university

1 Where were you? Bhavna and Akshar.
2 a ના, કાલે ભાવનાબેન અહીં જ હતાં. nā, kāle Bhāvnāben ahīṃ j hatāṃ. **b ના, સવારે ફિરદોસ ઘેર જ ન હતા. તેઓ બજારમાં હતા.** nā, savāre Phirdos gher j na hatā. Teo bajārmāṃ hatā. **3 a ચોપડી નવી છે.** copḍī navī che. **b કાલે ભાવનાબેન બજારમાં ન હતાં. તેઓ અહીં જ હતાં.** kāle Bhāvnāben bajārmāṃ na hatāṃ. teo ahīṃ j hatāṃ.

Language discovery

a છે, છો, હતા, હતો **b** કેમ, કયાં, કેવી, કોણ, કેટલા **c** યા

1 a A કેવી kevī B હતી hatī **b** A સારું sāruṃ B છે che **c** A કેટલાં keṭlāṃ B હતાં hatāṃ **d** A સાજો sājo B હતો hato

2 a Where was I yesterday? **b** The notebook is in the cupboard **c** Tea is in the market. **d** Yesterday the student was not in the market.

3 a આજ માં → આજે તે માંદો છે āj māṃ → āje te māṃdo che **b** છોકરું રસ્તો → રસ્તા પર છે chokruṃ rasto → rastā par che **c** મોટો → મોટા ઓરડામાં moto → moṭā orḍāmāṃ

In the university 2

1 ઘેર gher, બજાર bajar, દુકાનો dukano.

2 a ના, આજે ઘણા લોકો અહીં છે. nā, āje ghannā loko ahīṃ che. **b** ના, શૈલેશ રોજ અહીં આવતો નથી. એ દર અઠવાડિયે બેત્રણ વાર આવે છે. nā, Śaileś roj ahīṃ Hvto nathi. e dar aṭhvāḍiye betraṇ vār āve che.

3 a જુઈ બજારે જાય છે. Jūī bajāre jāy che. **b** બજાર સારી છે. bajār sārī che.

Language discovery

a આજે, અઠવાડિયે, બપોરે, સવારે, સાંજે, અહીંથી, બજારે **b** લોકો. દુકાનો

4 a તું પાણી પીએ છે. tuṃ pāṇī pīe che. **b** તમે પાણી પીતા નથી. tame pāṇī pītā nathī. **c** તે કચરો રસ્તો પર નાખે છે. te kacaro rasto par nākhe che **d** તેઓ પૈસા વાપરે છે. teo paisā vāpre che.

5 a Let's go! **b** May I come in? **c** Shall we go? **d** Should/may he come home?

Practice

1 a આજે બહુ ગરમી છે ને? āje bahu garmī che ne? **b** ગઈ કાલે ઠંડી હતી, ને? gai kāle ṭhaṃḍī hatī, ne? **c** ફિરદોસ કોણ છે? ફિરદોસ વિદ્યાર્થી છે? Phirdos koṇ che? Phirdos vidyārthi che? **d** નીલા કયાં જાય છે? કોણ ગામ જાય છે? Nīlā kyāṃ jāy che? kop gāṃ jay che? **e** તમે નથી આવતાં કે? tame nathi āvtāṃ ke?

2 a શહીનાઃ ચોપડી કેવી છે? Śahīnā: copḍī kevī che? **b** શહીનાઃ ગઈ કાલે તમે કયાં હતાં? Śahīnā: gaī kāle tame kyāṃ hatāṃ? **c** શહીનાઃ તમે કયારે દુકાને જાઓ છો ? Śahīnā: ame kyāre dukāne jāo cho? **d** શહીનાઃ પેલું કોણ છે? Śahīnā: pelum koṇ che?

3 a નીનાઃ ના, કાલે તેઓ અહીં નહોતા. Nīnā: nā kāle teo ahīṃ nahotā. **b** નીનાઃ ના, એ સારી નથી. Nīnā: nā, e sārī nathī. **c** નીનાઃ ના, હું રોજ નથી આવતી. Nīnā: nā, huṃ oj nathī āvtī. **d** નીનાઃ ના, તેઓ મુંબઈમાં રહેતા નથી. Nīnā: nā, teo Muṃbaīmāṃ ehetā nathī.

4 a તે માંદો હતો. te māṃdo hato. **b** તે લોકો અહીં હતા. te loko ahīṃ hata. અમે ખુશ છીએ. ame khuś chīe. **d** તમે મજામાં હતા? tame majāmāṃ hata?

5 a કેમ છે? બસ, સારું છે. kem che? bas, sāruṃ che. **b** હું અભ્યાસ કરું છું. huṃ bhyās karuṃ chuṃ. **c** ના, આજે બે ગુજરાતી વર્ગ છે. nā, āje be gujarāti varg che. આવજો! āvjo!

a ગરમી garmī **b** આવતી āvtī **c** હતા hatā? **d** રહેતી rahetī **e** ભારત Bhārat

7 ગયે અઠવાડિયે મારો મિત્ર અહીં હતો. પણ, તે આ ગામમાં નથી રહેતો અને હવે તે અહીં નથી. પણ હવે પેલા મોટા મકાનમાં એક નાનો છોકરો રહે છે. હું રોજ એ ઘેર જાઉં છું અને અમે ખુશ છીએ. gaye aṭhvāḍiye māro mitra ahīṃ hato. paṇ, te ā gāmmāṃ nathī raheto ane have te ahīṃ nathī. paṇ have pelā moṭā makānmāṃ ek nāno chokro rahe che. huṃ roj e gher jāuṃ chuṃ ane ame khuś chīe.

Do you understand?

a શૈલેશ લંડનમાં રહે છે. Śaileś Laṃḍanmāṃ rahe che. **b શૈલેશ દુકાનમાં કામ નથી કરતો. એ અભ્યાસ કરે છે.** Śaileś dukānmāṃ kām nathī karto. e abhyās kare che. **c એ સવારે યુનિવર્સિટીમાં જાય છે.** e savāre yunivarsiṭīmāṃ jiy che. **d બપોરે એ ઘેર જાય છે.** bapore e gher jāy che. **એ સાંજે એ અભ્યાસ કરે છે.** sāṃje **e** abhyās kare che.

Test yourself

1 તમે કેમ છો?

2 બહેન ગઈ કાલે તમે કયાં હતા?

3 પાણી મેજ પર છે.

4 સારા છોકરાઓ નિશાળમાં છે.

5 રમેશભાઈ, તમે રોજ યુનિવર્સિટીમાં આવો છો?

6 શું હવે હું જઈ શકું છું?

UNIT 3

What's your house like?

1 Where do you live? Areas in which they live, shopping, meeting friends, size of house, number of rooms, condition of the house, rent.

2 a જગદીશ ભારતમાં નથી રહેતો, એ વેંબલીમાં રહે છે. Jagdīś Bhāratmāṃ nathī raheto, e Veṃblīmāṃ rahe che. **b જગદીશને બહુ પૈસા નથી મળતા.** Jagdīśne bahu paisā nathī maḷtā. **c મોહમ્મદને ત્યાં નવો સામાન છે.** Mohammadne tyāṃ navo sāmān che.

3 a મોહમ્મદનું ઘર નવું છે. Mohammadnuṃ ghar navuṃ che. **b વેંબલી સરસ છે. ઘણા ગુજરાતી લોકો ત્યાં રહે છે.** Veṃblī saras che. ghaṇā gujarātī loko tyāṃ rahe che.

Language discovery

a personal pronouns **b** tamar<u>a</u>, tamar<u>u</u>

1 a છોકરી ભાઈને ગીત ગાવે છે. cokrī bhāīne gīt gāve che **b હું લીલાને વાર્તા સંભળાવું છું.** huṃ Līlāne vārtā saṃbhaḷāvūṃ chuṃ **c આ વાંદરો છોકરાને કેળું આપે છે.** ā vāndro cokrāne keluṃ āpe che

2 a ની બહેન / મારા ભાઈને nī bahen / mārā bhāīne **b મારી પત્ની નો** mārī patnī no **c મને** mane **d અમારું** amārūṃ

3 a આ છોકરી મને નથી ગમતી, પણ એ છોકરીઓ મને ગમે છે. ā chokrī mane nathī gamtī, paṇ e chokrīo mane game che. **b હું દીપકભાઈને ઘેર નથી મળતો/મળતી.** huṃ Dīpakbhāīne gher nathī maḷto/maḷtī **c દીપકભાઈને સમજ નથી પડતી.** Dīpakbhāīne samaj nathī paḍtī **d દીપકભાઈ ને લાગે છે.** Dīpakbhāīne lāge che **e તેને વાર્તા નો અર્થ સમજ પડતો નથી.** tene vārtā no arth samaj paḍto nathī **f મને સારું લાગતું નથી.** Mane sāruṃ lāgtuṃ nathī.

4 a હું ત્યાં ન હતો/હતી. huṃ tyāṃ na hato/hatī **b દીપક ઘરે રોજ આવતો નથી.** Dīpak ghare roj āvto nathī **c આ ખુરશી નથી** ā khurśī nathī **d ના, આ છોકરી ભારતીય નથી.** nā, ā cokrī bhāratīy nathī

a ચિંતા ન કરો, દીપકભાઈ, લીલાબેન અહીં રોજ આવે છે. cimtā na karo, Dīpakbhāī, ilāben ahīṃ roj ave che. **b** દીપકા મને પાણી આપજે! Deepak! Give me water! દીપકભાઈ, તમે અને લીલાબેન આજે મારા ઘેર આવશો! Dīpakbhāī, tame ane Līlāben je mārā gher āvśo! **d** Don't go home! Come inside, don't worry, I am also oming (I am coming as well).

low many brothers and sisters do you have?

How many brothers and sisters do you have? Sailesh, Kamlesh nd Anuj. **2 a** નલિનીને બે ભાઈ છે. Nalinīne be bhaī che. **b** ગોપી એકની એક દીકરી . Gopī eknī ek dīkrī che. **c** ગોપીના કાકાના દીકરાનું નામ અનુજ છે. Gopīnā kākānā ikrānum nāṃ Anuj che. **3 a** શૈલેષ અને કમલેશ નલિનીના ભાઈઓ છે. śaileś ane amaleś Nalinīnā bhāio che. **b** અનુજ પાસે નવી ગાડી છે. Anuj pāse navī gāḍī che.

anguage discovery

Family and relationship. **b** Joint family સંયુકત કુટુંબ.

a Leelaben comes/is coming home with Deepakbhai.

Those girls do not come with their brothers.

ractice

a મને સારું લાગે છે. mane sāruṃ lage che. **b** હા, એ મોટું છે. Ha, e motu che. દસ ઓરડા છે. 10 orḍā che. **d** ઓરડાઓનાં નામોઃ સૂવાનો ઓરડો, બેઠક કે રહેવાનો ઓરડો, સોડું અને નાહવાનો ઓરડો છે. orḍāonāṃ nāmo suvāno orḍo, beṭhak ke rahevāno rdo, rasoḍuṃ ane nāhvāno orḍo che. **e** હા, મને આ ઘર ગમે છે. hā, mane ā ghar ame che.

a હું તારા ભાઈને સાંભળું છું. huṃ tārā bhāīne sāṃbhaḷuṃ chuṃ. **b** એ મને સારું ગે છે. e mane sāruṃ lāge che. **c** આ ઘર મારી પત્નીને નથી ગમતું. ā ghar mārī atnīne nathī gamtuṃ. **d** મારા ઘરમાં ચાર ઓરડા છે. mārā gharmāṃ cār orḍā che. શોભાઃ કયાં જાય છે અનાહિતા? Śobhā: kyāṃ jāy che Anāhitā? અનાહિતાઃ હું બજારે ઉં છું. Anāhitā: huṃ bajāre jāuṃ chuṃ. શોભાઃ શહેરના બજારમાં વેપારીઓ સારો પણ ઘો માલ રાખે છે. Śobhā: Śahernā bajārmāṃ vepārīo sāro paṇ moṃgho māl khe che. અનાહિતાઃ મને ખબર છે. મારી પાસે થોડા પૈસા છે. Anāhitā: mane khabar ne. mārī pāse thoḍā paisā che. શોભાઃ આજે મારે કંઈ કામ નથી. હું તારી સાથે આવું? obhā: āje māre kaṃī kāṃ nathī. huṃ tārī sāthe avuṃ? અનાહિતાઃ કેમ નહીં? લો જઈએ! Anāhitā: kem nahīṃ? cālo jaīe!

a કેમ છો, વિરેન? kem cho, Viren? **b** હા, હું ગુજરાતી શીખું છું, બહુ અઘરું છે ને? hā, huṃ ujarātī Śīkhuṃ chuṃ, bahu aghruṃ che ne? **c** શું કહો છો? મને નથી આવડતું. ધીમે લજો! Śuṃ kaho cho? mane nathī āvaḍtuṃ. dhīme boljo! **d** હા, મને ગુજરાતી હુ જ ગમે છે. hā, mane gujarātī bahu j game che.

a દીપકભાઈ મારે ત્યાં આવશો! Dīpakbhāī māre tyāṃ āvśo! **b** શોભા કામ કર! Sobha am kar! **c** આનલ અને ઉદિતા મારી વાત સાંભળો! Ānal ane Uditā mārī vāt sāṃbhaḷo! રચનાબેન, જરા સામાન આપશો! Racnāben, jarā sāmān āpśo! **e** નીલા ઘેર ન જા! lā gher na jā!

6 a દુકાનમાં કંઈ મળતું નથી. dukānmāṃ kaṃī maḷtuṃ nathī. **b કંઈ કામ રહે છે?** kaṃī kām rahe che? **c કેટલાકને શહેર ગમે છે.** keṭlākne śaher game che. **d કંઈ દહાડે મારે ત્યાં આવજો!** kaṃī dahāḍe mare tyāṃ āvjo! **e તે કશો અભ્યાસ કરતો નથી.** te kaśo abhyās karto nathī.

Do you understand?

1 આ મકાનમાં ચાર માણસ રહે છે. ā makānāṃ cār māṇas rahe che. **2 મહેર અને ફિરદોસ શિક્ષકો છે.** Maher ane Phirdos siksako che. **3 એમના દીકરાનું નામ રેશાદ છે.** emnā dīkrānuṃ nām reśad che **4 અનાહિતાને કોઈ બહેન નથી.**! Anāhitāne koī bahen nathī!

Test yourself

1 તમે કયાં રહો છો?
2 મને લંડન ગમે છે.
3 દીપકભાઈ મેજ પર શું છે?
4 દીપકભાઈ, બજારમાં કંઈ નથી.
5 સમીર, તમે શું કરો છો?
6 દીકરી મારું નવું ખમીસ ધોઈ નાખ.

UNIT 4

Ahmedabad

1 Ahmedabad. See the city and visit Gandhi Ashram. By train. **2 a ના, આ લોકો ગાડીમાં અમદાવાદ નહિ જશે. તેઓ ટ્રેનમાં જશે.** nā, ā loko gāḍīmāṃ Amdāvād nahi jaśe. teo ṭrenmāṃ jaśe. **b ના, અમદાવાદમાં તેઓ લીનાના કાકાને ત્યાં નહિ રહેશે. તેઓ શાંતામાસી અને વિનોદમામાને ત્યાં રહેશે.** nā, Amdāvādmāṃ teo Līnānā kākāne tyāṃ nahi raheśe. teo Śāṃtāmāsī ane Vinodmāmāne tyāṃ raheśe. **c ના, લીનાની મા અમદાવાદ થોડા દિવસો પછી આવશે.** nā, Līnānī mā Amdāvād thoḍā divaso pachī āvśe. **3 a લીના અમદાવાદમાં ગાંધીના આશ્રમમાં જશે.** Linā Amdāvādmāṃ Gāṃdhīnā āśrammāṃ jaśe. **b હા, પ્રબોધને લાગે છે કે લીનાને અમદાવાદ ગમશે.** hā, Prabodhne lāge che ke Lināne Amdāvād gamśe.

Language discovery

1 a હું તમને વાર્તા કહીશ. huṃ tamne vārtā kahīś **b તે ઘેર જશે નહી.** te gher jase nahī **c દીપકભાઈ બજાર માં હશે, પણ લીલાબેન નહિ હશે.** Dīpakbhāī bajār māṃ haśe, paṇ Līlāben nahi haśe **d આપણે ગુજરાત જઈશું.** āpṇe gujarāt jaīśuṃ

2 a તેઓ વાર્તા સાંભળવા જશે. teo vārtā sāṃbhaḷvā jaśe **b દીપકભાઈ અને લીલાબેન ખમીસ ધોવા ઘેર ગયાં.** Dīpakbhāī ane Līlāben khamīs dhovā gher gayāṃ **c બહેનોને મળવા હું ઘેર રોજ નથી જતી.** bahenone maḷvā huṃ gher roj nathī jati

3 a Deepakbhai does not like that his sister will not be in Ahmedabad. **b** Leelaben's little notebooks are new. **c** What kind of story will you tell, old or new? **d** I know that my daughter was at home!

Do you like Gujarati food?

1 Invite Steve for a meal. Who will cook? Do you like vegetarian food? What kind of sweets do you like? **2 a ના, આશિષને ભૂખ લાગે છે.** nā, Āśiṣne bhūkh lāge che. **b ના, સ્ટીવને ગુજરાતી ખોરાક બહુ ભાવે છે.** nā, Śṭivne gujarātī khorāk bahu bhāve che. **c ના, સ્ટીવને ખાંડ નથી ભાવતી.** nā, Śṭivne khāṃḍ nathī bhavtī.

3 a આશિષ શાકાહારી (ગુજરાતી) ખાવાનું બનાવશે. Āśiṣ śākāhārī (gujarātī) khāvānuṃ banāvśe. b સ્ટીવને ખાંડ વગરની ચા ભાવે છે, પણ હવે એને તરસ નથી લાગતી. Sṭivne khāṃḍ vagarnī cā bhāve che, paṇ have ene taras nathī lagtī.

Language discovery

a Words related to food and cooking. b bhavvuṃ ભાવવું is only used for food c Cook his own (Gujarati) vegetarian food.

a You do not know this lesson. b The girl does not know this work. c Deepakbhai knows Leelaben. d They know that you had known (used to know) this story. e They will know Gujarati (lit. they will be knowing Gujarati)!

Practice

1 a કાલે સવારે જાવેદ ઘેર જ રહેશે. kāle savāre Jāved gher j raheśe. b કાલે સાંજે તે ઘેર જ નહિ રહેશે. તે અક્ષયને ત્યાં જશે. kāle sāṃje te gher j nahī raheśe. te Akṣayne tyām jase. c હા, તેને રજા મળશે. hā, tene rajā maḷśe. d તે સાંજે અક્ષયને ત્યાં વિરેન અને અક્ષયની સાથે શાકાહારી ખાવાનું ખાશે. te sāṃje Akṣayne tyaṃ Vīren ane Akṣaynī sāthe śākāhārī khāvānuṃ khāśe. e હા, ખૂબ જ મઝા આવશે. hā, khūb j majhā āvśe.

2 a મને ખાંડ નથી ભાવતી. mane khāṃḍ nathi bhāvtī. b આપણે ફરવા જઈશું. āpṇe pharvā jaīśuṃ. c તમને ખબર છે કે એ આવશે કે નહિ? tamne khabar che ke e āvśe ke nahi? d ગઈ કાલે તેઓ મારે ત્યાં હતાં. gai kāle teo māre tyim hatāṃ. e એ પોતે ચા બનાવશે. e pote cā banāvśe.

a સારું છે. કેમ છો? sāruṃ che. kem cho? b ના, મને ભૂખ નથી લાગતી. nā, mane bhūkh nathī lāgtī. c ના, મને તરસ નથી લાગતી. nā, mane taras nathi lāgtī. d ખાસ કંઈ નહિ. તમારો દીકરો આજે કયાં છે? khās kaṃī nahi. tamāro dīkro āje kyām che? e ચાલો, આપણે સ્ટીવને મળવા જઈએ. સ્ટીવ અમેરીકન છે પણ એને ગુજરાતી બોલતાં આવડે છે. cālo, āpṇe Sṭīvne maḷvā jaīe. Sṭīv amerikan che paṇ ene gujrātī boltāṃ avde che.

સ્ટીવઃ કેમ છો વિરેનભાઈ?/ Sṭīv: kem cho Vīrenbhāi?

સ્ટીવઃ મારી પત્ની ગુજરાતી છે. એ હમેશાં ગુજરાતી જ બોલે છે./Sṭīv: mārī patnī gujarātī che. e hameśāṃ gujarātī j bole che.

સ્ટીવઃ તમને ખબર છે કે ગુજરાતી બહુ અઘરું નથી./ Sṭīv: tamne khabar che ke gujarātī bahu aghruṃ nathī.

સ્ટીવઃ અહીંથી બહુ દૂર નથી. તમે મારી સાથે શીખવા આવશો!/Sṭīv: ahithi bahu dūr nathi. tame mārī sathe śīkhvā āvśo!

સ્મિતાઃ હા, હું જલદી આવું./Smitā: hā, huṃ jaldī āvuṃ.

સ્મિતાઃ હા, હુ જલદી કપડાં પહેરું./Smitā: hā, huṃ jaldi kapḍāṃ paherum.

સ્મિતાઃ હા, હું જાઉં./Smitā: hā, huṃ jāuṃ.

સ્મિતાઃ હું શહેર જઈશ./Smitā: huṃ śaher jaīś.

સ્મિતાઃ હું અહીં આવીશ./Smitā: huṃ ahīṃ āvīś.

Do you understand?

Kish, apje, sivshe.

Test yourself

1 દીપકભાઈ, તમને ગુજરાતી ખોરાક ભાવે છે?
2 લીલાબેન હું ગુજરાતી બોલી શકું છું અને વાંચી શકું છું.
3 લીલાબેનની દીકરીને અમદાવાદ ગમશે.
4 મને ભૂખ લાગી છે પણ હું ખાંડ નહીં લઉં.
5 મને ખબર છે કે બજારમાં ઘણી નાની નાની ચોપકીઓ છે.
6 રેખા તને બુરખો પહેરવો ગમે છે?

UNIT 5

I need some new clothes

1 Buying clothes. **2 a** **મુંબઈમાં મોટી દુકાનો હોય છે.** Mumbaīmāṃ moṭī dukāno hoy che. **b** **મીનાને મોંઘું કાપડ જોઈતું નથી.** Mīnāne moṃghuṃ kāpaḍ joītuṃ nathī. **c** **વીણા પાસે રોકડા પૈસા નથી.** Vīṇā pāse rokḍā paisā nathī.
3 a **મને લાગે છે કે મીના પાસે બહુ પૈસા નથી.** mane lāge che ke Mīnā pāse bahu paisā nathī. **b** **મીનાને કાપડ જોઈએ છે.** Mīnāne Kāpaḍ joie che.

Language discovery

a express their needs. **b** Suit, bank, hotel
1 a **પેસી નાની છોકરીઓને નવી ચોપડીઓ જોઈએ છે.** **b** What else do you need/want? There is a lot of stuff at home! **c** **મારે નવી ખમીસ બજારથી જોઈએ** māre navī khamīs bajārthī joīe **d** Deepakbhai does not need any new clothes.
2 a **હોય છે.** hoy che **b** **હોય છે.** hoy che! **c** **જતી હોતી નથી.** jatī hotī nathī.
3 a **મને ખાંડ ભાવતી નથી, મને ખાંડ વગરની ચા આપજો** mane khāṃd bhāvtī nathī, mane khāṃd vagarnī cā āpjo **b** **મુંબઈ તરફની બસ ક્યાં છે?** mumbāī taraph nī bas kyāṃ che? **c** **મારી દીકરીને નવો પંજાબી સૂટ જોઈએ** mārī dikrīe navī paṃjābī sūṭ joīe

I should go home now

1 Akshay's parents are returning home from India, so he has to clean the house before they arrive home. **2 a** **અક્ષયના માબાપ ઘેર નથી. તેઓ ભારતમાં છે.** Akṣaynāṃ mābāp gher j nathī. teo bhāratmāṃ che. **b** **કાલે અક્ષય ઘેર જ નહિ રહેશે. એને વિમાનમથક જવું પડશે.** kāle Akṣay gher j nathi raheśe. ene vimanmathak javuṃ paḍśe. **c** **અલી અક્ષયના માબાપને ઓળખે છે.** Alī Akṣaynāṃ mābāpne oḷakhe che. **3 a** **અક્ષયને ઘરના બધા ઓરડા સાફ કરવા પડશે.** Akṣayne gharnā badhā orḍā saph karvā paḍśe. **b** **અલીને અક્ષયની મદદની જરૂર નથી.** Alīne Akṣaynī madadni jarūr nathī.

Language discovery

a Need, necessity and wanting. **b** **ચા પીવી છે, કરવું પડશે, આવાવું જોઈએ, જવું જોઈએ**
4 a **મારે અમેરિકા જવું નથી, મારે ભારત જવું છે.** māre amerikā javuṃ nathī, māre bhārat javuṃ che **b** The students had to go to class every day. **c** **ગુજરાત માં તમારે ગુજરાતી બોલવી પડે છે** gujarāt māṃ tamāre gujarātī bolvī paḍe che **d** I have to go home.

Practice

1 a હા, મારે વહેલા ઊઠવું પડે છે. hā, māre vahelā ūṭhvuṃ pade che. **b** હા, મારે ખાવાનું તૈયાર કરવું પડે છે. hā, māre khāvānuṃ taiyār karvuṃ paḍe che. **c** ના, મારે આવ–જા કરવી પડતી નથી. nā, māre āv-jā karvī paḍtī nathī. **d** ના, મારે ઘર સાફ કરવું પડતું નથી. nā, māre ghar sāph karvuṃ paḍtuṃ nathī. **e** હા, મારે વહેલા સુઈ જવું છે. hā, māre vahelā sūī javuṃ che.

2 a સુથાર વહેલું કામ શરૂ કરે છે. suthār vahelum kām śarū kare che. **b** મારે ઘણો અભ્યાસ કરવો પડે છે. māre ghaṇo abhayās karvo paḍe che. **c** પ્રબોધ અને એની દીકરીને વહેલા નીકળવું પડે છે. Prabodh ane enī dīkrīne vahelā nīkaḷvuṃ paḍe che. **d** ચાલો, મારે જવું જોઈએ. cālo, māre javuṃ joīe. **e** તમારે હાથ ધોવા જોઈએ, એમ છોકરીઓને કહો! tamāre hāth dhovā joīe, em chokrīne kaho!

3 અલીઃ તારું ગુજરાતી હવે ઘણું સારું છે. તારે હવે થોડા વખતમાં ગુજરાત જવું જોઈએ.
હેલનઃ મારે જવું છે. આવતા વરસે હું જવા ધારું છું. તું ઉનાળામાં જાય છે ને?
અલીઃ હા, કારણ કે ઉનાળામાં મને રજા મળે છે. પણ ત્યારે ત્યાં ભારે ગરમી હોય છે. તારે શિયાળામાં જવું જોઈએ.
હેલનઃ મારી મા નાતાલમાં મારે ત્યાં આવે છે તેથી મારે અહીં રહેવું પડશે.
અલીઃ તારી સાથે લાવજે ને! મઝા આવશે!

Alī: tāruṃ gujarātī have ghaṇuṃ sāruṃ che. tāre have thoḍā vakhtmāṃ gujarāt javuṃ joīe.
Helen: māre javuṃ che. āvtā varse huṃ javā dhāruṃ chuṃ. tuṃ unāḷāmāṃ äy che ne?
Ali: hā, kāraṇ ke unāḷāmāṃ mane rajā maḷe che. paṇ tyāre tyāṃ bhāre garmī hoy che. tāre śiyāḷāmāṃ javuṃ joie.
Helen: māri mā Nātālmāṃ māre tyāṃ āve che tethī māre ahiṃ rahevuṃ paḍśe.
Ali: tārī sāthe lāvje ne! majhā āvśe!

4

ીનાઃ માશી, મારે નાનાં કપડાં ખરીદવાં છે.
ીલાઃ તારે ભારતીય કપડાં પહેરવાં જોઈએ.
ીનાઃ કાલે મારે બજારે જવું છે.
ીલાઃ તારે વહેલી સવારે નીકળવું જોઈએ.
ીનાઃ મારે નીલાને મળવું છે.
ીલાઃ અત્યારે તે ઓફીસે જતી હોય છે.
ીનાઃ મારે અહીં થોડી વાર રહેવું છે.
ીલાઃ તારે ઘેર પાછા જવું પડે છે.

īnā: māśī, māre nanāṃ, kapḍāṃ kharīdvāṃ che.
ā: tāre bhāratīy kapḍāṃ pahervāṃ joīe.
īnā: kāle māre bajāre javuṃ che.
ā: tāre vahelī savāre nīkaḷvuṃ joīe.
īnā: māre Nīlāne maḷvuṃ che.

Līlā: atyāre te ophise jatī hoy che.
Mīnā: māre ahīṃ thoḍī vār rahevuṃ che.
Līlā: tāre gher pāchā javuṃ paḍe che.

Do you understand?

1 **આ સ્ત્રી ગામડામાં રહે છે.** ā strī gāmḍāmāṃ rahe che. **2** **એનો પતિ ખેતરના જોઈતાં કામ કરે છે પણ એ ખેડૂત નથી, એ સુથાર છે. એ વાણિયો નથી.** eno pati khetarnuṃ joītaṃ kāṃ kare che paṇ e kheḍūt nathi, e suthār che. e vāṇiyo nathī **3** **તે મંદિરમાં પૂજા કરે છે.** te maṃdirmāṃ pūjā kare che. **4** **ના, તે બપોરે ઘેર જમવા નથી આવતી.** nā, te bapore gher jamvā nathī āvtī. **5** **ના, બસમાં તે મજામાં નથી કારણ કે બસો ચિકકાર હોય છે અને લોકો બહુ ગડબડ કરે છે.** nā, basmāṃ te majāmāṃ nathī kāraṇ ke baso cikār hoy che ane loko bahu gaḍbaḍ kare che. **6** **ના, તેને એ નોકરી નથી ગમતી. એણે નોકરી છોડવી છે.** nā, tene ā nokri nathī gamtī. eṇe nokrī choḍvī che.

Test yourself

1 **દીપકભાઈને નવા જોડા જોઈએ છે.**
2 **છોકરીઓને રોજ વર્ગમાં વહેલું જવું પડશે.**
3 **મને આજે બજારમાંથી તાજું દૂધ જોઈએ છે.**
4 **અમને વહેલા સુવાની ફરજ પડાય છે.**
5 **દીપકભાઈ હું ચામાં ખાંડ લેતો નથી.**
6 **મને ખમીસ માટે નવું કાપડ જોઈએ છે.**

UNIT 6

I went to India

1 Samir tells Leela that he went to India. He stayed a night at a hotel in Mumbai. In Vadodra he stayed with his uncle. His uncle is a grocer who has a manual system of keeping account books. Then he went to Rajkot and bought a hat for his brother and sarees for his sister. He fell ill because of heat and had to stay in a hospital. **2 a** **સમીર પહેલી વાર ભારત ગયો.** Samīr pahelī vār Bhārat gayo. **b** **સમીર મુંબઈથી વડોદરા ગયો.** Samīr Muṃbaīthī Vaḍodarā gayo. **c** **ભારતમાં સમીરની તબિયત સારી ન હતી.** Bhāratmāṃ Samīrnī tabiyat sārī na hatī.

3 a **સમીરને ભારત દેશ બહુ ગમ્યો.** Samīrne Bhārāt desh bahu gamyo. **b** **સમીર મજાક કરે છે કારણ કે એને લીલાને ત્યાં નાસ્તો કરવો છે.** Samīr majāk kare che kāraṇ ke ene Līlāne tyāṃ nāsto karvo che.

Language discovery

We haven't met for a long time. Mumbai (satyed in a hotel), Vadodra (stayed with uncle), Rajkot (stayed with Sureshmama)

1 a **તે ઘેર આવ્યો.** te gher āvyo **b** **શું થયું પછી?** shuṃ thayuṃ pachī?
c Where did she go to eat?
2 a I had gone home but my brother has gone to the the city.
b What have you brought? **c** What had happened? **d** That girl has come.
e Leelaben was sitting down at home.

3 a દીપકભાઈ, રસ્તા પર ધીમે ધીમે/ધીરે ધીરે જાઓ ! Dīpakbhāī, rāstā par dhīme dhīme/dhīre dhīre jāo! **b** લીલા ઉપર રહે છે, તમે ક્યાં રહો છો? Līlā upar rahe che, tame kyāṃ raho cho? **c** ના, ત્યાં ન જાઓ ડાબી બાજુ જાઓ! nā, tyāṃ nā jāo ḍābī bāju jāo!

What did you do today?

1 Perfective **2 a** આજે લીલાએ બહુ કામ કર્યું. āje Līlāe bahu kām karyuṃ. **b** લીલા ટ્રેનમાં આવ–જા કરે છે. Līlā trenmāṃ āv-jā kare che. **c** કારકુને ચોરને પૈસા ન આપ્યા. kārkune corne paisa na apya. **3 a** લીલાને બેન્કમાં જવું પડયું કારણ કે ગઈ કાલે એણે ઓછા પૈસા લીધા. Līlāne beṃkmāṃ javuṃ paḍyuṃ kāraṇ ke gaī kāle eṇe ochā paisā līdhā. **b** આજે પ્રબોધે એક બહુ સરસ ફિલ્મ જોઈ. āje Prabodhe ek bahu sara film joī.

Language discovery

a perfective with negative

b ending in -dhu

4 a દીપકભાઈની પત્નીએ વિદ્યાર્થીને ચોપડી આપી. Dīpakbhāī nī patnīe vidyārthīne chopḍī āpī. **b** આપણે જૂની ફિલ્મ જોઈ. āpṇe jūnī philm joī. **c** આણે ગુજરાતી ખોરાક જમ્યો. āṇe gujaratī khorāk jamyo.

Practice

1 a ફારૂક ગુજરાતમાં એક અઠવાડિયું રહ્યો. Phārūk Gujarātmāṃ ek aṭhvāḍiyuṃ rahyo. **b** ર ફારુક રાજકોટ અને ભાવનગરમાં રહ્યો. આવતે અઠવાડિયે એ મુંબઈ જશે. Phārūk Rājkoṭ ane Bhāvnagarmāṃ rahyo. āvte aṭhvāḍiye e Mumbaī jase. **c** હા, એને ભારત દેશ ગમ્યો. hā, ene Bhārat desh gamyo. **d** હા, એણે ફરીથી જવું છે. hā, eṇe pharīthī javuṃ che **e** હા/ના, હું ગુજરાત ગઈ/ગયો છું / નથી. hā/nā, huṃ Gujarāt gaī/gayo chuṃ/nathī.

2 a લીલાએ પરમ દિવસે એના ભાઈને જોયો. Līlāe param divase enā bhāīne joyo. **b** કોણે તમને આ ખબર કહી? koṇe tamne ā khabar kahi? **c** તમે આ ચોરીની બાબતમાં કંઈ વાંચ્યું? tame ā corīnī bābatmāṃ kaṃi vāṃcyuṃ? **d** તેં એની વાત સાંભળી? teṃ enī vāt sāṃbhaḷi? **e** નીલા મારા ભાઈને નથી મળી. Nīlā mārā bhāīne nathī maḷī.

3 તમેઃ તને મળીને મને ઘણો આનંદ આવ્યો. મેં તને ગયા વરસથી જોયો જ નથી. /tame: tane maḷine mane ghaṇo ānaṃd āvyo. meṃ tane gayā varasthī joyo j nathī. તમેઃ હું ભારત ગયો હતો અને પરમ દિવસે જ પાછો આવ્યો છું./tame: hum Bhārat gayo hato ane param divase j pācho āvyo chuṃ. તમેઃ માફ કરો. મને ખબર છે કે હું બહુ આળસુ છું. /tame: māph karo. mane khabar che ke huṃ bahu āḷsu chuṃ. તમેઃ આજે કંઈ ખાસ કામ નથી. કેમ?/tame: āje kaṃī khās kām nathī. kem? તમેઃ હા, જરૂર! tame: hā, jarūr!

શ્રીમતી પટેલ મોડાં જાગ્યાં અને ખુશ નહોતાં. બસ ભરચક હતી અને એક છોકરો એમની સાડી પર ઊભો રહ્યો અને એણે માફી ન માગી, એ શાકમારકેટ ગયાં, શાકભાજી વાસી હતી. એમનાં સેક્રેટરી ગુસ્સે હતાં કારણ કે કમ્પ્યુટર બગડી ગયું. જોકે સાંજે એમના મિત્રે એક નવી ફિલ્મ જોવા એમને બોલાવ્યાં તેથી શ્રીમતી પટેલ આનંદમાં આવ્યાં./Śrīmatī Paṭel moḍāṃ jāgyāṃ ane khuś nahotāṃ.

bas bharcak hatī ane ek chokro emni sāḍī par ūbho rahyo ane eṇe māphī na māgī, e śākmārkeṭ gayāṃ, śākbhājī vāsī hatī. emnāṃ sekreṭarī gusse hatāṃ kāraṇ ke kampyuṭar bagḍi gayuṃ. joke sāṃje emnā mitre ek navī philm jovā emne bolāvyāṃ tethi Śrīmatī Paṭel ānaṃdmāṃ āvyāṃ.

5 માઇકઃ સાંભળો ભાઈ, હું હરે કૃષ્ણ હરે રામનું મંદીર શોધું છું, એ કઇ બાજુમાં છે?
નટુભાઈ: જુઓ, જમણી બાજુમાં પોસ્ટ ઓફિસ છે. તમારી સામે જુહુ બજાર છે. સીધા જાઓ અને બજાર પહેલાં ડાબી બાજુ જાઓ. તમે હિંદુ ધર્મમાં વિશ્વાસ ધરાવો છો?
માઈકઃ ના, ભાઈ, હું ખ્રિસ્તી છું પણ લોકો કહે છે કે ત્યાંનું ખાવાનું બહુ સરસ છે અને એ લોકો બહુ માયાળુ છે.
Māīk: sāṃbhaḷo bhāī, huṃ Hare Kṛṣṇa Hare Rāmnuṃ maṃdir śodhuṃ chuṃ, e kaī bājumāṃ che?
Naṭubhāī: juo, jamnī bājumāṃ posṭ ophis che. tamari sāme Juhu bajār che. sīdhā jāo ane bajār pehelāṃ dābī bāju jāo. tame Hiṃdu ḍharmmāṃ viśvās dharāvo cho?
Māīk: nā, bhāī, huṃ Khristī chuṃ paṇ loko kahe che ke tyāṃnuṃ khāvānuṃ bahu saras che ane e loko bahu māyāḷu che.

Do you understand?

1 a તારીક અને કાસિમ ભાઈઓ નથી. તેઓ મિત્ર છે. Tārīk ane Kāsīm bhāīo nathī. teo mitro che. **b આ લોકો સાથે રહેતા નથી. તેઓ સામસામે રહે છે.** ā loko sāthe rahetā nathī. teo sāmsāme rahe che. **c તારીકની પત્ની બહાર ગઇ ન હતી. એ અંદર હતી.** Tārīknī patnī bahār gaī na hatī. e aṃdar hatī.

2 a નસરીન અંદર જાય છે કારણ કે ખુરશીદા અંદર છે અને એણે ખુરશીદા સાથે વાત કરવી છે. Nasrīn aṃdar jāy che kāraṇ ke Khurśīdā aṃdar che ane eṇe Khurśīdā sāthe vāt karvī che.
b આ લોકોનો ધર્મ ઈસ્લામ છે. તેઓ મુસલમાન છે. તેઓ કૃષ્ણ ભગવાનમાં વિશ્વાસ નથી ધરાવતા. ā lokono dharm Islām che. teo musalmān che. teo Kṛṣṇa Bhagvānmāṃ viśvās nathī dharāvtā.

Test yourself

1 હું ભારત ગયો અને મારી બહેનને મળ્યો.
2 દીપકભાઈ આજે તમે શું કર્યું?
3 હું આવી ગયો છું અને મારે હમણાં જમવું છે.
4 પહેલાં ડાબી બાજુ પછી જમણી બાજુ અને પછી સીધા – પણ ધીમેથી.
5 નીલા, છોકરાએ મને પૈસા આપ્યા પણ તે ઓછા હતા.
6 મેં ઠંડું પણી પીધું.

UNIT 7

What's the time?

1 Ashish lives in London and he travels by tube. **2 a આશિષ સવા નવની ટ્યૂબમાં આવે છે.** Āśiṣ savā navnī ṭyūbmāṃ āve che. **b સવારના વર્ગો દસ વાગ્યે શરૂ થાય છે.**

savārnā vargo das vāgye śarū thāy che. **c બપોરના વર્ગો અઢી વાગ્યે શરૂ થાય છે.** bapornā vargo adhī vāgye śarū thāy che.

3 a આશિષ વિદ્યાર્થી છે. Āśiṣ vidyārthī che. **b આશિષને લંડન ગમે છે. પણ એની પાસે વખત નથી તેથી લંડન જોવા નથી ગયો.** Āśiṣne Laṃḍan game che paṇ eni pāse vakht nathī tethī Laṃḍan jovā nathī gayo.

Language discovery

The words refer to time.

1 a દીપકભાઈ, તમે અહીં રોજ નવ વાગ્યા (ના સમયે) આવો છો? Dīpakbhāī, tame ahīṃ roj nav vage (nā samaye) avo cho? **b દીપકભાઈ, કાલે તમે કેટલા વાગ્યે** (or **વાગે**) **જશો?** Dīpakbhāī, kāle tame keṭlā vagyā keṭlā vāgye (or vāge) jaśo? **c દીપકભાઈ, બે વાગ્યે** (or **વાગે**) **અમે શું કરીશું?** Dīpakbhāī, be vāgye (or vāge) ame shuṃ karīśuṃ? **d દીપકભાઈ, આ ખમીસના એક સો રૂપિયા છે!** Dīpakbhāī, ā khamīsna ek so rūpiyā che!

I've heard you're going to India

1 I came to see you yesterday but could not meet you. Your father told me that you are going to India. **2 a નિશાએ ચાર દિવસ પહેલાં એનો સામાન તૈયાર કરવા માંડયો.** Nisā cār divas pahelāṃ eno sāmān taiyār karvā māṃḍyo. **b લીલાનો ભાઈ બહારગામ ગયા હશે.** Līlāno bhāī bahārgām gayā hase. **c લીલાએ કહ્યું કે પ્રબોધ બજારમાં ગયા હશે.** Līlāe kahyuṃ ke Prabodh bajārmāṃ gayā hase. **3 a પ્રબોધનું કામ પુરું થયું નથી કારણ કે એ નથી આવ્યો.** Prabodhnuṃ kaṃ puruṃ. thayuṃ nathī kāraṇ ke e nathī āvyo. **b લીલાને નથી જ લાગતું કે વરસાદ પડશે.** Līlane nathi j lāgtuṃ ke varsad paḍse.

Language discovery

સોચીને, સાંભળીને, બેસીને

a મેં ઘેર જઈને એને ફોન કર્યો. meṃ gher jaīene ene phon karyo. **અમારા સમાચાર સાંભળીને તેઓ રાજી થયા.** amārā samācār sāṃbhaḷine teo rājī thayā. **અહીં બેસીને એમની રાહ જોઈએ.** ayāṃ besine emnī rāh joīe.

a Start/begin the (your) work! **b** He/she/it began to drink water. It began to rain

a That person must be angry. **b આજે મને પત્ર મળશે.** āje mane patra maḷśe This boy must be clever. **d તે હમણાં ઘેર આવશે.** te hamaṇāṃ gher āvśe.

Practice

ગામડામાં અમારે થોડી જમીન છે, પણ તેઓ ખેડૂત નથી. તેઓ સુથાર છે. તેઓ પોતે ખેતરનું ઈતું કામ કરે છે. અમારા ખેતરમાં અમે મગફળીનો પાક લઈએ છીએ. ચાર વરસથી હું બેન્કમાં કરી કરું છું. હું વહેલી સવારે ઊઠી દાતણ કરીને સ્નાન કરું છું. ઘરમાં અંબાજીનુ મંદિર છે અને હું ની પૂજા કરું છું. પછી એમને માટે નાસ્તો તૈયાર કરીને ઓફિસ જવા નીકળું છું. હું બસમાં આવ–જા છું અને રોજ બસો ચિકકાર હોય છે અને લોકો બહુ ગડબડ કરે છે. રાતે હું કોઈ ચોપડી વાંચીને સુઈ ઉં છું. મારે નોકરી છોડવી છે પણ ગામડામાં લોકોને બહુ ઓછા પૈસા મળે છે અને બેચાર વરસ સુધી કરી કરવી પડે એમ છે.

gāmḍāmāṃ amāre thoḍī jamīn che, pan teo kheḍūt nathī. teo suthār che. teo pote khetarnuṃ joītuṃ kām kare che. amārā khetarmāṃ ame magphaḷīno pāk laīe chīe. cār varasthī huṃ beṃkmāṃ nokrī karuṃ chuṃ. huṃ vahelī savāre ūṭhī dātaṇ karīne snān karuṃ chuṃ. gharmāṃ Aṃbājīnuṃ maṃdir che ane huṃ enī pūjā karuṃ chuṃ, pachī emne maṭe nāsto taiyār karīne ophis javā nīkaḷuṃ chuṃ, huṃ basmaṃ āv-jā karuṃ chuṃ ane roj baso cikār hoy che ane loko bahu gaḍbaḍ kare che. rāte huṃ koi copḍī vāṃcīne sūī jāuṃ chuṃ. māre nokrī choḍvī che paṇ gāmḍāmāṃ lokone bahu ochā paisā maḷe che ane māre becār varas sudhī nokrī karvī paḍe em che.

2 a ગુજરાતની વસ્તી ચાર કરોડ અને વીસ લાખની છે. Gujarātnī vastī cār karoḍ ane vīs lākhnī che**. b ગુજરાતનો કિનારો એક હજાર છસો કિલોમીટર લાંબો છે.** Gujarātno kināro ek hajār chaso kilomīṭar lāṃbo che. **c ગુજરાતમાં એક વરસમાં વરસાદ એક હજાર પાંચસો મિલિમીટર પડે છે.** Gujarātmāṃ ek varasmāṃ varsād ek hajār pāṃcso milimīṭar paḍe che. **d ગુજરાતના પચાસ ટકા લોકોને (એટલે લગભગ બે કરોડ) લખતાં વાં ચતાં આવડે છે.** Gujarātnā pacās ṭakā lokone (eṭle lagbhag be karoḍ) lakhtāṃ vāṃctāṃ āvaḍe che. **e ભારતની વસ્તી લગભગ પચાસી કરોડની છે.** Bhāratnī vastī lagbhag pacāsī karoḍ che.

3 12.45 **પોણો વાગ્યો છે.** poṇo vāgyo che; 2.30 **અઢી વાગ્યા છે.** aḍhī vāgyā che; 7.45 **પોણા આઠ વાગ્યા છે.** poṇā āṭh vāgyā che; 5.15 **સવા પાંચ વાગ્યા છે.** savā pāṃc vāgyā che; 9.10 **નવ ને દસ (મિનિટ) થઈ છે.** nav ne das (miniṭ) thaī che; 1.30 **દોઢ વાગ્યો છે.** doḍh vāgyo che.

4 તમેઃ હું નવ વાગ્યે નીકળું છું. tame: huṃ nav vāgye nīkaḷuṃ chuṃ. **તમેઃ હું ટ્રેનમાં આવ–જા કરું છું.** tame: huṃ ṭrenmāṃ āv-jā karuṃ chuṃ. **તમેઃ હું લગભગ સાડા દસ વાગ્યે ઓફિસમા પહોંચું છું.** tame: huṃ lagbhag sāḍā das vāgye ophisma pahoṃcuṃ euṃ. **તમેઃ હું રાતે છ વાગ્યા સુધી કામ કરું છું.** tame: huṃ rāte cha vāgyā sudhī kām karuṃ chuṃ.

Do you understand?

1 a અઠવાડિઆના આઠ દિવસ નથી. સાત દિવસ હોય છે. b **ગુજરાતમાં પાંચ ઋતુ નથી. ત્રણ ઋતુ હોય છે. c ચોમાસાના છેલ્લા બે મહિનામાં વરસાદ નથી પડતો. વરસાદ પહેલા બે મહિનામાં પડે છે.**
2 a ચોમાસું લગભગ જુનમાં બેસે છે. b ચોમાસું લગભગ ઓકટોબર સુધી ચાલે છે.

Test yourself

1 યાના કેટલા રૂપિયા થયા અને કેટલા વાગયા છે.
2 દીપકભાઈ હું રોજ સવારે ઘરેથી કામે જવા છ વાગે નીકળું છું.
3 લીલા કુંટુંબને મળવા અઠવાડિયામાં કેટલી વાર તેના ગામ જાય છે?
4 મેં યા પીછા પછી કામ શરૂ કર્યું.
5 મેં પાંચ વાગ્યા સુધી કામ કર્યું અને પછી ઘેર જઈને ખાધું.
6 આ કઈ ઋતુ છે અને વરસનો કયો મહીનો છે?

ગુજરાતી–અંગ્રેજી શબ્દાવલિ
Gujarati-English vocabulary

સંભળાવવું	saṃbhaḷāvvuṃ	*to tell* (a story)
પાઠ	pāṭh	*lesson* (m.)
મેલું	meluṃ	*dirty*
ક્લાસ	klās	*class*
નવું	navuṃ	*new*
જુનું	jūnuṃ	*old*
વાર્તા (f.)	vārtā	*story*
ચોકખું	cokkhuṃ	*clean*
કેળું (n.)	keḷuṃ	*banana*
ગાવું	gāvuṃ	*to sing*
ગીત	gīt	*song*
અલમારી (f.)	almārī	*cupboard*
આપવું	āpvuṃ	*to give*
ોન કરવો	phone karvo	*to call on the phone*
ાંડો હોવું	gāṃḍo hovuṃ	*to be mad*
ગરબત્તી (f.)	agarbattī	*incense stick*
ઘરું	aghruṃ	*difficult*
ઠવાડિયું (n.)	athvāḍiyuṃ	*week*
ઢી	aḍhī	*two and a half, two and a half times*
ત્યારે	atyāre	*now*
દા (f.)	adā	*graceful movment, acting*
દ્ભુત	adbhut	*wonderful*
ધ્યાપક (m.)	adhyāpak	*teacher, professor*
ધ્યાપિકા (f.)	adhyāpikā	*teacher, professor*
ને	ane	*and*
નેક	anek	*several, many*
્યાસ (m.)	abhyās	*study*
્યાસક્રમ (m.)	abhyāskram	*curriculum, course*
ે	ame	*we* (exclusive)
ેરિકન (m./f./adj.)	amerikan	*American*
જી (f.)	arjī	*application, prayer, complaint*
જી કરવી	arjī karvī	*apply*
બી (f.)	arbī	*Arabic*
!	are!	*oh!*
(m.)	arth	*meaning*
	ardhuṃ	*half*
સાન (n.)	avsān	*end, death*

અવળુંસવળું	avaḷuṃ-savaḷuṃ	*topsy-turvy*
અવાજ (m.)	avāj	*sound, voice*
અશક્ય	aśakya	*impossible*
અહીં	ahiṃ	*here*
અંગ્રેજ (m./f.)	aṃngrej	*English person*
અંગ્રેજી	aṃngrejī	*English*
અંગ્રેજી (f.)	aṃngrejī	*English* (language)
અંત (m.)	aipt	*end, boundary*
અંતે	aipte	*at last, in the end*
અંદર	aṃdar	*inside*
આ	ā	*this, these*
આકાશ (n.)	ākāś	*sky*
આકાશવાણી (f.)	ākāśvāṇī	*radio*
આખરઘડી (f.)	ākharghaḍī	*last moment*
આખું	ākhuṃ	*whole, all*
આગ (f.)	āg	*fire*
આગગાડી (f.)	āggāḍī	*train*
આગળ	āgaḷ	*formerly, before*
આગળ જવું	āgaḷ javuṃ	*be fast* (of watch, etc.)
આજ	āj	*today*
આજુબાજુ	ājubāju	*on all sides*
આત્મા (m.)	ātma	*soul, life*
આદત (f.)	ādat	*habit, practice*
આધુનિક	ādhunik	*modern*
આનંદ (m.)	ānamd	*joy, delight*
આનો (m.)	āno	*anna* (coin)
આપણે	āpṇe	*we* (inclusive)
આપવું	āpvuṃ	*give*
આરતી (f.)	ārtī	*arti, ceremony with lights*
આરામ (m.)	ārām	*rest*
આરામ કરવો	ārām karvo	*have a rest*
આરોગ્ય (n.)	hrogya	*health*
આવ-જા (f.)	āv-jā	*coming and going*
આવ-જા કરવી	āv-jā karvi	*commute*
આવજો	āvjo	*goodbye*
આવડવું	āvaḍvuṃ	*know, know how to*
આવતું	āvtuṃ	*coming*
આવવું	āvvuṃ	*come*
આશા (f.)	āśā	*hope*
આશીર્વાદ (f.)	āśīrvād	*blessing; Yours ...*
આશ્રમ (m.)	āśram	*ashram*
આસપાસ(માં)	āspās (māṃ)	*near by, around, in the area*
આસમાની	āsmānī	*sky-blue, blue*

આળસુ	āḷsu	*lazy*
ઈચ્છવું	icchvum	*wish*
ઈનામ (n.)	inām	*reward, gift, prize*
ઈમારત (f.)	imārat	*building*
ઈસ્પિતાલ (f.)	ispitāl	*hospital*
ઈસ્લામ (m.)	Islām	*Islam*
ઉઘાડું	ughāḍuṃ	*open*
ઉતારુ (m.)	utāru	*passenger*
ઉત્તર (f.)	uttar	*north;* (adj.) *northern*
ઉધરસ (f.)	udhras	*cough*
ઉનાળો (m.)	unāḷo	*summer*
ઉનાળો બેસવો	unāḷo besvo	*summer sets in*
ઉપર	upar	*above*
ઉપરવાળો (m.)	uparvāḷo	*God* (colloquial)
ઉપરાંત	uparāṃt	*moreover, in addition, besides*
ઉમર (f.)	umar	*age*
ઉર્દૂ (f.)	urdū	*Urdu*
ઊગવું (intr.)	ūgvuṃ	*come up, grow, rise* (of sun)
ઊજવવું (tr.)	ūjavvuṃ	*celebrate*
ઊઠવું	ūṭhvuṃ	*rise, get up*
ઊતરવું (intr.)	ūtarvuṃ	*descend, alight*
ઊનું	ūnaṃ	*warm, hot*
ઊપડવું (intr.)	ūpaḍvuṃ	*start, depart*
ઊભા રહેવું (intr.)	ūbhā rehevum	*stop, wait*
ઊભું	ūbhuṃ	*standing*
ઊંચું	ūṃcuṃ	*high*
ઋતુ (m.)	ṛtu	*season*
એ	e	*this, those, he, she, it, they*
એ.સી.	e.sī.	*air-conditioned*
એક	ek	*one; a*
ેકટાણું (n.)	ekṭāṇuṃ	*vow of eating only once a day*
ેકદમ	ekdum	*at once, completely*
ેકલું	ekluṃ	*alone, lonely*
ેકસ રે (m.)	eks re	*X-ray*
ેના એ જ	enā e j	*the same old story*
ેમ	em	*thus*
ેરપોર્ટ (n.)	erporṭ	*airport*
વું	evuṃ	*of that sort, such*
શઆરામ (m.)	eśārām	*comforts of life*
ોછામાં ઓછું	ochāmāṃ ochum	*at least*
ોછું	ochuṃ	*few, less, insufficient, incomplete*
ોટલો (m.)	oṭlo	*verandah, porch*
ઢણી (f.)	oḍhṇi	*scarf, veil*

ઓપરેશન (n.)	opareśan	*operation*
ઓફિસ (f.)	ophis	*office*
ઓરડો (m.)	orḍo	*room*
ઓશીકું (n.)	ośīkuṃ	*pillow, cushion*
ઓહો!	oho!	*oh!*
ઓળખવું (tr.)	oḷakhvuṃ	*know, recognize*
ઔપનિવેશિક	aupaniveśik	*colonial*
કચરો (m.)	kacro	*rubbish*
કઠિન	kaṭhin	*hard, strong, difficult*
કડક	kaḍak	*hard, harsh, cruel*
કથા (f.)	kathā	*story, tale*
કથ્થાઈ	kaththāī	*maroon*
કદાચ	kadāc	*perhaps*
કપડાં (n.pl.)	kapḍāṃ	*clothes*
કમ	kam	*less, wanting, deficient*
કમ્પ્યુટર (n.)	kampyuṭar	*computer*
કયું (કઈ)	kayiṃ (kaī)	*which?*
કરકસર (f.)	karaksar	*thrift, frugality*
કરતૂક (n.)	kartūk	*misdeed, bad behaviour*
કરવું	karvuṃ	*do, make*
કરોડ (m.)	karoḍ	*crore, ten million*
કલમ (f.)	kalam	*pen*
કલાક (m.)	kalāk	*hour*
કહેવું	kahevuṃ	*say, tell*
કંઈ	kaṃī	*some, something*
કંઈ નહિ	kaṃī nahi	*nothing*
કંકોતરી (f.)	kaṃkotrī	*invitation* (to wedding or similar)
કંજૂસ	kaṃjūs	*miserly, mean*
કંટાળવું (intr.)	kaṃṭāḷvuṃ	*bored, weary*
કંટાળો (m.)	kaṃṭāḷo	*weariness, boredom, disgust*
કંબલ (m.)	kaṃbal	*blanket*
કંસારી (f.)	kaṃsarī	*cricket, type of insect*
કાકા (m.pl.)	kākā	*uncle, father's brother*
કાગળ (m.)	kāgaḷ	*paper, letter*
કાજુ (n.)	kāju	*cashew nut*
કાઢવું	kāḍhvuṃ	*take, draw out*
કાપડ (n.)	kāpaḍ	*cloth*
કાપવું (tr.)	kāpvuṃ	*cut*
કામ (n.)	kām	*work, task, use*
કામ (m.)	kām	*desire; sex*
કામનું	kāmnuṃ	*useful*
કાયમ	kāyam	*permanent*
કારકુન (m.)	kārkun	*clerk*

કારખાનું (n.)	kārkhānum	*factory, business establishment*
કારણ (n.)	kāraṇ	*cause, reason*
કારણ કે	kāraṇ ke	*because*
કાલ (f.)	kāl	*yesterday; tomorrow*
કાળું	kāḷuṃ	*black*
કાંટાળું	kāṃṭāḷuṃ	*thorny, full of difficulties*
કાંટો (m.)	kāṃṭo	*fork*
કિરમજી	kiramjī	*crimson*
કિલો (m.)	kilo	*kilo*
કિલોમીટર (n.)	kilomītar	*kilometre*
કિંમત (f.)	kiṃmat	*price, value*
કુટુંબ (n.)	kuṭuṃb	*family*
કુત્તો (m.)	kutto	*dog*
કુશળ	kuśaḷ	*well, healthy*
કુંવારી (f.)	kuṃvārī	*unmarried, single*
કૂવો (m.)	kūvo	*well*
કૃપા (f.)	krpi	*kindness, favour, pity*
કે	ke	*either; that; or*
કેટલુંક	keṭluṃk	*some, a few*
કેટલું	keṭluṃ?	*how many?*
કેમ?	kem?	*how?*
કેમકે	kem ke	*because*
કેવું?	kevuṃ?	*what sort of?*
કેસરી	kesari	*saffron*
કોઈ	koī	*some, someone*
કોણ?	kop?	*who?*
કોમ (f.)	kom	*community*
કોયલ (f.)	koyal	*koel, cuckoo*
કોલેજ (f.)	kolej	*college*
કોશિશ (f.)	kośiś	*effort*
ક્યારે?	kyāre?	*when?*
ક્યારેય	kyarey	*ever*
ક્યાં?	kyāṃ?	*where?*
ખણખણાટ (m.)	khaṇkhaṇāṭ	*clanking sound*
ખબર (f.)	khabar	*knowledge, news, information*
ખમીસ (n.)	khamīs	*shirt*
ખરચાળ	kharcāḷ	*costly, extravagant*
ખરાબ	kharāb	*bad*
ખરીદવું (tr.)	kharidvum	*buy*
ખરીદી (f.)	kharidi	*buying, purchases*
ખરું	kharum	*true, real, genuine*
ખરેખર	kharekhar	*truly, indeed*
ખાટલો (m.)	khāṭlo	*bed, charpoy*

ખાતરી (f.)	khltrl	*trust, conviction, certainty*
ખાલી	khālī	(adj.) *empty, vacant;* (adv.) *only, merely*
ખાવું	knāvuṃ	*eat*
ખાવાનું (n.)	khāvānuṃ	*food*
ખાસ	khās	*particular, special*
ખાંડ (f.)	khāṃḍ	*sugar*
ખાંસવું (intr.)	khāṃsvuṃ	*cough*
ખીચડી (f.)	khīcḍī	*khicheree*
ખીલો (m.)	khilo	*peg, post, nail*
ખુરશી (f.)	khurśī	*chair*
ખુશ	khuś	*happy*
ખૂબ	khūb	*very, much*
ખૂલતું	khūltuṃ	*loose; light-coloured*
ખેતર (n.)	khetar	*field*
ખેતીવાડી (f.)	khetīvāḍī	*fields and gardens, agriculture*
ખેડૂત (m.)	kheḍūt	*farmer, peasant*
ખોટ (f.)	khoṭ	*deficit, loss, error*
ખોટું	khoṭuṃ	*false, bad*
ખોટું (n.)	khoṭuṃ	*loss, wrong*
ખોરાક (m.)	khorāk	*food*
ખોલવું (tr.)	kholvuṃ	*open*
ખ્યાલ (m.)	khyāl	*guess, idea*
ખ્રિસ્તી	khristī	*Christian*
ગઈ	gaī	*see* ગયું
ગરબડ (f.)	garbaḍ	*noise*
ગણવું (tr.)	gaṇvuṃ	*count, reckon, regard, value*
ગમવું	gamvuṃ	*to be pleasing, to like*
ગરમ	garam	*hot*
ગરમી (f.)	garmī	*heat*
ગરીબ	garīb	*poor*
ગર્જના (f.)	garjnā	*thunder, roar*
ગયું (ગઈ)	gayuṃ (gaī)	*past, gone*
ગંદું	gaṃduṃ	*dirty*
ગાડી (f.)	gāḍī	*car, vehicle*
ગાદીતકિયો (m.)	gādītakiyo	*cushion*
ગામ (n.)	gām	*village*
ગામડું (n.)	gāmḍuṃ	*village*
ગાય (f.)	gāy	*cow*
ગાયન (n.)	gāyan	*singing, music, song*
ગાવું	gāvuṃ	*to sing*
ગાળ (f.)	gāḷ	*abuse*
ગિરદી (f.)	girdī	*crowd, crowding*
ગીત (n.)	gīt	*song*

ગુજરવું (intr.)	gujarvuṃ	*pass away*
ગુજરી જવું	gujrī javuṃ	*die*
ગુજરાતી (m.f./adj.)	gujarātī	*Gujarati*
ગુજરાતી (f./n.)	gujarātī	*Gujarati* (language)
ગુફા (f.)	guphā	*cave*
ગુરુવાર (m.)	guruvār	*Thursday*
ગુલાબી	gulābī	*pink*
ગુસ્સે થવું	gusse thavum	*become angry*
ગોઠવવું (tr.)	goṭhavvuṃ	*arrange, settle*
ગોઠવેલું લગ્ન (n.)	goṭhveluṃ lagan	*arranged marriage*
ગોરજ (f.)	goraj	*twilight*
ગ્રહશાંતિ (f.)	grahaśāṃti	*type of ceremony*
ગ્લાસ (m.)	glās	*glass*
ઘટના (f.)	ghatnl	*composition, incident*
ઘડિયાળ (f.)	ghaḍiyāḷ	*watch*
ઘડિયાળ (n.)	ghaḍiyāḷ	*clock*
ઘડી (f.)	ghaḍi	*moment, opportunity*
ઘણું	ghaṇuṃ	*much, many, quite*
ઘણું બધું	ghaṇuṃ badhnṃ	*many, lots of*
ઘર (n.)	ghar	*house, home*
ઘરખર્ચ (m./n.)	gharkharc	*household expenses*
ઘરેણા (n.pl.)	ghareṇāṃ	*jewellery*
ઘંટડી (f.)	ghaṃṭaḍī	*little bell*
ાઘરો (m.)	ghāghro	*skirt*
ેરું	gheruṃ	*deep* (colour)
ોડો (m.)	ghoḍo	*horse*
ડવું (tr./intr.)	caḍvuṃ	*go up, get on*
ડાવવું (tr.)	caḍāvvuṃ	*load, put on; flatter*
ણિયો (m.)	caṇiyo	*petticoat, skirt*
મકવું (intr.)	camakvuṃ	*shine, twinkle*
મચો (m.)	camco	*spoon*
લણી	calṇī	*current*
(f.)	cā	*tea*
કર (m.)	cākar	*servant*
ખવું (tr.)	cākhvuṃ	*taste*
દર (f.)	cādar	*sheet*
પાણી (n. pl.)	cāpāṇī	*tea and refreshments*
મડું (n.)	cāmḍuṃ	*leather*
રપાઈ (f.)	cārpāī	*charpoy, cot*
લ (m.)	cāl	*custom*
લતી પકડવી	cāltī pakaḍvī	*walk away, run away*
લવું	cālvuṃ	*go, walk*
લુ	cālu	*present, continuing*

ચાલો	cālo	*let's go; well then*
ચાર	cār	*four*
ચાવવું	cāvvuṃ	*chew*
ચાંદ (m.)	cāṃd	*moon*
ચિકાર	cikār	*crowded*
ચિરંજીવ	ciraṃjīv	*Dear ...*
ચિંતા (f.)	ciṃtā	*care, thought, anxiety*
ચીજ (f.)	cīj	*thing, substance*
ચીનો (m.)	cīno	*Chinese person*
ચીસ (f.)	cīs	*whistle, shriek, loud cry*
ચુંબન (n.)	cuṃban	*kiss*
ચૂકવું	cūkvuṃ	*to miss (train, etc.); err*
ચૂલો (n.)	cūlo	*fireplace, hearth*
ચૂંદડી (f.)	cūṃdḍī	*silk garment, scarf*
ચોક (m.)	cok	*square (in town), open space*
ચોકકસ	cokas	*certainly, sure*
ચોથું	cothuṃ	*fourth*
ચોપડી (f.)	copḍī	*book*
ચોપડો (m.)	copḍo	*ledger*
ચોમાસું (n.)	comāsuṃ	*rainy season*
ચોર (m.)	cor	*thief*
ચોરી (f.)	corī	*theft*
ચોળી (f.)	coḷī	*bodice*
છ	cha	*six*
છઠ્ઠું	chaṭhṭhuṃ	*sixth*
છત (f.)	chat	*ceiling, terrace*
છત્રી (f.)	chatrī	*umbrella*
છરી(f.)	charī	*knife*
છાપરું (n.)	chāpruṃ	*roof*
છાપું (n.)	chāpuṃ	*newspaper*
છીએ	chīe	*(we) are*
છીંકણી (f.)	chīṃkṇī	*snuff*
છું	chuṃ	*(I) am*
છૂટાછેડા (m.pl.)	chūṭācheḍā	*divorce*
છૂટી (f.)	chūṭī	*leave, remission*
છૂટું (n.)	chūṭuṃ	*small change*
છૂટવું (intr.)	chūṭvuṃ	*leave, go out*
છે	che	*(he, she, it) is; (you) (informal) are*
છો	cho	*(you) (formal) are*
છોકરી (f.)	chokri	*girl*
છોકરું (n.)	chokruṃ	*child*
છોકરો (m.)	chokro	*boy*
છોડવું (tr.)	choḍvuṃ	*leave, let loose, give up, dismiss*

જ (enclitic)	j	*only*
જગાવવું (tr.)	jagāvvuṃ	*wake* (someone) *up*
જગ્યા (f.)	jagyā	*place, room*
જચવું (intr.)	jacvuṃ	*suit, look nice*
જણ (n./m.)	jaṇ	*person*
જણાવવું	jaṇāvvuṃ	*inform, tell, report*
જનમ (m.)	janam	*birth*
જનમવું (intr.)	janamvuṃ	*be born*
જમણું	jamṇuṃ	*right* (not left)
જમવું	jamvuṃ	*eat, dine*
જમીન (f.)	jamīn	*land, ground, floor*
જય શ્રીકૃષ્ણ	jay Śri Krṣṇa	*Glory to Lord Krishna*
જય સ્વામિનારાયણ	jay Śvāmināràyaṇ	*Glory to Swami Narayan*
જરા	jarā	*just, a little*
જરૂર (f.)	jarūr	*necessity; certainly; yes please!*
જરૂર પડવી	jarūr paḍvī	*be necessary*
જલદી	jaldī	*quickly*
જવાબ (m.)	javāb	*reply*
જવું	javuṃ	*go*
જાંબુડું	jāṃbuḍuṃ	*purple*
જાગવું	jāgvuṃ	*wake up*
જાડું	jāḍuṃ	*fat*
જાણવું	jāṇvuṃ	*know, understand, believe*
જાણીજોઈને	jāṇi joīne	*deliberately*
જાત (f.)	jāt	*kind, type; caste*
જાતે	jāte	*personally, of one's own accord*
જામવું (intr.)	jāṃvuṃ	*gather, be in full swing*
જંતુ (m./n.)	jāṃtu	*insect*
જાંબલી	jāṃblī	*violet*
જિલ્લો (m.)	jillo	*district*
જી હા	jī hā	*yes* (formal)
જીવતું જાગતું	jīvtuṃ jāgtuṃ	*lively*
જીવન (n.)	jīvan	*life*
જીવવું (intr.)	jīvvuṃ	*live*
જુદું	juduṃ	*different*
જુવાન	juvān	*young*
જૂનું	jūnuṃ	*old, ancient*
જોવા જેવું	jovā jevuṃ	*worth seeing*
જોઈએ	joīe	*need*
જોકે	joke	*although*
જોખવું (tr.)	jokhvuṃ	*weigh*
જોડણી (f.)	joḍṇi	*spelling*
જોડો (m.)	joḍo	*shoe*

જોવું	jovuṃ	*see*
જૈન (m.f/adj.)	jain	*Jain*
ઝટપટ	jhaṭpaṭ	*quickly, without delay*
ઝાડ (n.)	jhāḍ	*tree*
ઝીણું	jhīṇuṃ	*small, pointed, sharp*
ઝૂડી (f.)	jhūḍī	*bundle*
ઝૂલો	jhūlo	*swing*
ઝૂલો ખાવો	jhūlo khāvo	*swing*
ટકો (m.)	ṭako	*percentage*
ટકોરો (m.)	ṭakoro	*knock, blow*
ટપાલી (m.)	ṭapālī	*postman*
ટૂંકું	ṭūṃkuṃ	*short*
ટેક્સી (f.)	ṭeksī	*taxi*
ટેવ (f.)	ṭev	*habit, addiction*
ટોપી (f.)	ṭopī	*hat*
ટોળું (n.)	ṭoḷuṃ	*crowd, multitude*
ટ્યૂબ (f.)	ṭyūb	*tube, underground*
ટ્રેન (f.)	ṭren	*train*
ઠરવું	ṭharvuṃ	*be fixed, be resolved*
ઠંડી (f.)	ṭhaṃḍī	*cold, coldness*
ઠંડું	ṭhaṃḍuṃ	*cold*
ઠંડું (n.)	ṭhaṃḍuṃ	*cold drink*
ઠીક	ṭhīk	*all right, good, OK*
ડબ્બો (m.)	ḍabbo	*box; train compartment, carriage*
ડરવું (intr.)	ḍarvuṃ	*fear, to be afraid of*
ડાબું	ḍābuṃ	*left* (not right)
ડિગ્રી (f.)	ḍigrī	*degree*
ડિઝાઈન	dijhāīn	*design*
ડોક્ટર (m.)	ḍokṭar	*doctor*
ડ્રાઈવર (m.)	ḍrāīvar	*driver*
ઢગલો (m.)	dhaglo	*heap, pile*
ઢાળવું (n.)	ḍhāḷvuṃ	*put down, spread cot* (to sit on), *make bed*
ઢોર (n.)	ḍhor	*cattle*
તક (f.)	tak	*opportunity, chance*
તકલીફ (f.)	taklīph	*labour, exertion, trouble*
તજવું (tr.)	tajvuṃ	*leave, forsake*
તથાપિ	tathāpi	*nevertheless*
તપખીરી	tapkhīrī	*brown*
તપાસ (f.)	tapās	*inspection, inquiry*
તમાકુ (f.)	tamāku	*tobacco*
તમે	tame	*you* (formal)
તબિયત (f.)	tabiyat	*health*

તરત	tarat	*quickly*
તરસ (f.)	taras	*thirst*
તહેવાર (m.)	tahevār	*festival*
તળાવ (n.)	taḷāv	*tank, pond*
તંગ	taṃg	*tight*
તાજું	tājuṃ	*fresh*
તારા (f.)	tārā	*star*
તારીખ (f.)	tārīkh	*date, whole day*
તાલીમી	tālīmi	*educational*
તીખું	tīkhuṃ	*pungent, fiery, hot*
તું	tuṃ	*you* (informal)
તે	te	*he, she, it*
તેઓ	teo	*they*
તેથી	tethī	*therefore*
તેલ (n.)	tel	*oil*
તૈયાર	taiyār	*ready, prepared*
તો	to	*then*
તોફાન (n.)	tophān	*mischief, disturbance, fight*
ત્યાં	tyāṃ	*there*
ત્રણ	traṇ	*three*
ત્રીજું	trījuṃ	*third*
થઈને	thaīne	*via, having become*
થવું	thavuṃ	*become, happen* (irreg. as javuṃ)
થાક (m.)	thāk	*exhaustion, tiredness*
થાક લાગવો	thāk lāgvo	*be tired*
થાન (n.)	thān	*bale* (*of cloth*)
થાળી (f.)	thāḷī	*thali, plate*
થી	thī	*from*
થેલી (f.)	thelī	*beg*
થોડું	thoḍuṃ	*little, few*
થોડુંઘણું	thoḍuṃghaṇuṃ	*little*
થોડાંક	thoḍāṃk	*some, a few*
દક્ષિણ (f.)	dakṣiṇ	*south;* (adj.) *southern*
દયા (f.)	dayā	*pity, compassion, mercy*
દર	dar	*each, every*
દરજી (m.)	darjī	*tailor*
દરિયો (m.)	dariyo	*sea, ocean*
દવા (f.)	davā	*medicine*
દહાડો (m.)	dahāḍo	*day*
દાખલ તરીકે	dākhal tarīke	*e.g., for example*
દાગીનો (m.)	dāgīno	*thing; package; jewel*
દાતણ (n.)	dātaṇ	*toothbrush, twig for cleaning teeth*
દાતણ કરવું	dātaṇ karvuṃ	*clean one's teeth*

દાળ (f.)	dāḷ	*lentils, pulses*
દિવસ (m.)	divas	*day*
દિશા (f.)	diśā	*side, direction*
દીકરી (f.)	dīkrī	*daughter*
દીકરો (m.)	dīkro	*son*
દુકાન (f.)	dukān	*shop*
દુકાનદાર (m.)	dukāndār	*shopkeeper*
દુખ, દુઃખ (n.)	dukh, duḥkh	*pain, grief, sorrow*
દુખવું (intr.)	dukhvuṃ	*ache, pain, feel pain*
દુનિયા (f.)	duniyā	*world*
દુઃખ (n.)	duḥkh	*pain, sorrow, grief*
દુઃખદ	duḥkhad	*giving pain, aching*
દુઃખી	duḥkhī	*sad*
દૂધ (n.)	dūdh	*milk*
દૂર	dūr	*far, distant*
દ્રશ્ય (n.)	dṛśya	*scene, sight*
દેખાડવું (tr.)	dekhāḍvuṃ	*show*
દેખાડવું	dekhāvḍvuṃ	*beautiful, handsome*
દેખાવું	dekhāvuṃ	*be seen, appear, seem*
દેડકું (n.)	deḍkuṃ	*frog*
દેશ (m.)	deś	*country, native place, India*
દોઢ	doḍh	*one and a half, half again*
દોડવું	doḍvuṃ	*run*
ધમાલ (f.)	dhamāl	*bustle, activity*
ધરમ (m.)	dharam	*dharma, religion*
ધરવું (tr.)	dharvuṃ	*catch, put on, take*
ધરાવવું	dharāvvuṃ	*hold*
ધર્મ (m.)	dharma	*dharma, religion*
ધંધો (m.)	dhaṃdho	*business, profession*
ધીમે	dhime	*slowly*
ધીરે	dhīre	*slowly, patiently*
ધૂપ (m.)	dhūp	*incense*
ધૂમ્રપાન (n.)	dhūmrapān	*smoking*
ધૂળ (f.)	dhūḷ	*dust*
ધોતિયું (n.)	dhotiyuṃ	*dhoti*
ધોબી (m.)	dhobī	*dhobi, washerman*
ધોળું	dhoḷuṃ	*white*
ધ્યાન (n.)	dhyān	*meditation, attention*
ધ્યાન રાખવું	dhyān rākhvuṃ	*look after, attend to*
ધ્યાનમંત્ર (m.)	dhyānmaṃtra	*motto*
નજર (f.)	najar	*seeing, sight; evil eye*
નજરે પડવું	najare paḍvuṃ	*be seen*
નથી	nathī	*is not*

નદી (f.)	nadī	*river*
નમસ્તે	namaste	*hello; goodbye* (Hindu and Jain)
નમવું (tr.)	namvuṃ	*bend down*
નર્સ (f.)	nars	*nurse*
નવાઈ (f.)	navāī	*newness, wonder*
નવાઈ લાગવી	navāī lāgvī	*feel surprised*
નવું	navuṃ	*new*
નવેસર(થી)	navesar(thī)	*over again, anew*
નળ (m.)	naḷ	*tap*
નંખાવું (intr.)	naṃkhāvuṃ	*become pale or weak; vomit*
નંબર (m.)	naṃbar	*number*
ના	nā	*no*
ના જી	nā jī	*no* (formal)
ના પાડવી	nā pāḍvī	*refuse, deny*
ાચવું (intr.)	nācvuṃ	*dance*
ાટક (n.)	nāṭāk	*play, drama*
ાતાલ (f.)	nātāl	*Christmas*
ાનપણ (n.)	nānpaṇ	*childhood*
ાનું	nānuṃ	*small, little, young*
ામ (n.)	nām	*name*
ાયક (m.)	nāyak	*actor; hero*
યીકા (f.)	nāyikā	*actress; heroine*
રંગી	nāraṃgī	*orange*
સ્તો (m.)	nāsto	*breakfast; snack*
હવું (intr.)	nāhvuṃ	*bathe*
રાંત (f.)	nirāṃṭ	*leisure; comfort; peace*
શાળ (f.)	niśāḷ	*school*
શ્ચય (m.)	niścay	*determination, resolve*
ષ્કાસન (n.)	niṣkāsan	*expulsion*
કળવું	nīkaḷvuṃ	*set out, depart*
વડવું	nīvaḍvuṃ	*turn out, prove to be*
સાનકારક	nuksānkārak	*harmful*
	ne?	*isn't it?*
કરી (f.)	nokrī	*service, employment*
ટ (f.)	noṭ	(bank)*note*
ડવું	pakāḍvuṃ	*catch, hold; arrest*
(m.)	pag	*foot; leg*
પાળું	pagpāḷum	*on foot, walking, pedestrian*
ડવું	pachāḍvuṃ	*knock to the ground; defeat*
પછી	(nī) pachī	*after, afterwards*
ું	padvuṃ	*fall, happen*
	paṇ	*but; also*
(m.)	pati	*husband*

પત્ની (f.)	patnī	*wife*
પત્ર (m./n.)	patra	*letter*
પધારવું	padhārvuṃ	*to come, give (someone) the pleasure of one's company*
પર	par	*on*
પરણવું	paraṇvuṃ	*marry*
પરમ દિવસ (m.)	param divas	*the day before yesterday; the day after tomorrow*
પરમપૂજ્ય	parampūjya	*Dear ...*
પરસ (f.)	pars	*handbag*
પરંતુ	paraṃtu	*but*
પરંપરાગત	paraṃparāgat	*traditional*
પરિચય (m.)	paricay	*acquaintance; habit*
પરિવાર (m.)	parivār	*family*
પરીક્ષા (f.)	parīkṣā	*exam*
પરીક્ષા આપવી	parīkṣā āpvi	*sit an exam*
પરું (n.)	paruṃ	*suburb*
પશ્ચિમ	paścim	*western*
પશ્ચિમ (f.)	paścim	*west; name of a train*
પસરવું (intr.)	pasarvuṃ	*spread, extend*
પસંદ	pasaṃd	*pleasing*
પહેરવું	pahervuṃ	*put on, wear* (clothes)
પહેરવેશ (m.)	paherveś	*dress, costume*
(ની) પહેલાં	(nī) pahelāṃ	*before*
પહેલું	paheluṃ	*first*
પહોર (m.)	pahor	*period of three hours*
પહોળું	paholuṃ	*broad*
પહોંચવું	pahoṃcvuṃ	*reach, arrive*
પંજાબી (m.f./adj.)	paṃjābī	*Panjabi*
પંજાબી સૂટ (n.)	paṃjābī sūṭ	*Panjabi suit, salwar-kameez*
પા	pā	*quarter*
પાઉંભાજી (f.)	pāuṃbhājī	*name of a snack*
પાક (m.)	pāk	*crop*
પાકિસ્તાની (m.f./adj.)	pākistānī	*Pakistani*
પાકું	pakuṃ	*ripe, mature; fast* (of colour)
પાછળ જવું	pāchaḷ javuṃ	*be slow* (of watch)
પાછું	pāchuṃ	*returned*
પાટીદાર	pāṭīdār	*Patidar* (surname often Patel)
પટિયું (n.)	pāṭiyuṃ	*plank, shelf*
પાઠ (m.)	pāṭh	*recitation; lesson; homework*
પાણી (n.)	pāṇī	*water*
પાતળું	pātḷuṃ	*thin*
પાથરવું (tr.)	pātharvuṃ	*spread on the ground*

પાન (n.)	pān	*paan*
પારસી	pārsī	*Parsi*
પાલન (n.)	pālan	*protecting, supporting*
(ની) પાસે	(ni) pāse	*near; with; in the possession of*
પાંચ	pāṃc	*five*
પાંચમું	paṃcmuṃ	*fifth*
પિતા (m.)	pitā	*father*
પીઠી (f.)	pīṭhī	*name of part of a wedding ceremony*
પીવું	pīvuṃ	*drink*
પીળો	pīḷo	*yellow*
પુરુષ (m.)	puruṣ	*man*
પુસ્તકાલય (n.)	pustakālaya	*library*
પૂછપરછ (f.)	pūchparach	*inquiry*
પૂછવું	pūchvuṃ	*ask, inquire*
પૂજા (f.)	pūjā	*worship*
પૂરતું	pūrtuṃ	*enough*
પૂરી (f.)	pūrī	*poori*
પૂરું કરવું (tr.)	pūruṃ karvuṃ	*finish*
પૂરું થવું (intr.)	pūruṃ thavuṃ	*finish*
પૂર્વ (f.)	pūrva	*east* (adj.) *eastern*
પૂર્વે	pūrve	*formerly*
પૂંજી (f.)	pūṃjī	*capital, wealth*
પૃથ્વી (f.)	pṛthvī	*the earth*
પેટી (f.)	peṭī	*box*
પેઢી (f.)	peḍhī	*generation; house of business*
પેલું	peluṃ	*that*
પૈસા (m.pl.)	paisā	*money*
પૈસા ભરવા	paisā bharvā	*pay*
પોણું	poṇuṃ	*three-quarters, minus a quarter*
પોતાનું	potānuṃ	*one's own, own*
પોતે	pote	*oneself, self*
પોપટી	popaṭī	*green-yellow*
પોલીસ (m.)	polīs	*police*
પોસાવું (intr.)	posāvuṃ	*afford*
પ્રકાશ (m.)	prakāś	*light*
પ્રજાસત્તાક દિવસ (m.)	prajāsattāk din	*Republic Day*
પ્રમાણ (m. pl.)	praṇām	*Yours ...*
પ્રદેશ (m.)	pradeś	*country, land, region, state in country, province*
પ્રયત્ન (m.)	prayatna	*effort*
પ્રશ્ન (m./n.)	praśna	*question*
પ્રસાદ (m.)	prasād	*food from deity*

પ્રસારવું (tr.)	prasārvuṃ	*spread*
પ્રાર્થના (f.)	prārthnā	*request, prayer*
પ્રિય	priya	*Dear...*
પ્રેમ (m.)	prem	*love, affection, liking*
પ્લાસ્ટર (n.)	plāsṭar	*plaster*
ફકત	phakat	*only, merely, simply*
ફરવું	pharvuṃ	*walk, stroll; tour*
પ્રમાણ (n.)	pramāṇ	*evidence, proof; standard*
પ્રભુ (m.)	prabhu	*God (usually Krishna)*
ફરક (m.)	pharak	*change, difference*
ફરિયાદ (f.)	phariyād	*complaint*
ફરિયાદ કરવી	phariyād karvī	*complain*
ફરીથી	pharīthī	*again*
ફળ (n.)	phaḷ	*fruit*
ફાઈન	phāīn	*fine, nice*
ફાટવું (intr.)	phāṭvuṃ	*be torn, be split, be broken*
ફાવવું	phāvvuṃ	*like; be suitable*
ફિલ્મ (f.)	philm	*film*
ફૂલ (n.)	phūl	*flower*
ફૂંકવું (tr.)	phūṃkvuṃ	*blow; smoke*
ફેલાવું (intr.)	phelāvuṃ	*spread*
ફોટો (m.)	phoṭo	*photograph, picture*
ફોન (m.)	phon	*telephone*
ફોન કરવો	phon karvo	*telephone*
ફ્લેટ (m.)	phleṭ	*flat*
બકરું (n.)	bakruṃ	*goat*
બગડવું (intr.)	bagaḍvuṃ	*be spoilt; be out of order*
બગડી ગયું	bagḍī gayuṃ	*out of order*
બચત (f.)	bacat	*savings*
બચાવવું (tr.)	bacāvvuṃ	*save, protect*
બજાર (m.)	bajar	*snuff*
બજાર (m.,f., n.)	bajār	*market, bazaar*
બટાટો (m.)	baṭāṭo	*potato*
બતાવવું	batāvvuṃ	*show*
બધું	badhuṃ	*all*
બનારસી	banārsī	*Banarsi sari*
બનાવવું	banāvvuṃ	*make, do; form*
બપોર (m.)	bapor	*noon; afternoon*
બમણું	bamṇuṃ	*double*
બસ!	bas!	*enough!*
બસ (f.)	bas	*bus*
બસ કરો!	bas karo!	*stop it!*
બહુ	bahu	*very, much*

બહેન (f.)	bahen	*sister*
બહેનપણી (f.)	bahenpaṇī	*friend*
બળદ (m.)	baḷad	*bullock*
બળાત્કાર (m.)	baḷātkār	*force, violence; rape*
બંગાળી (m.f./adj.)	baṃgāḷī	*Bengali*
બંધ	baṃdh	*shut, closed*
બંધન (n.)	baṃdhan	*prohibition*
બાઈ (f.)	bāī	*woman; servant*
બાકી (f.)	bākī	*balance, remainder; deficient*
બાજુ (f.)	bāju	*side*
બાધા (f.)	bādhā	*vow to abstain from certain foods*
બાપ રે બાપ!	bāp re bāp!	*goodness!*
બાપુજી (m.)	bāpujī	*father*
બાબત (f.)	bābat	*subject, matter*
(ની) બાબત	(nī) bābat	*about, concerning*
બારણું (n.)	bārṇuṃ	*door, gate, entrance*
બારી (f.)	bārī	*window*
બાળક (m./n.)	bāḷak	*child*
બાંધણી (f.)	bāṃdhṇī	*tie-dye*
બાંધવું (tr.)	bāṃdhvuṃ	*bind, build, etc.*
બાંધી દેવું (tr.)	bāṃdhī devuṃ	*wrap* (purchases)
બિચારું	bicāruṃ	*poor, helpless, miserable*
બીક (f.)	bīk	*fear*
બીજું	bījuṃ	*second; other; next*
બીડી (f.)	bīḍī	*beedi*
બુધવાર (m.)	budhvār	*Wednesday*
બે	be	*two*
બેટા	beṭā	*my child* (term of address)
બેઠક (f.)	beṭhak	*living room*
બેન (f.)	ben	*sister, Ms*
બેરોજગાર	berojgār	*unemployed*
બેન્ક (f.)	beṃk	*bank*
બોલવું	bolvuṃ	*speak*
બોલાવવું	bolāvvuṃ	*call, invite, summon*
બોલી (f.)	bolī	*dialect*
ભગવાન	bhagvān	*God* (usually Krsna)
ભણવું	bhaṇvum	*study*
ભરચક	bharcak	*full*
ભરત (n.)	bharat	*embroidery*
ભરતકામ (n.)	bharatkam	*embroidery work*
ભરવું (tr.)	bharvuṃ	*fill up*
ભલું	bhaluṃ	*good, kind, polite*
ભલે!	bhale!	*good! OK!*

ભળવું (intr.)	bhaḷvuṃ	*mix with, mingle*
ભાઈ (m.)	bhāī	*brother, Ms*
ભાગ (m.)	bhāg	*part, portion, share*
ભાડું (n.)	bhāḍuṃ	*rent*
ભાત (f.)	bhāt	*rice*
ભારત (m.)	bhārat	*India*
ભારતીય (m.f./adj.)	bhārtīy	*Indian*
ભારે	bhāre	*very; heavy*
ભાવ (m.)	bhāv	*being, nature; feeling; price*
ભાવવું	bhāvvuṃ	*like, be fond of* (food)
ભાષણ (n.)	bhāṣaṇ	*speech, lecture, discourse*
ભાષા (f.)	bhāṣā	*language*
બીમાર	bīmār	*ill, sick*
ભજન (n.)	bhajan	*bhajan* (song in praise of God)
ભાંગવું (intr./tr.)	bhāṃgvuṃ	*be broken into pieces, break*
ભીનું	bhīnuṃ	*wet, moist*
ભૂખ (f.)	bhūkh	*hunger*
ભૂરું	bhūruṃ	*blue*
ભૂલ (f.)	bhūl	*mistake, error*
ભૂલવું (intr.)	bhiilvum	*forget; make a mistake*
ભેગું	bheguṃ	*together, collected, mixed*
ભોળું	bhoḷuip	*artless, credulous*
મ.પ.	ma. pa.	*p.m.*
મ.પૂ.	ma. pū.	*a.m.*
મકાન (n.)	makān	*house*
મગફળી (f.)	magphaji	*groundnut, peanut*
મજદૂર (m.)	majdūr	*labourer*
મજાક (f.)	majāk	*joke*
મજામાં	majāmāṃ	*well* (only as a reply to 'how are you?')
મઝા (f.)	majhā	*pleasure*
મદદ (f.)	madad	*help, aid*
મધ્યાહ્ન (m.)	madhyāhn	*midday, noon*
મધરાત (f.)	madhrāt	*midnight*
મનાઈ (f.)	manāī	*prohibition*
મફત	maphat	*free of charge, gratis*
મરાઠી (f.)	marāṭhī	*Marathi* (language)
મશીન (n.)	maśīn	*machine, engine*
મહારાજ (m.)	mahārāj	*king; term of address for Brahmin, often Brahmin cook*
મહારાણી (f.)	mahārāṇi	*queen*
મહિનો (m.)	mahino	*month; menstrual period*
મહેનત (f.)	mahenat	*labour, exertion, effort*
મહેમાન (m.)	mahemān	*guest*

મહેરબાની (f.)	maherbānī	*kindness, favour*
મહેરબાની કરીને	maherbānī karine	*please*
મળવું	maḷvuṃ	*meet; get*
મંગળવાર (m.)	maṃgaḷvār	*Tuesday*
મંદી (f.)	maṃdī	*recession* (economic)
મંદિર (n.)	mamdir	*temple, area of worship in house*
મા	mā	*mother*
માગવું (tr.)	mfgvum	*ask for, demand*
માટલું (n.)	māṭluṃ	*earthenware pot*
(ને) માટે	(ne) māṭe	*for, for the sake of*
શા(ને) માટે?	śā (ne) māṭe?	*why?, for what reason?*
માણસ *(m., n.)*	mfpas	*man; person, human*
માતૃભાષા (f.)	mātṛabhāśa	*mother tongue*
માધ્યમ (n.)	mādhyam	*medium*
માનવું (tr.)	mānvuṃ	*agree, accept; consider, believe*
માબાપ (n. pl.)	mābāp	*parents*
માફ કરો!	māph karo!	*Excuse me! Forgive me!*
માફી માગવી	māphī māgvī	*apologize*
મામા (m.)	māmā	*uncle, mother's brother*
માયાળુ	māyāḷu	*kind, affectionate*
માસી/માશી (f.)	māsī/māśī	*aunt, mother's sister*
માસ્તર (m.)	māstar	*teacher*
માં	mām	*in*
માંડવું	māṃḍvuṃ	*start, begin; place, put*
માંદું	māṃḍuṃ	*ill*
માંસાહારી	māṃsāhāī	*non-vegetarian*
મિત્ર (m.)	mitra	*friend*
મિનિટ (f.)	miniṭ	*minute*
યાં (m.)	miyāṃ	*Muslim gentleman, Mr*
ટર (n.)	mīṭar	*metre*
ઠાઇ (f.)	mīṭhāī	*sweets*
કયું	mukhya	*chief, major*
જબ	mujab	*like, according to*
રબ્બી	murabbī	*Dear ...*
શ્કેલ	muśkel	*difficult*
સલમાન (m.f./adj.)	musalmān	*Muslim*
કવું	mūkvuṃ	*place, put*
ર્	mūrkh	*foolish, stupid*
ર્ખાઇ (f.)	mūrkhāī	*stupidity*
યુ (n.)	mṛtyu	*death*
જ (n.)	mej	*table*
	mete	*by oneself*
(m.)	meḷ	*agreement, union*

મેળ ખાવો	meḷ khāvo	*suit, agree*
મેળો (m.)	meḷo	*meeting, fair*
મોકલવું	mokalvuṃ	*send*
મોકો (m.)	moko	*occasion, chance*
મોચી (m.)	mocī	*cobbler, shoemaker*
મોટું	moṭuṃ	*big, large; old; important*
મોડું	moḍuṃ	*late*
મોઢું (n.)	moḍhuṃ	*mouth; face*
મોતિયો (m.)	motiyo	*cataract* (of eye)
મોદી (m.)	modī	*grocer*
મોર (m.)	mor	*peacock*
મોરપીંછ	morpīṃch	*peacock blue*
મોહક	mohak	*fascinating; beautiful*
મોંઘવારી (f.)	moṃghvārī	*expensiveness, high price(s)*
મોંઘું	moṃghuṃ	*expensive*
યંત્ર (n.)	yaṃtra	*machine, engine*
યાદ (f.)	yād	*remembrance, memory*
યાદ આવવું	yād āvvuṃ	*remember* (NB IFN is neuter here)
યુનિવર્સિટી (f.)	yunivarsiṭī	*university*
યોગ્ય	yogya	*appropriate, suitable*
રડવું (intr.)	raḍvuṃ	*cry, weep*
રજા (f.)	rajā	*holiday, leave*
રવિવાર (m.)	ravivār	*Sunday*
રસ (m.)	ras	*juice, sap; taste, liking; emotion*
રસોડું (n.)	rasoḍuṃ	*kitchen*
રસ્તો (m.)	rasto	*road*
રહેવું	rehevuṃ	*remain, stay; live*
રંગ (m.)	raṃg	*colour*
રંગીન	raṃgīn	*coloured, brightly coloured*
રાખવું	rākhvuṃ	*put, keep*
રાજનીતિ (f.)	rājnītī	*politics*
રાજી	rājī	*pleased, willing*
રાત (f.)	rāt	*night*
રાષ્ટ્રભાષા (f.)	rāṣṭrabhāṣā	*national language*
રાષ્ટ્રવાદી (m.)	rāṣṭravādī	*nationalist*
રાહ (m.)	rāh	*road, way*
રાહ (f.)	rāh	*waiting*
રાહ જોવી	rāh jovī	*wait for*
રાંધવું (tr.)	rāṃdhvuṃ	*cooked*
રિક્ષા (f.)	rīkśā	*autorickshaw*
રીત (f.)	rīt	*way, manner*
રીતરિવાજો (m. pl.)	rītrivājo	*manners and customs*
રૂપ (n.)	rūp	*form, beauty*

રૂપિયો (m.)	rūpiyo	*rupee*
રેડિયો (m.)	reḍiyo	*radio*
રેશમ (n.)	reśam	*silk*
રેશમી	reśmī	*silken, of silk*
રોકડા પૈસા (m. pl.)	rokḍā paisā	*cash*
રોકવું (tr.)	rokvuṃ	*stop; employ, occupy*
રોકાયેલું	rokāyeluṃ	*busy*
રોકાવું	rokāvuṃ	*stay*
રોજ	roj	*everyday*
રોજગાર (m.)	rojgār	*employment*
રોટલી	roṭlī	*thin bread, chapati*
લઈ આવવું	laī āvvuṃ	*bring*
લઈ જવું	laī javuṃ	*take*
લાઈન (f.)	lāīn	*line, queue*
લઈ લેવું	lāi levuṃ	*get; take*
લખવું	lakhvuṃ	*write*
લગ્ન (n.)	lagan	*wedding, marriage*
લગભગ	lagbhag	*approximately*
લત્તો (m.)	latto	*area of town*
લપ (f.)	lap	*trouble, bother; boring person*
લાગવું	lāgvuṃ	*strike, seem*
લાકડી (f.)	lākḍī	*stick*
લાકડું (n.)	lākḍuṃ	*wood*
લાખ (m.)	lākh	*lakh, 1,000,000*
લાવવું	lāvvuṃ	*bring*
લાલ	lāl	*red*
લાલન (n.)	lālan	*caressing, cuddling*
લાંબું	lāṃbuṃ	*long, tall*
લીલું	līluṃ	*green*
લેવું	levuṃ	*take*
લોકપ્રિય	lokpriya	*popular*
લોકો (m. pl.)	loko	*people*
લોટ (m.)	loṭ	*flour*
લોન્ડ્રી	loṃḍrī	*laundry*
વકીલ (m.)	vakīl	*lawyer*
(ના) વગર	vagar	*without*
વગેરે	vagere	*etc.*
વખત (m.)	vakhat	*time, opportunity*
વખતસર	vakhatsar	*at the proper time*
વજન (n.)	vajan	*weight*
વટાણો (m.)	vaṭāṇo	*pea*
વડું	vaḍuṃ	*big, great, chief*
વણવું (tr.)	vaṇvuṃ	*weave; roll dough*

વતન (n.)	vatan	*native place*
વરસ (m.)	varas	*year*
વરસાદ (m.)	varsād	*rain*
વરસાદ પડવો	varsād paḍvo	*rain*
વર્ગ (m.)	varg	*class*
વર્ણન (n.)	varṇan	*description*
વર્તન (n.)	vartan	*behaviour*
વસાણું (n.)	vasāṇuṃ	*grocery item; goods*
વસાવવું (tr.)	vasāvvuṃ	*settle*
વસંત (m./f.)	vasaṃt	*spring* (caitra and Vaisakh)
વહેલું	vaheluṃ	*early*
વળવું (intr.)	vaḷvuṃ	*bend, turn; return*
વંદન (n. pl.)	vaṃdan	*Yours ...*
વાગવું	vāgvuā	*sound*
વાજબી	vājbī	*reasonable*
વાણિયો (m.)	vāṇiyo	*merchant, bania*
વાત (f.)	vāt	*thing; speech; story; subject*
વાત કરવી	vāt karvī	*chat*
વાતચીત (f.)	vātcīt	*conversation, chat*
વાતાનુકૂલિત	vātānukūlit	*air-conditioned*
વાતાવરણ (n.)	vātāvaraṇ	*atmosphere, weather*
વાદવિવાદ (m.)	vādvivād	*debate, discussion*
વાદળ (n.)	vādaḷ	*cloud; rain*
વાપરવું	vāparvuṃ	*make use of, use, consume*
વાર (f.)	vār	*time*
વારુ	vāru	*well, all right; yes*
વાવું (intr.)	vāvuṃ	*blow*
વાહ!	vāh!	*bravo! good!*
વાંચવું	vāṃcvuṃ	*read*
વાંધો (m.)	vāṃdho	*objection; quarrel; problem*
વિચાર (m.)	vicār	*thinking, thought, opinion; anxiety*
વિચિત્ર	vicitra	*strange; wonderful*
વિડિયો (f.)	viḍīo	*video*
વિકસવું (intr.)	vikasvuṃ	*open, bloom; develop*
વિદેશી	videśī	*foreign*
વિદ્યાર્થિની (f.)	vidyārthīnī	*student*
વિદ્યાર્થી (m.)	vidyārthī	*student*
વિધિ (m/f.)	vidhi	*rite*
વિભાગ (m.)	vibhāg	*part, section, department*
વિભાગના વડા (m.)	vibhāgnā vaḍā	*head of department*
વિમાન (n.)	vimān	*aircraft*
વિમાનમથક (n.)	vimānmathak	*airport*
વિરમવું (intr.)	viramuṃ	*stop*

વિશ્વાસ (m.)	viśvās	*belief, faith, confidence*
વિષય (m.)	viṣay	*subject, sense object*
(ના) વિષે	(nā) viṣe	*about*
વીજળી (f.)	vījḷī	*lightning, electricity*
વીતવું (intr.)	vītvuṃ	*pass away; occur; experience*
વેચવું	vecvuṃ	*sell*
વેપાર (m.)	vepār	*trade, commerce, business*
વેપારી (m.)	vepārī	*trader, merchant*
વેલણ (n.)	velaṇ	*rolling pin*
વ્યવસ્થા (f.)	vyavasthā	*arrangement*
વ્યાધિ (m./f.)	vyādhi	*disease; problem*
શક્તિ (f.)	śakti	*strength, power, ability*
શનિવાર (m.)	śanivār	*Saturday*
શરમ (f.)	śaram	*shyness, modesty*
શરૂ કરવું	śarū karvuṃ	*begin*
શરૂઆત (f.)	śarūāt	*beginning*
શહેર (n.)	śaher	*city*
શાક (n.)	śāk	*vegetable*
શાકભાજી (n.pl.)	śākbhājī	*vegetables*
શાકમારકેટ (f./n.)	śākmarkeṭ	*vegetable market*
શાકાહારી	śākāhārī	*vegetarian*
શાસક (m.)	śāsak	*ruler, governor*
શાસ્ત્રીયસંગીત (n.)	śāstrīyasaṃgīt	*classical music*
શાંતિ (f.)	śāṃti	*peace*
શિક્ષક (m.)	śikṣak	*teacher*
શિક્ષિકા (f.)	śikśikā	*teacher*
શિયાળો (m.)	śiyāḷo	*winter*
ીખવું	śīkhvuṃ	*learn, study*
ુક્રવાર (m.)	śukravār	*Friday*
ુભાશિષ (f.)	śubhāśiś	*blessing; Yours ...*
ું?	śuṃ?	*what?*
ોધવું	śodhvuṃ	*look for, examine*
ોખ (m.)	śokh	*liking, fondness; fashion*
ોર (m.)	śor	*noise*
ખત	sakhat	*hard, cruel, severe*
ગાંવહાલાં (n. pl.)	sagāṃvahālāṃ	*relations*
ગુંવહાલું (n.)	saguṃvahāluṃ	*member of family*
ત્ર (n.)	satra	*session, term*
દાકાળ	sadākāḷ	*always*
ફર (f.)	saphar	*travel, journey*
ફળ	saphaḷ	*fruitful, successful, accomplished*
ફળતા (f.)	saphaḷtā	*success*
ફાઈ (f.)	saphāī	*cleanliness*

સફેદ	saphed	*white*
સમજ (f.)	samaj	*understanding*
સમજ પડવી	samaj paḍvī	(be able to) *understand*
સમજાવવું (tr.)	samjāvvuṃ	*explain*
સમય (m.)	samay	*time*
સમાચાર (m.pl.)	samācār	*news*
સમાજિક	samājik	*social*
સમું કરવું	samuṃ karvuṃ	*mend*
સમો (m.)	samo	*time, season*
સરખું	sarkhuṃ	*equal, alike, even; fit, proper*
સરસ	saras	*interesting, excellent*
સરળ	saraḷ	*straightforward, simple*
સલાહ (f.)	salāh	*advice, opinion*
સવા	savā	*one and a quarter, plus a quarter*
સવાર (f., n.)	savār	*morning*
સવાલ (m.)	savāl	*questions*
સસ્તું	sastuṃ	*cheap*
સહન (n.)	sahan	*bearing, enduring, patience*
સહેલું	sahelum	*easy*
સહેવું (intr.)	sahevuṃ	*suffer*
સળગાવવું (tr.)	saḷgāvvuṃ	*light, set fire to*
સંદેશો (m.)	saṃdeśo	*message, news*
સંભાળવું (tr.)	saṃbhāḷvuṃ	*take care of*
સંયુકત	saṃyukta	*joint*
સંવાદ (m.)	saṃvād	*conversation, dialogue*
સંશોધન (n.)	saṃśodhan	*research*
સંસ્કૃત (f/n.)	saṃskṛt	*Sanskrit*
સંસ્કૃતિ (f.)	saṃskṛti	*culture*
સાચું	sācuṃ	*true*
સાજું	sājuā	*well; in good health*
સાજુંતાજું	sājuṃtājuṃ	*hale and hearty*
સાડી (f.)	sāḍī	*saree*
સાત	sāt	*seven*
સાતમું	sātmuṃ	*seventh*
સાદું	sāduṃ	*plain, simple*
સાધારણ	sādhārāṇ	*ordinary, general*
સાફ	sāph	*clean*
સાફ કરવું	sāph karvuṃ	*clean*
સામાન (m.)	sāmān	*luggage; furniture*
સામું	sāmuṃ	*opposite*
સારું	sāruṃ	*good, well*
સાહિત્ય (n.)	sāhitya	*literature*
સાહેબ (m.)	sāheb	*Sir, master*

સાલવું	sālvuṃ	*pinch; feel pain*
સાંજ (f.)	sāṃj	*evening*
સાંભળવું	sāṃbhaḷvuṃ	*hear, listen to*
સિગરેટ (f.)	sigāreṭ	*cigarette*
સિગરેટ પીવી	sigāreṭ pīvī	*smoke*
સીઝન (f.)	sījhan	*season*
સીધું	sīdhuṃ	*straight ahead*
સીવવું	sīvvuṃ	*sew*
સુકાવું (intr.)	sukāvuṃ	*dry, become dry*
સુખી	sukhī	*happy*
સુગમ	sugam	*light, accessible*
સુગંધ (m./f.)	sugaṃdh	*fragrance, good smell*
સુથાર (m.)	suthār	*carpenter*
સુધી	sudhī	*until, up to*
સુંદર	suṃdar	*beautiful*
સુઈ જવું	sūī javuṃ	*go to bed*
સૂતર (n.)	sūtar	*thread, cotton*
સૂર્યાસ્ત(m.)	sūryāst	*sunset*
સૂર્યોદય(m.)	sūryoday	*sunrise*
સૂંઘવું (tr.)	sūṃghvuṃ	*smell*
સેકંડ(f.)	sekaṃḍ	*second*
સેક્રેટરી (f./m.)	sekreṭarī	*secretary*
સેંકડો (m.)	seṃkḍo	*hundred, century; hundreds*
સેંડલ (.)	seṃḍal	*sandal*
સો (m.)	so	*hundred*
સોનેરી	sonerī	*golden*
સોમવાર(m.)	somvār	*Monday*
સોસાયટી (f.)	sosāyaṭī	*society; housing association*
સૌ	sau	*all*
સ્ત્રી (f)	strī	*woman*
સ્થિતિ(f.)	sthiti	*state, condition, status*
નાન (n.)	snān	*bath*
નાન કરવું	snān karvuṃ	*take a bath, bathe*
નેહી	snehī	*Dear ...*
પષ્ટ	spaṣṭ	*clear, evident, plain*
મરણ (n.pl.)	smaraṇ	*Yours ...*
વભાવ (m.)	svabhāv	*character, nature*
વરાજ (n.)	svarāj	*self-government*
વર્ગવાસી	svargvāsī	*living in heaven, deceased, late*
ીકારવું (tr.)	svīkārvuṃ	*accept, receive*
કીકત (f.)	hakīkat	*fact, news, detailed account*
જાર (m.)	hajār	*thousand*
જી (પણ)	hajī(paṇ)	*still, yet, even now*

હજી સુધી	hajīsudhī	*still, yet, up till now*
હતું	hatuṃ	*was*
હમાલ (m.)	hamāl	*coolie, porter*
હમેશાં	hameśāṃ	*always*
હવા (f.)	havā	*wind, breeze*
હવા ખાવી	havā khātvī	*get some fresh air*
હવે	have	*now*
હસવું	hāsvuṃ	*laugh*
હસ્તમેળાપ(m.)	hastmeḷāp	*joining hands* (name of part of wedding ceremony)
હળવું (intr.)	haḷvuṃ	*be familiar, be friendly*
હળવુંમળવું (tr.)	haḷvuṃmaḷvuṃ	*mix; meet*
હા	hā	*yes*
હા જી	hā jī	*yes* (formal)
હાડકું (n.)	hāḍkuṃ	*bone*
હાથ (m.)	hāth	*hand, arm*
હાથ જોડવા	hāth joḍvā	*join hands in greeting or supplication*
હાફપેંટ	hāphpeṃṭ	*shorts*
હાલચાલ (f.)	hālcāl	*movement; manners*
હાસ્ય (n.)	hāsya	*laugh, laughing*
હિસાબ (m.)	hisāb	*calculation, account*
હિંદુ (m. f./adj.)	hindu	*Hindu*
હિંસા (f.)	hiṃsā	*violence*
હીંચકો (m.)	hīṃcko	*swing*
હું	huṃ	*I*
હોટલ/હોટેલ (f.)	hoṭal/hoṭel	*hotel, café*
હોવું	hovuṃ	*be*
હોશિયાર	hośiyār	*clever*